CONVEYANCING 2008

CONVEYANCING 2008

Kenneth G C Reid WS

Professor of Scots Law in the University of Edinburgh

and

George L Gretton WS

Lord President Reid Professor of Law in the University of Edinburgh

with a contribution by Alan Barr of the University of Edinburgh

Avizandum Publishing Ltd
Edinburgh
2009

Published by
Avizandum Publishing Ltd
58 Candlemaker Row
Edinburgh EH1 2QE

First published 2009

ISBN 978-1-904968-11-5

British Library Cataloguing in Publication Data
A catalogue record for this book is available from the British Library.

Typeset by Waverley Typesetters, Fakenham
Printed and bound by Bell & Bain Ltd, Glasgow

CONTENTS

PREFACE

This is the tenth annual update of new developments in the law of conveyancing. As in previous years, it is divided into five parts. There is, first, a brief description of all cases which have been reported or have appeared on the Scottish Courts website (www.scotcourts.gov.uk) or have otherwise come to our attention since *Conveyancing 2007*. The next two parts summarise, respectively, statutory developments during 2008 and other material of interest to conveyancers. The fourth part is a detailed commentary on selected issues arising from the first three parts. Finally, in part V, there are three tables. New this year is a cumulative table of decisions, usually by the Lands Tribunal, on the variation or discharge of title conditions. This covers all decisions since the revised jurisdiction in part 9 of the Title Conditions (Scotland) Act 2003 came into effect. Next is a cumulative table of appeals, designed to facilitate moving from one annual volume to the next. Finally, there is a table of cases digested in earlier volumes but reported, either for the first time or in an additional series, in 2008. This is for the convenience of future reference.

We do not seek to cover agricultural holdings, crofting, public sector tenancies (except the right-to-buy legislation), compulsory purchase or planning law. Otherwise our coverage is intended to be complete.

We gratefully acknowledge help received from Alan Barr, John Glover, Brian Hamilton, Richard Miller, Roddy Paisley, Neil Tainsh and Scott Wortley.

Kenneth G C Reid
George L Gretton
15 March 2009

TABLE OF STATUTES

TABLE OF ORDERS, RULES AND REGULATIONS

TABLE OF CASES

PART I
CASES

CASES

The full text of all decisions of the Court of Session and of many decisions of the sheriff court is available on the Scottish Courts website: http://www.scotcourts.gov.uk.

Since 1 January 2005 all Court of Session opinions are numbered consecutively according to whether they are decisions of the Outer House or Inner House. Thus '[2008] CSOH 4' refers to the fourth Outer House decision of 2008, and '[2008] CSIH 15' refers to the fifteenth Inner House decision of 2008. This 'neutral' method of citation is used throughout this volume.

MISSIVES OF SALE

(1) McDougall v Heritage Hotels Ltd
[2008] CSOH 54, 2008 SLT 494

Circumstances in which **held** that the 'reservation' of a new house accompanied by payment of a deposit did not oblige the builder to issue an offer to sell or prevent the builder from selling the house to someone else. See **Commentary** p 81.

(2) Gray v Welsh
[2008] CSIH 11, 2008 GWD 5-84

A house, bought off-plan by the pursuers, bordered the River Clyde. When, subsequently, the pursuers were faced with carrying out works to prevent flooding, they sought to recover the cost from the builder, basing their claim both in contract and in delict.

So far as contract was concerned, the argument was as follows. (i) The missives, in standard form, provided for the purchase of a numbered plot on the defender's layout plan 'which plan is demonstrative only and not taxative and may be varied by you as circumstances require'. (ii) Certain variations were agreed by an agent of the defender, both orally and by letter. (iii) These included an obligation to construct the garden by use of artificial 'made' ground. (iv) There was to be implied into such an obligation a further obligation to construct the ground with the reasonable care and skill to be expected of a competent contractor. (v) In fact it had not been conducted with such care and skill. In particular, the materials used were likely to render the ground unstable in the event of changing water levels in the Clyde.

As well as attacking the factual basis of the pursuers' case, the defender argued (para 8) that: 'A contract for the sale of land did not carry with it any warranty as to the quality of the land or its suitability for any particular purpose and so, absent any contractual obligation to carry out a work of construction on the garden ground, there could be no contractual liability upon the defender.'

The Lord Ordinary had allowed proof before answer – see [2007] CSOH 64 – and the First Division has now upheld this disposal. It seems worth mentioning that the supposed absence of a warranty of quality in the sale of heritable property has been contested: see R Black, 'Practice and precept in Scots law' 1982 *Juridical Review* 31 at 47–50.

(3) Aisling Developments Ltd v Persimmon Homes Ltd
[2008] CSOH 140, 2008 GWD 36-542

Between 2001 and 2006 the pursuer and defender were sporadically engaged in negotiations for the sale by the defender to the pursuer of a 35-acre site at Old Craighall, Musselburgh. Matters were complicated by the fact that, at one stage, this was part of a tripartite arrangement whereby (i) the pursuer would also buy an additional (and adjacent) site from the defender, (ii) that site would be sold to Queen Margaret University College in exchange for its existing site at Clermiston in Edinburgh, and (iii) the Clermiston site would be sold to the defender. The pursuer hoped that the relocation of QMUC would result in the adjacent site being released from its green belt status, at least to the extent of allowing the building of a business park.

At a 40-minute meeting involving all three parties held on 5 March 2002 it was agreed that QMUC would deal directly with the defender, as would the pursuer in respect of the 35-acre site. When, in August 2006, the defender withdrew from further negotiations, the pursuer argued (a) that an oral contract of sale was agreed upon at the meeting of 5 March 2002, and (b) that the subsequent actings of the parties, in the course of which the pursuer spent some £500,000, were sufficient to set up the contract under s 1(3), (4) of the Requirements of Writing (Scotland) Act 1995. In this action the pursuer sought declarator that the defender was bound by the contract.

After proof, Lord Glennie was satisfied as to (b) but unconvinced in respect of (a). In order to conclude that an oral contract had been formed on 5 March 2002, it was necessary to show both that the parties intended to enter into such a contract and that they had reached agreement on its essential terms. In seeking to explain the relationship of these two requirements, Lord Glennie relied on the analysis of the New Zealand Court of Appeal in *Fletcher Challenge Energy Ltd v Electricity Corporation of New Zealand Ltd* [2002] NZLR 433, delivered by Blanchard J, and especially on the following passages (paras 53 and 58):

The prerequisites to formation of a contract are therefore:

(a) An intention to be immediately bound (at the point when the bargain is said to have been agreed); and

(b) An agreement, express or found by implication, or the means of achieving agreement (eg an arbitration clause), on every term which:
  (i) was legally essential to the formation of such a bargain; or
  (ii) was regarded by the parties themselves as essential to their particular bargain.

A term is to be regarded by the parties as essential if one party maintains the position that there must be agreement upon it and manifests accordingly to the other party....

The Court has an entirely neutral approach when determining whether the parties intended to enter into a contract. Having decided that they had that intention, however, the Court's attitude will change. It will then do its best to give effect to their intention and, if at all possible, to uphold the contract despite any omissions or ambiguities.

Lord Glennie found that the pursuer had failed 'by some margin' to prove any contractual intention on 5 March 2002 (para 57). In any event, there was an awkwardness in saying that parties intended to be bound in circumstances where both parties knew perfectly well that only a written contract would do (para 58). It followed that the pursuer must fail.

(4) Carmarthen Developments Ltd v Pennington
[2008] CSOH 139, 2008 GWD 33-494

A letter indicating that suspensive conditions had been purified was **held** to be served at the time when a bag containing the letter was collected from the Post Office by the addressee. It was not served earlier, at the time of posting, because the postal rule only applied to the acceptance of offers. See **Commentary** p 88.

(5) Parvaiz v Thresher Wines Acquisitions Ltd
[2008] CSOH 160, 2008 GWD 40-592

After concluding a contract for the purchase of a shop, the pursuer discovered that the seller did not have title to the internal toilets. As the toilets could only be accessed by means of the shop, this came as a considerable surprise to the pursuer. In the normal case the pursuer's remedy would lie in warrandice, for the seller would be in breach of its obligation to exhibit a good and marketable title to the subjects (assuming that the subjects were described in such a way as to include the toilets). But this was not a normal case. The shop had been sold at auction, and the contract took the form of articles of roup which contained the standard provision that the subjects were 'sold *tantum et tale* as they exist with no warranty as to descriptions, extents, boundaries'. Accordingly, the pursuer's case was based on error, and he sought reduction of the contract and repayment of the deposit (£26,200 being 10% of the price).

A proof before answer was allowed. On the authority of cases such as *Hamilton v Western Bank of Scotland* (1861) 23 D 1033 and *Young v McKellar* 1909 SC 1340, the *tantum et tale* clause did not prevent a claim founded on error, at least where this was in respect of a material matter. If the pursuer could prove mutual error, he was entitled to decree if the error was sufficiently material. And even if he could prove only unilateral error, this might still be relevant if, as the pursuer averred, he could show bad faith on the part of the defender, in the sense that the defender 'knew that it did not have title to the toilet area, knew that the appearance of the subjects indicated that the toilet area was included, did nothing to draw this to the pursuer's attention, but, rather, relied on the exclusion provisions in the Conditions incorporated in the Articles of Roup to throw the risk of eviction from what is averred to be a material part of the subjects of sale on to the pursuer' (para 20 *per* Lord Brodie).

(6) Connell v Hart
[2008] CSIH 67, 2009 GWD 1-12

Buyers were entitled to resile in the event that their surveyor decided that matters disclosed in a coal mining report 'would' affect the property's stability. In the event, the surveyor's letter merely indicated that the stability *might* be affected. **Held**: The buyers, who had purported to resile, were not entitled to do so. See **Commentary** p 85.

(7) Simmers v Innes
[2008] UKHL 24, 2008 SC (HL) 137

This was a dispute about whether an option to purchase land (and shares) had been validly exercised. The terms of the agreement were, as Lord Neuberger said (at para 25), 'inartistically drafted'. **Held**: (i) that the option had been duly exercised by service of a notice, being a notice which was served within the required time frame; (ii) that, the option having been exercised, there was nothing in the contract to displace the usual rule of the common law, set out in *Rodger (Builders) Ltd v Fawdry* 1950 SC 483, that time was not of the essence for payment of the purchase price. Accordingly, the buyer was entitled to enforce the contract despite having delayed in paying.

TENEMENTS

(8) Crolla v Hussain
2008 SLT (Sh Ct) 145

When the owner of a shop at the foot of the tenement at 5 Merchiston Place, Edinburgh caused works to be carried out to replace a load-bearing wall with a steel beam, serious cracking appeared on the walls of the flat above. The owner of the flat sued for damages on the basis (i) that the shop owner was liable for the negligent actings of an independent contractor in circumstances where the operation was inherently hazardous, or alternatively (ii) that the damage was caused by a nuisance committed by the defender. In attacking the relevancy of the pleadings, the defender argued that (a) in principle there was no liability for the negligence of an independent contractor (a proposition which was not in dispute), and (b) the exception in respect of inherently hazardous activities might be English law but was not Scots. **Held**: That the exception was indeed part of Scots law, and proof before answer allowed.

The foundation of the averments in support of (i) was the statement that 'The defender was subject to an obligation to provide support to the tenements in the upper floors.' It might be added that that obligation, formerly attributable to common interest, is now statutory: see Tenements (Scotland) Act 2004 ss 8 and 9.

(9) Stewart v Malik
2008 GWD 14-252, Sh Ct

The facts were broadly the same as in the previous case, although the pursuers did not additionally sue in nuisance. In allowing a proof before answer the sheriff principal (B A Lockhart) said (at para 42) that:

> In my opinion the law to which I have been referred, and which I have set out in full, allows a remedy to a party whose property is damaged by an independent contractor instructed by another if the operation can be described as inherently hazardous.

For that statement the sheriff principal relied in particular on D M Walker, *The Law of Delict in Scotland* (2nd edn 1981) pp 154 and 159; *Duncan's Hotel (Glasgow) Ltd v J & A Ferguson Ltd* 1972 SLT (Notes) 74; and *Dalton v Angus* (1881) 6 App Cas 740 *per* Lord Watson. An appeal was refused: see 2009 SLT 205 (to be covered in next year's volume).

(10) Dalby v Bracken
13 June 2008, Lands Tr

An application to the Lands Tribunal by the owners of an upper flat to discharge a right of common property in the roof held by the owner of the lower flat was dismissed as incompetent.

[A fuller account of this case can be found at Case (29).]

SERVITUDES

(11) Aberdeen City Council v Wanchoo
[2008] CSIH 6, 2008 SC 278, 2008 SLT 106

For 20 years the defender (and before him, his predecessor) took access over land belonging to the pursuer, on the basis of an informal agreement set up by *rei interventus*. The pursuer sought a declarator that no servitude existed in favour of the defender. **Held**: that the possession was 'as of right' and hence a servitude had been established by prescription. This affirms the decision of the Lord Ordinary: [2006] CSOH 196, 2007 SLT 289 (*Conveyancing 2006* Case (16)). See **Commentary** p 105.

(12) Neumann v Hutchison
2008 GWD 16-297, Sh Ct

For more than 20 years the pursuer took access to the rear of his house by means of property belonging to the defenders. He claimed a servitude by prescription. At first instance the sheriff held that, as the pursuer was unable to prove an absence of tolerance on the part of the defenders and their predecessors, no servitude had been established. See 2006 GWD 28-628 (*Conveyancing 2006* Case (17)). On appeal to the sheriff principal, it has now been **held** that there was no need for the pursuer to prove a negative and that, in the absence of evidence of tolerance, it could be taken that the possession was as of right and that a servitude had been established. See **Commentary** p 102.

(13) Chalmers Property Investment Co Ltd v Robson
2008 SLT 1069, HL

Although decided in the 1960s, this decision was only properly reported in 2008. A split-off feu disposition of land in Mull, granted in 1943, conferred a right 'to draw water for domestic purposes from the spring or well situated some ninety-five yards or thereby to the north east side of the said subjects'. In fact there was no 'spring or well' at that point but only a burn, which was fed by springs and by surface water higher up the hill. Nonetheless, a system of water supply was put in place by which water was taken from the burn at the stipulated point. When the servient owner challenged the right to do so, the dominant owner sought interdict against interfering with the supply.

On the main issue, the First Division and, on appeal, the House of Lords had little difficulty in concluding that withdrawal of water from the burn was within the terms of the servitude. In the Division, Lord Guthrie expressed matters thus (pp 1072–1073):

> I agree with counsel that it is a general rule in the construction of dispositions that they are to be construed strictly against restriction of the right of an owner to the possession and enjoyment of his property, and that a clause creating a servitude will, therefore, be strictly construed. But in this case the question is not as to the scope of the clause, but as to its validity, and, in addition, to the rule of strict construction, other principles of interpretation come into operation. There can be no doubt that the original grantor and disponee intended that the latter should have the right to draw water from a source of supply on the grantor's property, and that the deed specified that the source was to be found at a point approximately 95 yards north east of the subject disponed. Therefore, if the respondents' contention were accepted, it would mean that the intention of parties, clearly expressed in the deed, would be defeated. That is not a result which the court would willingly reach, and I do not think that the rule of strict construction requires us to arrive at that conclusion. This case seems to me to be a clear example of the application of the maxim *falsa demonstratio non nocet dummodo constet de re*. In *Trayner's Latin Maxims* at p 218 the maxim is translated and explained thus: 'An erroneous description does not injure. Where the description is merely expository, an error in it will not vitiate, if there be no doubt as to the identity of the person or thing intended to be specified.' The application of this principle is

generally to be found in the interpretation of testamentary writings, but it is obviously equally applicable in dealing with contracts and dispositions of property.

For Lord Reid in the House of Lords, the discrepancy was easily explained (para 6):

> There is no spring in the ordinary sense of the word anywhere near the point marked by the dot on the plan. It is fairly obvious that the person who made the plan saw the water coming down the hill in a water course but did not trouble to go to the top to find out where it came from. And the conveyancer in Glasgow took his description from the plan adopting the word 'spring' on the plan and for some reason adding to it the words 'or well'.

The difficulty could readily be accommodated by the principle *falsa demonstratio* (para 9):

> This seems to me to be a simple case of *falsa demonstratio*. The right is a right to draw water at a particular place, and there is running water there. The fact that it does not come direct from a spring but is already in a watercourse seems to me to be wholly immaterial.

A separate issue was whether the servitude entitled the holder to make installations on the servient tenement. There was an express right to lay pipes, but in addition the pursuer had installed a small dam and a settling tank. It was **held** that there was such a right. See **Commentary** p 111.

An important issue at first instance had been whether a servitude could be regarded as having been created by the defender's acquiescence in the pursuer's installations: see 1965 SLT 381. As matters turned out, this was not necessary for the decision, because a servitude was held to exist on other grounds, and the issue was little discussed on appeal. Only Lord President Clyde touched on the subject (p 1072), indicating that, had it been necessary to do so, he would have followed the Lord Ordinary in deciding that a servitude had been created by acquiescence.

(14) Fyvie v Morrison
30 May 2000, Arbroath Sheriff Court

The defenders' property comprised two separate plots, one feued in 1903 and the other feued (by the same granter) in 1932. The 1903 feu charter conferred on the feuar 'an entrance from his Feu' by means of ground which was now the property of the pursuer. In the 1932 feu charter it was stated that 'as the said piece of land hereby feued is to form an addition to the said piece of ground feued to the said William Elder [ie in 1903] ... no access is required or given for the ground hereby feued'.

After 1903 a wall was built by the defenders' predecessors which separated the 1903 feu from the servient tenement, but left a gap with a gate by which access could be taken. In 1996 the defenders built a house on the 1932 feu and formed an access to it from the servient tenement which ran through the 1903 feu. This involved demolition of part of the wall. The pursuer raised an action of interdict against taking this new access. The defenders counterclaimed for declarator of a right of access in respect of both the 1903 and 1932 feus.

The sheriff principal (R A Dunlop QC) affirmed the sheriff's decision to allow the counterclaim, on a number of grounds.

(1) '[T]he feuar was entitled to exercise the right of access over the whole of the servient tenement to whatever point of entry to the 1903 feu that he chose' (p 7). The sheriff principal continued (p 8):

> Counsel for the pursuer and appellant contended that, having formed an entrance in the wall once constructed, the proprietors of the 1903 feu were not entitled to alter that entrance. In my opinion there is no warrant for such a proposition upon a proper construction of the titles. The fact that the proprietor of a dominant tenement exercises a right of access in a particular way does not exclude his right to exercise it in a different way, provided it is warranted by the express terms of his grant. Once it is understood that the proper construction of the grant is to allow a right of access over the whole servient tenement to whatever point of entry is chosen by the feuar, in my opinion the feuar is entitled to change the entry from time to time as he chooses.

(2) On a proper construction of the deed, the 1932 feu was intended to be an addition to the 1903 feu and therefore to have the right of access which had been granted in 1903. Hence access to the 1932 feu could be taken from the servient tenement.

Had it been necessary to do so, the sheriff principal would also have found that the pursuer had acquiesced in the new access taken by the defenders and could not now challenge it. This final point, however, seems questionable – see E Reid and J W G Blackie, *Personal Bar* (2006) para 6-60 – for, so far as the judgment discloses, the building work was carried out only on the dominant tenement. What, then, was it that the pursuer failed to do? He could not have interdicted the building work, because the defenders were perfectly entitled to build on their own property. What he could do was to interdict access – but that was exactly what he had done in the present action.

[Although decided in 2000, this unreported decision has only recently been brought to our attention.]

(15) Romano v Standard Commercial Property Securities Ltd
[2008] CSOH 105, 2008 SLT 859

A disposition of 1962 separating the basement from the ground floor flat in a tenement purported to create a servitude right to place 'a shop front including fascia' on the front wall of the ground floor flat. As this wall was apparently the common property of all the owners in that and the adjoining tenement, the grant of servitude was ineffective, but there was argued to have been prescriptive possession. **Held**: That no servitude of signage was recognised in Scots law, but in any event there were no relevant averments of appropriate and sufficient possession for the purposes of positive prescription. See **Commentary** p 108. It is understood that the decision has been appealed.

(16) Elrig Estate Co Ltd v Wright
22 August 2008, Stranraer Sheriff Court

The property owned by the defender in Port William included a derelict cottage known as Strawfauld Croft. In advertising the cottage for sale, the defender undertook to grant a servitude of way over a private road. The basis for such a grant was that the defender held an existing servitude constituted by prescription. The pursuer, who held an express servitude over the road, disputed the defender's servitude and hence her title to grant. In this action the pursuer sought interim interdict against the granting of the servitude. The real concern seems to have been possible damage to the road from the construction traffic which any purchaser would be likely to introduce in order to renovate the cottage.

Reversing the sheriff, the sheriff principal (B A Lockhart) granted interim interdict. This is perhaps a surprising decision. No harm could come to the pursuer merely from words in the disposition of the cottage purporting to grant a servitude; for either the servitude already existed, in which case it would transmit without words, or it did not exist, in which case the words would be ineffectual. The proper time to bring an interdict would be if and when the disponee began to use the road. A further possible difficulty was whether, as a mere servitude holder, the pursuer had title to sue. In granting the interim interdict, the sheriff principal was evidently influenced by the desirability of getting the problem over access rights out in the open, and, hopefully, resolved by a proof, before any person was committed to the purchase.

REAL BURDENS

(17) Barker v Lewis
2008 SLT (Sh Ct) 17

The owner of one of the houses in a five-house development started up a bed-and-breakfast business, contrary to the deed of conditions. Her neighbours were refused interdict on the ground that they had no interest to enforce: see 2007 SLT (Sh Ct) 48 (*Conveyancing 2007* Case (7)). That decision has now been affirmed by the sheriff principal. See **Commentary** p 92.

(18) Teague Developments Ltd v City of Edinburgh Council
27 February 2008, Lands Tribunal

The validity of a notice registered under s 18B of the Abolition of Feudal Tenure etc (Scotland) Act 2000 (economic development burdens) was challenged on the basis that the feudal burden which the notice purported to preserve was not, as s 18B required, 'imposed for the purpose of promoting economic development'. **Held**: That the burden did indeed fall within s 18B, and further that the statutory presumption of interest to enforce a personal real burden was irrebuttable. See **Commentary** pp 90 and 95.

VARIATION ETC OF TITLE CONDITIONS
BY LANDS TRIBUNAL

The full opinions in some Lands Tribunal cases are available at http://www.lands-tribunal-scotland.org.uk/records.html. Section 98 of the Title Conditions (Scotland) Act 2003 provides that the Tribunal is to grant an application for variation or discharge of a title condition if it is reasonable to do so having regard to the 10 factors (factors (a)–(j)) set out in s 100. A table listing all the applications so far made under the 2003 Act, and their result, will be found in Part V.

(19) Ritchie v Douglas
2008 GWD 8-148, Lands Tribunal

In 1986 a substantial mansion house, Midfield House in Lasswade, was divided into 15 flats. The property was subject to a deed of conditions, one of the terms of which was:

> No proprietor shall be entitled to occasion any external alterations to their house without the unanimous consent of all the proprietors of the other houses and without prejudice to the foregoing generality shall not be entitled without such consent to affix any external television aerial or other structure, nor any advertisement signs or name plates other than a door plate indicating such proprietor's name.

The applicant, who owned a one-bedroom flat on the ground floor, sought variation of this condition to the extent of allowing her to convert one of the windows in her main room into a French door. The proposed door was to be in the same astragalled style as the window it was to replace, and the applicant had already obtained a building warrant and also planning and listed building consent. The application was opposed by the owners of no fewer than 10 of the other flats, although this opposition appeared 'to have been coloured by the feelings of the other proprietors about other events involving the applicant' (para 23). The application was disposed of by written submissions and a site visit.

The Tribunal had little difficulty in deciding to grant the application. While the purpose of the condition (factor (f)) was to preserve the external appearance of the building, the Tribunal felt it should also take notice of the possible effect on the communal garden to which direct access could be taken by the proposed door. In the event, the Tribunal concluded that the effect on the other proprietors in both these respects would be minimal (factor (b)). Conversely, the condition did present a material impediment to the applicant (factor (c)).

(20) Blackman v Best
2008 GWD 11-214 (merits), 2008 GWD 23-371 (expenses), Lands Tribunal

In 1934 a disposition of a nursery garden in Merchiston Bank Gardens, Edinburgh provided that:

> It shall not be in the power of my said disponee or his foresaids to erect on the subjects hereby disponed any buildings except a greenhouse (which greenhouse shall not exceed twenty feet in length ten feet in width and twelve feet in height)....

The applicant, who also owned the plot next door on which he had built a house, sought variation of this condition to the extent of allowing the erection of a double garage. Planning permission had already been obtained for a garage in substantially the same style as the house. The application was opposed by a number of neighbours, and in particular by those on the other side of the street who had a view over what was currently a garden.

The application was decided on the basis of written submissions and a site inspection. In granting the application, the Tribunal explained that (para 36):

> If the double garage would have any real detrimental effect, the respondents should be allowed to rely on the building restriction. In our view, however, in the particular circumstances which we have reviewed, including the changes at the subjects and in their setting, the effect on the amenity will be minimal. The benefit of the condition to the benefited proprietors in relation to this proposal is therefore also minimal.

One reason why the benefit to the respondents was so slight (factor (b)) was because the applicants were in any event allowed to build a greenhouse so large as to be half the size of the proposed double garage. Furthermore, there had been changes in the neighbourhood (factor (a)), not least the building of the applicant's own house, and the fact that what was formerly a nursery was now the house's front garden. As to factor (c), it was plain that, now that planning consent had been granted, the burden was a substantial impediment.

As the application had been completely successful, expenses were awarded to the applicants in full. The Tribunal did not accept that there had been a failure to negotiate by the applicants such that expenses should be reduced. On the contrary, the applicants had written to the respondents at the time of applying for planning permission and had visited personally those of the respondents who had voiced objections. There was no evidence that a compromise could have been reached which would have been acceptable to all parties.

(21) Verrico v Tomlinson
2008 SLT (Lands Tr) 2

Around 1950 a detached Victorian house at 3 Dundonald Road in the Dowanhill area of Glasgow was divided into flats. Among the restrictions imposed in the split-off dispositions was a requirement that 'the subjects hereby disponed shall be used as a private residence for the occupation of one family only, and for no other purpose'. Included as part of one of the ground and basement flats was what had come to be a separate mews cottage, at the rear of the building, with its own separate entrance. Its owner, wishing to sell the cottage separately, applied for variation of the burden to allow him to do so. Other owners in the building opposed the application.

The application was granted. In the Tribunal's view, the purpose of the condition (factor (f)) was 'to preserve the amenity of the building as a whole' (para 24). But that amenity would be little disturbed by the separate sale of the mews cottage (factor (b)). Conversely, 'the title restriction is a very significant impediment to the effective use and potential sale of the property having regard to its present layout' as two separate dwellings (para 27) (factor (c)). The time interval since the imposition of the condition was also relevant (factor (e)), particularly having regard to the fact that there is today a trend towards smaller flats (factor (a)).

Following its recent practice (see *Conveyancing 2007* p 94), the Tribunal emphasised that 'consideration of the motives of the applicant is not a matter that the tribunal can or should address' (para 22). Thus it did not matter if the applicant was a property developer whose primary motive was to make money.

(22) Cocozza v Rutherford
2008 SLT (Lands Tr) 6

The extensive grounds of Gleneagles Hotel contain a number of groups of privately-owned houses, ranging from the large and expensive to the (relatively) small and cheap. The applicant's house – one of 27 bungalows in Airlie Court – fell into the latter category. All the houses were subject to a Deed of Conditions dating from 1977. Clause (sixth) provided that:

> No alterations shall be made to the external appearance of any of the premises except with the prior written consent of the Superiors, such consent not to be unreasonably withheld.

Following the abolition of the feudal system, the provisions of the deed of conditions were enforceable, apparently for the first time, by neighbours by virtue of the Title Conditions (Scotland) Act 2003 s 53.

Most of the houses in Airlie Court had been altered over the years, sometimes quite substantially (eg two-storey extensions at the side). But the applicant's proposed alterations were of a quite different scale, involving more than a doubling of the house's footprint. Her application to the Tribunal for variation of clause (sixth) was opposed by several neighbours.

The application was refused. The purpose of the clause (factor (f)) was to preserve rough uniformity in the different groups of houses. Admittedly, 'it is not fatal if previous changes have not gone as far as the applicant's proposals: it is not uncommon for applications to our jurisdiction to involve going further than what has gone before and such applications may and sometimes do succeed' (para 26). But this alteration was quite different in kind from previous alterations. It would make the house out of character with its relatively modest neighbours (paras 25, 27). As to factor (b), 'the applicant's extended house would ... be so out of place as to stick out and substantially affect the amenity at least of the properties at this end of Airlie Court' (para 29). In addition, it would have specific adverse effects for particular neighbours (para 27), although the Tribunal accepted the applicant's argument that 'this title condition is directed more at the general amenity of the development than at the particular interests of immediate neighbouring proprietors' (para 25). As to factor (c), the fact that it was, in effect, open to the applicant to carry out a more modest alteration, in line with what others had done, meant that '[t]he extent of impediment to the applicant's enjoyment of her property is ... considerably reduced' (para 30).

(23) Esplin v Higgitt
2008 GWD 28-439 (merits), 18 September 2008 (expenses), Lands Tribunal

The south side of Inverleith Terrace, Edinburgh, comprises a terrace of late Georgian/Victorian houses. In many cases these have now been flatted. There is a lengthy garden at the rear of the houses, sloping down to a mews lane, which has now been adopted, Inverleith Terrace Lane. Many of the houses have garages abutting on to the lane, but so far there are no houses. The original houses were burdened by individual feu charters with similar but not identical conditions, and it was accepted that these were (and probably always had been) mutually enforceable among the owners of the different houses.

The applicants owned the lower half of number 14. They sought variation of two of the conditions in their feu charter (which dated from 1870) to the extent of allowing the building of a two-storey house at the end of the garden and fronting the lane (for which they had planning permission). One condition prohibited subdivision without the superior's consent. The other regulated the size of mews buildings:

> That any stables, offices and other buildings to be erected on the said area next to the Meuse Lane shall not exceed Twenty one feet in width, the side walls shall not exceed fifteen feet in height and the Buildings shall not exceed twenty two feet in height including the roof and that the gables thereof shall be mutual and paid for as such. ...

The application was opposed by the owners of the upper flat at number 14 as well as by the owners of upper flats in two adjoining properties and by the owner of number 13 (which was undivided).

The Tribunal granted the application. The titles already permitted quite a substantial mews building, and did not prevent that building from being used for residential purposes. So, while it was accepted that the building restriction (at least) was conceived with neighbours in mind, the benefit which it conferred was relatively modest (factor (b)). Further, the impact of the proposed building was quite small. It was some distance away. The slope of the ground reduced the visual impact. And there was already a much more significant visual disturbance in the form of a modern office block. Further, the impact of separate ownership on traffic in the lane was likely to be slight. By contrast, the impediment which the conditions created for the applicants was substantial (factor (c)). As to factor (j) (any other factor) the Tribunal acknowledged that a successful application would be likely to lead to other mews houses in the lane, as had already occurred in neighbouring streets.

The Tribunal also rejected the claims for compensation – which amounted to £100,000 in the case of the whole house (number 13) and £20,000–£60,000 in the case of the flats. Compensation was due only in respect of 'substantial loss or disadvantage': Title Conditions (Scotland) Act 2003 s 90(7)(a). As usual in such cases, expert witnesses for each side produced opposing opinions. The Tribunal emphasised again that the existing title did not prevent the building of a mews house of more modest proportions, and concluded that it was 'not persuaded that the market, as opposed to a more subjective viewer, would reflect the loss of protection against this development, in comparison with what is permitted under these title conditions, in any substantial way' (para 66).

Expenses were granted in full, from the date on which opposition to the application was intimated. The respondents argued that it was important for them to challenge an application which might set a precedent, and that they had sought to conduct their case reasonably and as simply as possible. But these factors were not, the Tribunal said, relevant to the question of expenses. 'In general, the applicants, like the respondents, conducted the case reasonably and with due regard for the need to avoid unnecessary expense' (para 4).

(24) Lackie v Sloss
1 May 2008 (merits), 11 July 2008 (expenses), Lands Tribunal

9 Carlton Terrace, a grade A listed building in the Edinburgh New Town, was divided into four flats in 1990. Among the provisions in the deed of conditions was a requirement that 'no structural or external alterations shall be made to any flat or to any part thereof except with the prior consent in writing of the superiors'. Following the abolition of the feudal system it was accepted that this provision was now mutually enforceable within the building by virtue of s 53 of the Title Conditions (Scotland) Act 2003.

The applicant, who owned the basement flat, sought variation of this condition to the extent of allowing various structural alterations. These comprised the demolition of a number of walls, two of which were plainly structural, in order to create more usable space. The application was opposed by the owners of the other three flats, who feared for the structural stability of the building. Although the Tribunal's opinion proceeded by reference to the s 100 factors in the usual way, in substance the question for the Tribunal was whether there was a material risk that the proposed alterations would create structural problems. This was no different from the question which an ordinary court would have to consider in the event that the upper proprietors had elected to enforce their right of support conferred by s 9 of the Tenements (Scotland) Act 2004 (which prohibits doing anything 'which would, or would be reasonably likely to, impair to a material extent the support or shelter provided to any part of the tenement building').

On the evidence, the Tribunal was generally satisfied that the work would be properly and safely carried out, with adequate professional supervision, and that the proposals for replacement support (involving beams and a central column) were sufficient. The Tribunal was unmoved by the fact that there was up to a 20% chance of minor cosmetic cracking of plasterwork at the upper levels, no doubt partly because the applicant accepted that she would be liable and offered to accept a condition that appropriate insurance should be taken out. Yet the Tribunal did not feel able to grant the application at the present time. This was because slight to moderate cracking had recently appeared towards the top of the back wall of the common stair. It might well be that structural work in the basement would have no effect on such cracking. But one could not be sure. Therefore the Tribunal offered, and the applicant accepted, that the application should be sisted for nine months to allow further investigation and monitoring. In those circumstances, the Tribunal decided that it was premature to deal with expenses.

(25) Council for Music in Hospitals v Trustees for Richard Gerard Associates
2008 SLT (Lands Tr) 17 and 44

In *Brown v Richardson* 2007 GWD 28-490 (*Conveyancing 2007* Case (20)), the Tribunal had to consider for the first time an application, under s 90(1)(b)(i) of the Title Conditions (Scotland) Act 2003, for the renewal of a real burden which, being more than 100 years old, had been the subject of a notice of termination served under the 'sunset' rule (ie s 20 of the 2003 Act). The application was refused, to the extent that the burden prevented the building work which was being proposed. This case is the second such application.

The only feature which distinguishes an application for renewal from a 'normal' Tribunal application for variation or discharge is a shift in the onus of proof. In the 'normal' case the onus is on the proprietor who is seeking to be relieved of the burden, whereas in renewal cases the onus is on the benefited proprietor who is seeking to have the burden continued. In the new case, the effect of this shift was described as follows (para 28):

> The benefited proprietors have to persuade us that it is reasonable to renew the burden. Onus is often not of great importance, and may not in the end of the day be important in this case, but it does mean that to the extent that questions about the original purpose, and the history of the operation, of the burden arise, there is at least an initial onus on the benefited proprietors to shed light on the matter. It seems consistent with the general scheme of the legislation that while older burdens may well be shown to have continuing current usefulness making it reasonable to renew them, if there is some obscurity about their original purpose and their operation over the years, the task of upholding them might be harder.

The case concerned an end-terraced house in the Edinburgh New Town, 10 Forth Street. Built originally as a single dwelling, the house had been the subject of multiple occupation, virtually room-by-room, in the 1960s and 1970s, after which it was divided into four flats. The property was burdened by conditions contained in an instrument of sasine of 1838 which followed a grant in feu. The owner of the basement flat, which included the substantial rear garden, served a notice of termination in respect of one of the 1838 conditions which, among other matters, provided that the feuars 'are hereby expressly limited and restricted from erecting any buildings behind the said dwellinghouse other than the walls of enclosure'. In serving this notice, the owner had no specific building project in mind, although it seems likely that, subject to the difficulty of obtaining planning permission, he wanted ultimately to build a house. In 1838 it seems that the only person with title to enforce the burden was the feudal superior, but, following subdivision, the other owners in the building would also have had title. It was those other owners who made the present application for renewal of the condition.

In refusing the application to renew, the Tribunal was influenced by the physical and occupational changes to the building, and by the fact that there had been building in the rear gardens of some other houses in the same street (factor (a)). This was in contrast to the position in *Brown v Richardson* (para 44). Further, while the applicants, certainly, gained some benefit from the burden (factor (b)), it should be borne in mind that they were also protected by planning law which, in the present case, would restrict, possibly severely, what could be built in the rear garden. As in previous cases of this kind, the Tribunal pointed out, by reference to factor (f), that the condition was in any event designed to benefit the superior and not the applicants, who were owners of properties which, in 1838, did not exist as separate units; but the Tribunal then repeated its recent practice of balancing this consideration with 'the evident statutory intention within the Act of giving the benefit of burdens previously enforceable by superiors to co-proprietors who usually have much better claims of legitimate interest' (para 43). See *Conveyancing 2007* p 92.

As to factor (c), the Tribunal considered that the need to get others' permission for building work was 'of some weight' (para 38). Interestingly, the absence of a particular proposal was not thought to reduce the force of this factor, as it had in *Hamilton v Robertson* 2008 SLT (Lands Tr) 25 (*Conveyancing 2007* Case (16)).

Finally, the Tribunal was influenced by the length of time since the condition had been imposed (factor (e)) (para 39):

> Despite the 'Sunset Rule', the fact that the burden is over 100 years old does not, apart from the change of onus, necessarily add to the applicants' task. Consideration of the purpose of the burden, along with the extent of change, is more important. In this case, we do consider that the lapse of 170 years adds at least a little, in a general way, to consideration of these factors. This burden was entered into in very different times. An impression which the applicants have been unable to dispel is that for a very long time it has had no real life.

Expenses were awarded against the applicants, but reduced by 25% in acknowledgement of the fact that the novelty of the case – the first application for renewal where no specific project was in contemplation – had necessitated an oral hearing (the applicants had sought to have the case decided on the basis of written submissions) and the employment of counsel by the respondent. The Tribunal added that, since this was the applicants' and not the respondent's case, it was less easy to argue for further modification of expenses on the basis of deficiencies in the way in which the case was pled.

(26) Jensen v Tyler
2008 SLT (Lands Tr) 39 (merits), 2008 GWD 25-393 (expenses)

So far, applications under the Title Conditions (Scotland) Act 2003 for variation of servitudes have been mostly for the re-routing of servitudes of way. All have succeeded: see the tables in Part V of this volume. This case is no exception.

In 1995 the then owners of the farm and lands of Mains and Mill of Rainnieston and Cairnhill Moss Croft in Udny, Ellon granted a feu of the farmhouse. Access was by a private road running through the farm, and the feu disposition included the grant of a servitude of way. The present application was by the current farm owner, who wished to vary the route away from the existing farm steading. His plan was to develop the steading as residential units, though he had not yet applied for planning permission. The application was opposed by the owners of the farmhouse.

The Tribunal granted the application without hesitation. On the one hand, the proposed variation would not result in any significant benefit being lost by the owners of the farmhouse (factor (b)); on the other, the existing route of the servitude substantially impeded enjoyment of the farm (factor (c)). In granting the application the Tribunal rejected the argument by the farmhouse owners (i) that an express maintenance obligation should be imposed on the applicant, and (ii) that they should have exclusive access over the re-routed section (in fact it would in practice be mainly for their use).

Since the split-off in 1995 the farmhouse had been augmented by a small additional area of land. Strictly, this was not part of the benefited property in the servitude, but it was now agreed between the parties that it should have this status. The Tribunal took the view that it could not give effect to this agreement, on the basis that its declaratory jurisdiction under s 90(1)(a)(ii) of the Act was only available in respect of real burdens. But this seems to overlook s 90(5)(a), which permits the addition of a new benefited property provided that this is agreed to by the burdened proprietor.

Expenses were awarded to the applicants from the date of the respondents' representations up to the site inspection but not for the subsequent proceedings. This was because of the 'sloppiness' of the applicant's approach in failing to inform either the Tribunal or the respondents, until the site inspection, that he had altered the proposed new route.

(27) Hooper v Sinclair
11 September 2008, Lands Tribunal

Originally, the tenement at 16 Queen Street/28 High Street, Lossiemouth, comprised a shop and a flat above the shop, both in the same ownership. When the shop was sold separately, in 1950, one of the real burdens imposed was that 'the subjects hereby disponed shall not be used, let or suffered to be used by my said disponees or his foresaids for the business of cooking and/or retailing fried fish and/or chips'. Since 2003, however, the shop had been used as a café/bistro, and a deep fat fryer and extractor unit had been installed following the granting of planning permission, without objection from the upper proprietor. The present application sought to regularise matters by varying the burden by deleting the reference to 'chips'. It was opposed by the upper owner. The application was disposed of on the basis of written submissions.

The Tribunal accepted the value to the upper proprietor in maintaining a prohibition against use as a fish-and-chip shop (factor (b)). But the limited nature of the burden should be acknowledged. It did not, for example, prevent use of the premises as a café (the current use) or as eg a pub. And in making what was a legitimate use of the premises, the applicants would have their business impeded if they were prohibited from frying chips 'on a modest basis' (para 14) (factor (c)). Further, modern techniques of ventilation and extraction rendered 'at least a small fryer very much more tolerable than might have been anticipated in 1950'. Accordingly, the Tribunal was willing to grant the application, but only to the extent of the current, modest use, ie by use of a deep fat fryer not exceeding an oil capacity of 30 litres accompanied by a metal flue which was fully compliant with environmental regulatory requirements.

This result seems a sensible compromise, although one wonders whether the reference to 'environmental regulatory requirements' is sufficiently specific to qualify as a real burden (on which see Title Conditions (Scotland) Act 2003 s 4(2) (a)).

(28) Ballantyne Property Services Trs v Lawrence
31 October 2008, Lands Tribunal

This is the first case in which the Tribunal has been asked to vary a one-family-only burden in a housing estate in order to allow multiple occupancy. The application was refused. See **Commentary** p 96. Along the way the Tribunal offered some general comments on how purpose (factor (f)) is to be determined (para 23):

> There is ... a distinction between the meaning and effect of the condition on the one hand, and its purpose on the other. A condition may be clear (and indeed it would not meet the test of validity if it were not), but that does not tell us its purpose. The purpose is often not expressed, particularly in older deeds where no requirement to do so would be perceived by the drafter. It can, however, often be discerned without much difficulty.

To which it may be added that, except perhaps where the Tribunal resorts to guesswork, any purpose so discerned may well be anodyne and of relatively little assistance. See *Conveyancing 2007* p 91.

(29) Dalby v Bracken
13 June 2008, Lands Tribunal

The applicants owned the upper flat at 30 Dungoyne Street, Glasgow and the respondent the lower flat. As part of converting the roof space into bedrooms, the applicants wished to put windows into the roof. But in terms of the titles the roof was the common property of the owners of the lower and upper flats. In this application the applicants sought the discharge of the respondent's right of common property. The application was refused. As the Tribunal pointed out, its jurisdiction is confined to the variation and discharge of title conditions, and a right of ownership is not a title condition.

(30) Hamilton v Robertson
14 May 2008, Lands Tribunal

An application to the Tribunal having been refused (see 2008 SLT (Lands Tr) 25; *Conveyancing 2007* Case (16)), one of the respondents, who was not legally represented, claimed expenses in respect of his work in preparing the case (which was disposed of by written submissions). In addition to the statutory fee for lodging representations (£25), which was not in dispute, he claimed for 10 hours' preparation (although he said he had done much more) at £50 an hour, ie £500. The Tribunal confirmed that it was entitled to award expenses to party litigants (Litigants in Person (Costs and Expenses) Act 1975), and awarded the respondent £360, based on 12 hours at £30 an hour.

(31) Anderson v McKinnon
20 August 2008, Lands Tribunal

The applicants had previously succeeded on the merits: see 2007 GWD 29-513 (*Conveyancing 2007* Case (12)). Expenses were now awarded but reduced by one quarter in recognition of the fact that the applicants conceded an alteration to their proposed building in the course of the hearing. On the other hand, the Tribunal was not willing to order a reduction because of the 19-month delay in applying for expenses (which was due to a different litigation continuing between the parties) or because the application succeeded only to the extent of the variation necessary to allow the building (because it could not be said that this caused any additional expense as, from the start, the argument focused on the particular building).

(32) Gallacher v Wood
2008 GWD 13-242, Lands Tribunal

The applicants had previously succeeded on the merits: see 2007 GWD 13-647 (*Conveyancing 2007* Case (15)). In awarding expenses, the Tribunal deducted one quarter to reflect the fact that the applicants had abandoned at very short notice their cases on the enforceability of the burdens and on complete discharge.

(33) Lawrie v Mashford
2008 GWD 16-289, Lands Tribunal

The applicants had previously succeeded on the merits: see 2008 GWD 7-129 (*Conveyancing 2007* Case (16)). Expenses were now awarded to the applicants, restricted to 80% because the respondents had been successful on one point (the imposition of certain conditions).

(34) Kirkwood v Thomson
24 April 2008, Lands Tribunal

The applicants sought the complete discharge of burdens, and also indicated what it was they were likely to seek to build. In response to the respondents' objections, the applicants gave notice that they might in fact seek to build something different. Shortly afterwards the respondents dropped their opposition, and the discharge was duly granted. The Tribunal refused to award expenses on the basis that (i) the period of opposition was brief, (ii) it had elicited a possible change in plans, and (iii) the applicants had failed to consult prior to making the application.

(35) Nott v Teasdale
13 October 2008, Lands Tribunal

An application for a ruling as to real burdens under s 90(1)(a)(ii) of the Title Conditions (Scotland) Act 2003 was withdrawn. The respondents sought expenses including the expenses of employing junior counsel. There was no dispute that expenses were due but the applicants challenged the use of counsel. The Tribunal responded as follows (para 3):

> The Tribunal accepts that much of the pleadings in this case related to what can properly be referred to as standard issues in relation to discharge or variation of title conditions. It is not our normal practice to sanction the employment of counsel in that type of case. What the applicants' position ignores, however, is that this was not an application for discharge or variation of a title condition. It was in fact an application for a determination as to the continuing validity and/or enforceability of a feuing condition. Following the abolition of feudal superiorities, that raised questions about the interpretation and application of provisions of the Act of 2003. These provisions, in particular section 53, are not easy to apply and there have, to date, been only a small number of cases addressing them. In these circumstances, while it may be hoped that the law will become clearer in time, we accept that the law is presently far from clear.

Hence the use of counsel was sanctioned.

(36) Sheltered Housing Management Ltd v Jack
[2008] CSIH 58, 2008 SLT 1058, 2008 Hous LR 85

This concerned the question of whether an appeal against two related decisions of the Lands Tribunal – for which see 2007 GWD 32-533 (*Conveyancing 2006* Case (35)) and decision of 11 October 2007 (*Conveyancing 2007* Case (21)) – was out of time. Under r 41.20(1)(b) of the Rules of the Court of Session 1994 an appeal must be brought within 42 days after intimation of the decision in question. Although the present appeal was brought within 42 days of the Tribunal's final order, it was not within 42 days of the two Tribunal opinions. **Held**: That the order could be regarded as including the reasons given in the opinions, and that the appeal had accordingly been made in time.

PUBLIC RIGHTS OF WAY AND ACCESS RIGHTS

(37) Hamilton v Dumfries and Galloway Council
[2008] CSOH 65, 2008 SLT 531

This is the latest decision in a long-running battle between the owner of a short stretch of road on the one hand and Dumfries and Galloway Council on the other. At one time public, the road was the subject of a stopping up order in 1983 and was finally removed from the list of public roads in 1989. It remained physically passable, however, and from 1999 onwards was used as the only access to a new 14-house residential development known as Townhead Park. When the owner sought to charge for use of the road, the Council searched for a solution which would allow access without payment of money. One possibility would have been compulsory purchase of the road, but that could not be done without compensation. Instead the Council re-adopted the road, thus returning it to the list of public roads. The precise thinking involved is not clear, but the view may have been taken – although it is not supported by the legislation – that if a road was 'public' in the sense of being adopted, then it became a road to which the public had a right of access.

The owner sought judicial review of the Council's decision. His initial line of attack was to focus on the definition of 'road' in s 151(1) of the Roads (Scotland) Act 1984. Naturally, the Council's powers under the Act, including the power to adopt, are limited to 'roads', and a 'road' is defined as 'any way (other than a waterway) over which there is a public right of passage'. Although central to the definition, and therefore to the Act as a whole, 'public right of passage' is a term of considerable obscurity and uncertainty. Its use in the Act would suggest that it was well-established – a term of art long familiar to the common law. Yet it is virtually unknown to the common law and has not previously appeared in statute. The courts now have the unenviable task of giving it some meaning.

It was initially argued for the owner of the road that, by analogy with public rights of way, a public right of passage required to be constituted by public use for 20 years. Since there had been no such use, there was no public right of passage. Consequently, the road was not a 'road' within the Act, and could not be adopted by the Council. This argument was rejected by Lord Kingarth back in 2006: see [2006] CSOH 110 (*Conveyancing 2006* Case (37)).

The owner's next argument was more successful. Under s 16 of the 1984 Act an application for adoption must be made by either a majority of frontagers or such number of frontagers as together own land which includes not less than half of the boundary fronting or abutting the road. In the present case, the application only complied with this definition if the frontagers included the owners of two houses which were adjacent to the road. These houses, however, were separated from the road by a pavement built by the original developer of the housing estate. The pavement was not in fact conveyed to the developer, and thus could not thereafter have been conveyed by the developer to the house buyers. However, the descriptions in the various deeds were capable of including the pavement, thus opening the way to the possibility of prescriptive acquisition. The disposition in favour of the developer, dated 13 and 15 May 1995, was recorded in the Register of Sasines on 2 June 1995, and on the day on which the road was adopted (26 May 2005), the period from the date of recording was fatally short – by one week – from the 10 years required for positive prescription. The court accepted that, for this reason, the adoption was flawed and fell to be reduced: see [2007] CSOH 96, 2007 GWD 20-347 affd [2007] CSIH 75, 2007 GWD 34-582 (*Conveyancing 2007* Case (22)).

By the time that this decision was reached, prescription of course had long since run, so that it would be possible for the Council to embark once again on the process of adoption. Before it could do so, however, the owner of the road wrote, through his solicitors, to the owners of the individual houses in the Townhead Park estate. The letter included the following passage:

> We are therefore writing to confirm that with immediate effect you should consider yourselves prohibited from using that area of road which was the subject of the previous purported adoption order, without Mr Hamilton's express permission. For the avoidance of doubt our client will be happy to grant such permission when met by your written intimation of a willingness to negotiate terms.

The thinking behind this letter appears to have been something like the following. (i) For as long as the road was still on the list of public roads, the right of the public to use the road could not be challenged. (ii) But the listing had now been reduced, and the public right lost. (iii) It was true that, as previously found by Lord Kingarth, the road was still subject to the 'public right of passage' which was sufficient for it to qualify as a 'road' under the 1984 Act. But there were indications both in Lord Kingarth's judgment and in previous cases that such a public right depended, or might depend, on the permission of the owner, and permission so given could always be withdrawn. (iv) The purpose of the letter was to make clear that there was now no permission to use the road. (v) Absent such permission, the road ceased to be subject to a public right of passage. Therefore it ceased to be a 'road' under the 1984 Act and could not be adopted of new by the Council.

The latest phase of the litigation involves the testing of this argument. The owner sought declarator that the road was not now a 'road' within the 1984 Act. This was because any public right of passage had ceased to exist following the sending of the letters to the owners of the houses.

From the petitioner's point of view, Lady Smith's opinion began unpromisingly (para 1): 'The petitioner's sole interest in this stretch of road is to seek to exploit it for financial gain; he sees it as a "ransom strip".' Lady Smith's starting point was the proposition that the road was a 'road' within the Act, ie was subject to a public right of passage, at the time when it was removed from the list of public roads. In her opinion, nothing had happened since to change its status. It was improbable that a public right of passage was extinguished either by de-listing or by the issue of a stopping up order (except where there was a physical stopping up of the road, which had not occurred in the present case). But even if this was incorrect, the fact was that, since de-listing and stopping up, the road had in fact been used by members of the public for a period of 18 years, and the volume of use was such as to indicate possession as of right. In the result, a public right of passage had been established, and such a public right could not be defeated by an owner's withdrawal of permission. In Lady Smith's words (para 46):

> If the prescriptive period has passed and passage has been exercised along an identifiable way between two public places, then it is too late for him [ie the owner] to prevent a public right of way being established. Similarly, if such a level of user has been arrived at over an identified way (which need not pass between two public places) at any point even if short of the prescriptive period, it will be too late for the owner to prevent a public right of passage having come into existence. Once that has occurred, the public right of passage can only be destroyed by a road authority in exercise of its statutory power to stop up the road.

Two aspects of this view are potentially contentious. First, it is unclear what rules govern the creation of public rights of passage except that they are less rigorous than those for public rights of way. The public, it seems, must use the road as of right and not merely by tolerance. But for how long? For 15 years or 10 or 5? Or will three months be enough? Secondly, if, as Lady Smith asserts, a public right of passage cannot be withdrawn by the owner of the road, it would follow that it is every bit as powerful as a public right of way. But in that case what is the point of public rights of way? And why have there been so many closely fought litigations seeking to establish public rights of way when the public could have won an easy but no less useful victory by showing the existence of a public right of passage? There is much here which does not make sense.

This decision has now been reversed: see [2009] CSIH 13. The appellate decision will be discussed in next year's volume.

(38) Snowie v Stirling Council
2008 SLT (Sh Ct) 61, 2008 Hous LR 46 (merits), 2008 GWD 27-427 (expenses)

The owners of a 70-acre estate sought a declaration that the whole estate was exempt from statutory access rights by virtue of the privacy exemption (Land Reform (Scotland) Act 2003 s 6(1)(b)(iv)). **Held**: That only the 12.6 acres nearest the house were so exempt. See **Commentary** p 113.

(39) Ross v Stirling Council
23 April 2008, Stirling Sheriff Court

This application for a declaration in respect of the privacy exemption concerned a small part of the same estate as in the previous case, but separately owned, and was heard at the same time. The sheriff's opinion in both cases is substantially identical.

The pursuers owned the West Lodge on the western edge of the estate. The Lodge's garden was bisected by a driveway which formed a principal access to the estate. The pursuers, presumably taking for granted that their garden fell under the privacy exemption, sought a declaration only in respect of the relevant stretch of driveway. It was refused. On a practical level it is easy to see why, for if even a small stretch was exempt, this would have the effect of preventing any public use of the driveway. Yet the driveway was close to the Lodge, and its use would plainly interfere with both privacy and enjoyment. The sheriff does not engage with these issues.

WARRANDICE

(40) MacPherson v Williams
[2008] CSOH 25, 2008 GWD 6-110

A year or so after moving in, the buyers of a house found that it was subject to a servitude of way in favour of a neighbour. The servitude had been registered, but only against the title of the dominant tenement. The buyers sued for damages for breach of missives, or alternatively for breach of the warrandice clause in the disposition. Although their pleadings were rather indistinct, they appeared to be seeking either (i) the cost of cure (which in this case involved an element of betterment as they had bought the dominant tenement), or (ii), what was averred to be a larger sum, the diminution in value resulting from the servitude. The sellers accepted that there was a breach of warrandice, but disputed the relevance of the sums sued for.

In allowing a proof before answer the temporary judge (C J MacAulay QC) made a number of general points. (i) Following on from *Welsh v Russell* (1894) 21 R 769 and *Palmer v Beck* 1993 SLT 485 (para 27):

> The purpose of an award of damages for a breach of warrandice is indemnification. If the purchaser, as a result of the defect in title, is totally evicted then the measure of damages is the market value of the property as at the date of eviction. On the other hand if the defect in title does not result in total eviction then the general rule is that the purchaser's loss is assessed by reference to the diminution in value of the property.

(ii) If the pursuers in fact cure the defect, and the cost of cure is less, then that is the correct measure of damages. 'The purchaser who manages to cure a title defect at a cost less than the loss ascertained by calculating the diminution in value with the title defect in place is mitigating his loss' (para 29).

(iii) 'The appropriate date for making such an assessment of the diminution in value is the date when the threat of eviction arises – in *Palmer v Beck* that occurred when the disposition was delivered' (para 28).

(iv) The pursuers sought additional damages for anxiety and distress and also for inconvenience. These two heads are not the same thing: *Mack v Glasgow City Council* 2006 SLT 556. Inconvenience is a standard head of damages. Anxiety and distress, however – sometimes unhelpfully known as 'solatium' – are relevant only if associated with averments of physical or psychiatric injury. In the absence of such averments in the present case, they cannot be admitted to probation.

The issue raised at (iii) is not straightforward. A claim in warrandice for absence of title is admissible only where there has been eviction. In such a case it is therefore correct that loss should be quantified as at the date of eviction. But where, as in the present case, the title is good and the claim relates merely to an unexpected encumbrance, eviction is not required. The mere existence of the encumbrance is enough to trigger a claim. (Unhelpfully, this is sometimes referred to as 'partial' eviction: see K G C Reid, *The Law of Property in Scotland* (1996) para 707 n 17.) So a claim arises as soon as warrandice is granted – that is to say, on delivery of the disposition. It seems to follow that loss should be quantified on that day also.

LAND REGISTRATION

Full opinions in some Lands Tribunal cases are available at http://www.lands-tribunal-scotland.org.uk/records.html.

(41) Turnberry Homes Ltd v Keeper of the Registers of Scotland
11 June 2008, Lands Tribunal

Problems arising from common areas in a housing development: see **Commentary** p 149.

(42) PMP Plus Ltd v Keeper of the Registers of Scotland
2009 SLT (Lands Tr) 2

Problems arising from common areas in a housing development. See **Commentary** p 133.

(43) McCoach v Keeper of the Registers of Scotland
19 December 2008, Lands Tribunal

On a first registration, more was registered to the buyers than the seller owned. The Keeper rectified despite the fact that the buyers were proprietors in possession. Was the Keeper entitled to do so? See **Commentary** p 121.

(44) Brown v Stewart
[2008] CSOH 155, 2008 GWD 39-581

Mr Stewart was the co-owner, with his wife, of a house in Kinglassie, Fife. He received intimation from Mr Brown of a claim for damages for injury caused by an alleged assault (ie an assault by Mr Stewart on Mr Brown). Following that intimation, Mr Stewart disponed his half share to his wife, for no consideration. Mrs Stewart was registered without exclusion of indemnity. Mr Brown subsequently raised the action and was awarded damages against Mr Stewart in the sum of £32,433. Mr Stewart did not pay, and not long after the decree he was sequestrated. In this action Mr Brown sought reduction of the disposition as a gratuitous alienation. Apart from Mr Stewart himself, Mrs Stewart and also Mr Stewart's trustee in sequestration were called as defenders. Since Mrs Stewart was presumably a proprietor in possession she presumptively had a defence under s 9(3) of the Land Registration (Scotland) Act 1979, but she failed to lodge proper defences and as a result decree in favour of the pursuer was granted.

Ever since the decision of the House of Lords in *Short's Tr v Keeper of the Registers of Scotland* 1996 SC (HL) 14 it has been established that, where there has been a gratuitous alienation and the property is in the Land Register, reduction will not normally lead to a rectification of the Register. The form of action in the present case is therefore a little surprising. However, we understand that the pursuer's pleadings (condescendence VI) averred that the second defender had been 'complicit in a fraud against the pursuer'. Whether the court would have upheld this can only be a matter of speculation.

The third conclusion was:

> For an order ordaining the Keeper of The Registers of Scotland to rectify the inaccuracies in the Land Register for the County of Fife in respect of the Subjects (FFE64534) arising from and following decree of reduction as first concluded for by deleting in its entirety the entry in the proprietorship section and substituting 'JAMES WEST STEWART and MARGARET STEWART, both 27 West End, Kinglassie, equally between them' therefor.

Inexplicably, the Keeper was not called as a defender. Obviously an order against someone who is not a party to an action is incompetent. However, we understand that the error was put right by amendment, with the Keeper being eventually convened as fourth defender. Despite decree being granted in favour the pursuer, at the time of writing the title sheet for FFE 64534 continues to show Mrs Stewart as sole proprietor.

RIGHT-TO-BUY LEGISLATION

Full opinions in some Lands Tribunal cases are available at http://www.lands-tribunal-scotland.org.uk/records.html.

(45) Lewis v South Lanarkshire Council
2008 GWD 9-169, Lands Tribunal

Right-to-buy missives were concluded. When the Council produced the proposed deed plan, the tenant/buyer alleged that too little garden ground had been included, and he refused to settle the transaction, whereupon the Council rescinded. The tenant then applied to the Lands Tribunal under s 71(2)(b) of the Housing (Scotland) Act 1987 on the ground that the Council had failed to make a proper offer to sell. The Tribunal **held** that, missives having been concluded, it had no jurisdiction. The ordinary courts now had jurisdiction. The Tribunal added that, in any case, it would have held against the tenant on the merits of the case.

(46) Robb v Tayside Police Board
2009 SLT (Lands Tr) 23

A retired policeman applied to buy his property which was rented from the police authority. The question was whether the special provision in Sch 2 para 7(a)(i) of the Housing (Scotland) Act 1987 about police tenants had the effect of excluding the right to buy. **Held**: that that provision was not applicable to the facts of the case and that accordingly there was a right to buy.

(47) Methven v Lothian and Borders Fire and Rescue Board
2008 GWD 9-169, Lands Tribunal

Schedule 1 para 9 of the Housing (Scotland) Act 2001 provides:

> A tenancy is not a Scottish secure tenancy if the house forms part of, or is within the curtilage of, a building which –
> (a) is held by the landlord mainly for purposes other than the provision of housing accommodation; and
> (b) mainly consists of accommodation other than housing accommodation.

A tenant applied to buy a property which had been built as part of a fire station at Marionville Drive, Edinburgh. **Held**: that the property was not a Scottish secure tenancy and so did not fall within the right to buy provisions.

(48) Rizza v Glasgow Housing Association
2008 SLT (Lands Tr) 13, 2008 Hous LR 54

Margaret Rizza, tenant of a house at Mosspark Drive, Glasgow, applied to the Tribunal for a finding in terms of s 71(2)(b) of the Housing (Scotland) Act 1987 that the landlords had served an offer to sell which was disconform to the requirements of the Act. The nub of the issue was whether she could bring into account the years in which her husband had been a tenant of another public sector landlord, ie whether she had a 'preserved' right to buy. It was held that the housing association had calculated the discount correctly.

(49) McLaughlin v Thenew Housing Association Ltd
2008 SLT (Sh Ct) 137

A public-sector tenant exercised her right to buy. The landlord made an offer at a figure of £21,000. Missives were concluded. At that point the landlord realised that it had made a mistake in applying the rules for calculating discount. The property should have been offered at a figure of £49,000. In this action by the tenant to enforce the missives it was **held** that the error had rendered the missives void. The decision of the sheriff, reported at 2007 Hous LR 18 (*Conveyancing 2007* Case (33)), was upheld.

LEASES

(50) Possfund Custodial Trustee Ltd v Kwik-Fit Properties Ltd
[2008] CSOH 79, revd [2008] CSIH 65, 2009 SLT 133, 2008 Hous LR 82

The landlord of commercial premises wished to send in contractors to carry out intensive investigations for the purpose of ascertaining whether fuel kept on site had caused contamination. The tenant refused access. Was it entitled to do so? See **Commentary** p 97.

(51) Tawne Overseas Holdings Ltd v The firm of Newmiln Farms
[2008] CSOH 12, 2008 Hous LR 18

A landlord raised an action of declarator of irritancy and removing and also an action to recover unpaid rent. The tenants were successful. See **Commentary** p 98.

(52) Primary Health Care Centres (Broadford) Ltd v Ravangave
[2008] CSOH 14, 2008 Hous LR 24

Leases to partnerships often give rise to difficulties. In this case the Medical Centre in Broadford, Skye was owned by Dr Humphreys. In 2000 he granted a 99-year lease to the pursuer and at the same time the pursuer granted a 33-year sub-lease to the medical partnership, which at that time consisted of Drs Humphrey and Ravangave. Later Dr Turville was assumed as a salaried partner. Thereafter the Medical Centre was taken over by the Highland Health Board, the three doctors became salaried employees, and the Board took over payment of rent to the pursuer. Later still Dr Humphreys retired and was granted a discharge by the pursuer. Thereafter Dr Ravangave left. By that stage the partnership had clearly been dissolved. The present action was not for payment of rent, or for irritancy, but simply for declarator that Drs Ravangave and Turville continued to be liable for the rent. Dr Ravangave was not involved in this particular phase of the litigation. Dr Turville's main argument was that, although there had never been a formal assignation to Highland Health Board, *de facto* the lease had been taken over by the Board. It was **held** that the lease had not been taken over by the Board, but that nevertheless Dr Turville had no ongoing liability for the rent. Where that leaves Dr Ravangave is unclear. If he is not liable either, then seemingly nobody is liable for the rent. If so, one wonders where that leaves the lease.

(53) Wolanski & Co Trustees Ltd v First Quench Retailing Ltd
[2008] CSOH 50, 2008 GWD 16-283

These parties have been in dispute a long time: for an earlier case see *Wolanski & Co Trustees Ltd v First Quench Retailing Ltd* 2004 GWD 33-678 (*Conveyancing 2004* Case (36)).

The pursuer owned premises in Glasgow's Renfield Street. It was leased in 1986, the ish being in 2010. In 1999 the tenant (the defender) sublet to Big Mammy K Ltd. In 2001 Big Mammy K Ltd assigned the sub-lease to Soulband Ltd. When Soulband Ltd went into liquidation in 2004 the premises were occupied by Soulband Ltd's guarantors, Degreefresh Ltd, in terms of the step-in provisions of the assignation. (This is only a partial account of what was a tangled tale.)

In the present action (para 3):

> The pursuer seeks declarator that the defender is tenant of the premises that are the subject of the lease. Secondly, declarator is sought that the defender is bound to use and occupy the premises until 31 July 2010 or until the lease is lawfully terminated or assigned. Thirdly, the pursuer seeks declarator as to the amount of rent from 1 August 2001 onwards, decree ordaining the defender to execute a minute of agreement recording that rent, and payment of arrears of rent.

The defender pled that the pursuer was in material breach, so that the defender was entitled to rescind the contract of lease. A central issue was whether or not the pursuer had consented to Degreefresh Ltd's acquisition of the sub-lease. The pursuer argued that the defender's pleadings were irrelevant. With certain qualifications it was **held** that they were relevantly pled, and also that the pursuer had indeed consented to Degreefresh Ltd's acquisition of the sub-lease.

(54) Killen v Dundee City Council
[2008] CSIH 43, 2008 SLT 739

An application was made for a multiple occupancy licence for a property in Dundee's Constitution Crescent. The application was refused. The main reason was that the area had been designated as a 'home zone' under s 74 of the Transport (Scotland) Act 2001. The owners appealed to the sheriff. They were unsuccessful. They appealed again, to the Inner House. They were successful. The 'home zone' designation was a traffic control matter and so the committee had erred in law in basing their decision on it. For discussion see Adrian Stalker, 'Houses in multiple occupancy' 2008 SCOLAG 260. This is not the first time that a refusal of an HMO licence has been successfully appealed. See *Valente v Fife Council* 2006 GWD 38-752 (*Conveyancing 2006* Case (72)).

(55) Holland House Property Investments Ltd v Crabbe
[2008] CSIH 40, 2008 SLT 777, 2008 SCLR 633

This was a dispute about a rent review for a property in Bath Street in Glasgow. The lease provided for a review every five years. The parties not agreeing on a new rental level, a surveyor was appointed to determine the appropriate new rent. The surveyor set the rent and, when the tenants failed to pay, the landlord sued. The tenant's defence was that the surveyor was acting as an arbiter and, in so acting, had been in breach of the principles of natural justice. This argument failed before the sheriff. The tenants appealed to the sheriff principal but failed again. The tenants now appealed to the Inner House where the argument once more failed. It was **held** that the surveyor was acting not as an arbiter but as an expert.

(56) Style Menswear Ltd Ptr
[2008] CSOH 149, 2008 Hous LR 66

Style Menswear Ltd was the tenant of a retail unit in the St Enoch Centre in Glasgow. The landlord was St Enoch Trustee Company Ltd. The annual rent was £169,141. When arrears developed the landlord sought to execute summary diligence. The tenant responded with this action of suspension and interdict. The tenant did not deny the arrears but argued that it was entitle to retain rent because of breach of contract by the landlord. What had happened was that the landlord had been carrying out works in the St Enoch Centre which, pled the tenant, had obstructed access to its unit and hence reduced turnover. Since these works had not been to the unit itself, the difficulty was in showing that these works amounted to a breach of the contract of lease. **Held**: (following *Huber v Ross* 1912 SC 898) that a landlord who carries out works to neighbouring property is liable only for physical damage to the subjects let, and that there was nothing in the lease to extend the scope of that common law duty. The lease had a clause whereby it was the landlord's obligation that the tenant 'shall and may peaceably and quietly possess and enjoy the Property'. The tenant argued that since the original landlord and tenant were both English, this clause fell to be construed according to English law. This argument failed. A weak argument at best, it was further weakened by the provision that 'the Lease shall be interpreted in accordance with the Law of Scotland'.

(57) Cathay Loon Fung Ltd v Purewal Enterprises Ltd
[2008] CSOH 129, 2008 SLT 1111, 2008 Hous LR 71

The pursuer had a lease of a restaurant in Sauchiehall Street, Glasgow. On 20 May 2008 the landlord, the defender, served a pre-irritancy notice for alleged rent arrears. The pursuer responded by raising an action for declarator that the notice was invalid and for interim interdict. Interim interdict was granted in these terms: 'Ad interim interdicts the defenders ... from performing any act which interferes with the pursuers' right to use and occupy the premises....'

On 1 July 2008 the defender's agents served an irritancy notice. The question at this particular point in the dispute was whether the service of this notice was a breach of the interim interdict. The position was complicated by the fact that the landlord was also seeking the winding up of the tenant and at one stage, at least, an interim liquidator was in office, but this complication – as to which see

[2008] CSOH 127 and [2008] CSOH 130 – can be ignored for present purposes. The Lord Ordinary (Glennie) held that the service of the irritancy notice was a breach of the interim interdict, but for reasons which do not seem to us entirely convincing.

(58) Gardner v Curran
2008 SLT (Sh Ct) 105

This was a crofting case, but may be of more general significance. A man held a croft. When he died his will left certain legacies, not including the croft, and the residue to his widow. The landlord argued that this was not a legacy of the croft for the purposes of s 10 of the Crofters (Scotland) Act 1993: such a legacy had to be specific. **Held** that there had been a valid legacy of the croft to the widow.

For a discussion, see an article by Hilary Hiram published at (2009) 13 *Edinburgh Law Review* 143.

(59) Trygort (No 2) Ltd v UK Home Finance Ltd
[2008] CSIH 56, 2008 SLT 1065, 2008 Hous LR 62

A lease of property in West George Street, Glasgow, had a break option:

> Declaring … (One) it shall be competent to determine These Presents as follows, namely (i) at the sole option of the Tenant on 31st March 2005 upon the Tenant providing not less than 3 months prior written notice to that effect to the Landlord time being of the essence and (ii) at the option of either or both of the Landlord or the Tenant at any date subsequent to 31st March 2005 on the party so determining providing the other party with not less than six months prior written notice to that effect to be issued on or any date subsequent to 1st October 2004 time being of the essence and (Two) the Tenant shall not be entitled to issue any notice determining These Presents in terms of this Clause 2 if the Tenant has been in breach of its obligations to the Landlord in terms of These Presents.

The tenant exercised the option and removed. The landlord raised an action of declarator that the lease was still in force. The landlord founded on the second part of the clause, arguing that the tenant had been late in making certain payments including rent. Admittedly, at the time when the tenant exercised the option, all payments were up to date, but the landlord argued that the second part of the clause meant that *any* breach resulted in the break option being forfeited. The tenant argued that all that the provision meant was that the tenant could not exercise the break option at a time when it was in default, and that since it had not been in default at the relevant time, the exercise of the option had been valid.

Held (affirming the decision of the sheriff): that the provision could be read either way and that accordingly the court should adopt the 'commercially sensible construction' (para 10) which was the construction advanced by the tenant.

(60) Wright v Shoreline Management Ltd
October 2008, Arbroath Sheriff Court

Section 20 of the Land Registration (Scotland) Act 1979 says that tenants-at-will have the right to buy their property at a discount of 96% below market value. Given that incentive, it seems likely that all have been purchased by now. Though cases continue to be brought, they all seem to fail, as did this one. See David Cabrelli, 'Tenancies-at-will: *Allen v McTaggart*' (2007) 11 *Edinburgh Law Review* 436.

This action concerned a property in Angus, which was not a promising start, since it appears that the courts have never recognised a tenancy-at-will outwith the counties of Aberdeenshire, Banffshire, Lanarkshire, Ross-shire and Sutherland. It also got off to a bad start in being raised in the sheriff court, for it was held that the sheriff court has no jurisdiction concerning tenancies-at-will. It was also held that, even if the court had had jurisdiction, this tenancy could not have been a tenancy-at-will, for a hallmark of such tenancies is fixed rent – *Allen v McTaggart* 2007 SC 482 (*Conveyancing 2007* Case (40)) – and it was a matter of concession that here the rent had varied over time. The sheriff (Hendry) observed (para 14): 'the situation is more readily explained by there being a year to year lease of the ground to the tenants and that the owner of the land was free to increase the rent at the end of each year leaving the "hutter" free to accept the increase or to give up occupation'.

STANDARD SECURITIES

(61) Royal Bank of Scotland v Wilson
2008 GWD 2-35, Sh Ct

The RBS raised an action to eject the debtors in a standard security. **Held**: that the bank was not entitled to this remedy. (a) The certificate of indebtedness that it had served had contained no demand for payment and hence there had been no default. (b) The certificate had been sent to only one of the two owners. (c) The action was procedurally flawed because it should have been taken under the Heritable Securities (Scotland) Act 1894.

(62) Wilson v Dunbar Bank plc
[2008] CSIH 27, 2008 SC 457, 2008 SLT 301

Section 25 of the Conveyancing and Feudal Reform (Scotland) Act 1970 says that if a standard security holder enforces the security by sale, then 'it shall be the duty of the creditor to … take all reasonable steps to ensure that the price at which all or any of the subjects are sold is the best that can be reasonably obtained'. The pursuer had carried out a development called 'The Harriers' at Fernieside Avenue, Edinburgh, with the assistance of secured finance from the defender. The pursuer's affairs having become embarrassed, the defender enforced the security and sold the flats. The pursuer argued that the flats had not been adequately marketed and had accordingly failed to achieve a fair value. He was successful in the Outer House: [2006] CSOH 105, 2006 SLT 775, 2007 SCLR 25 (*Conveyancing 2006* Case (77)). The defender reclaimed, not on the merits, but (i) on the way the Lord Ordinary had quantified damages, and (ii) on the way he had applied interest to the damages. **Held** (i) that the Lord Ordinary's approach to quantification was sound, but (ii) that the decision about interest had been incorrect, and accordingly the Lord Ordinary's decision reversed to that extent.

(63) Prosper Properties Ltd v Bell
26 March 2008, Dumfries Sheriff Court

For an earlier phase in this dispute, see *Bell v Inkersall Investments Ltd* [2006] CSIH 16, 2006 SC 507 (*Conveyancing 2006* Case (59)).

Land in Dumfriesshire was controlled by a Mr Woodcock, some being held in his own name, some in the name of one of his companies, Inkersall Investments Ltd, and some in the name of another, Prosper Properties Ltd. Mr Woodcock and his companies on the one hand and Mr Bell on the other had a complex business relationship, with Mr Bell at times acting as their agent. He was also their tenant. When the relationship broke down the question arose as to what he was the tenant of, and what type of tenant he was. The present action was one of four actions brought against Mr Bell, two by Prosper Properties Ltd and two by Inkersall Investments Ltd. In the present action declarator was sought that an annual grazing let was at an end and that Mr Bell accordingly no longer had any right to occupy the area in question. Mr Bell counterclaimed for reduction, *ope exceptionis*, of the let and declarator that he held as an agricultural tenant. The opinion of the sheriff (Kenneth Ross) runs to about 110,000 words. After a proof, he **held** in favour of the pursuer.

(64) Henderson v Royal Bank of Scotland plc (No 2)
[2008] CSOH 146, 2008 GWD 34-518

In 1997 the pursuers borrowed £800,000 from the defender to buy the Portree Hotel in Skye. The loans were to be repaid over 15 years with interest at 10.22%. The loan contract allowed early repayment, but only on condition of payment of breakage (ie the cost to the lender of early repayment, based on interest rates at time of repayment).

In 1998 the pursuers sold another hotel, the Park Hotel in Montrose. The net free proceeds amounted to £850,000. They considered using this to pay off the Skye loan early, and contacted the defender for the breakage charge. On being told that the figure would be £240,000 they decided not to pay off early. In fact there had been a mistake: the correct figure was £66,000.

Thereafter the pursuers' financial affairs deteriorated. They considered that had they paid off the loan in 1998 their affairs would have been much better, and they quantified this loss at £502,000, and sued the bank for this sum, basing their case alternatively in delict (breach of a duty of care not to make negligent misrepresentations) and contract (breach of an implied term in the contract that information about the breakage charge would be accurate). The Lord Ordinary (Woolman) agreed that the bank had an obligation to take reasonable care when providing a figure (para 32). Nevertheless, the action was dismissed. Lord Woolman said (para 19):

> Couched in the language of duty of care, it can be said that the loss was not reasonably foreseeable. From the standpoint of causation, there was not a sufficient causal connection with the subject matter of the duty. Alternatively, it can be simply said that the loss was too remote.

Moreover the pursuers' case fell to be rejected because their account of how the bank's mis-statement had supposedly caused the loss was 'impenetrable' (para 27).

SURVIVORSHIP CLAUSES

(65) Lavery v Lavery
2008 Fam LR 46, 2008 GWD 11-205, Sh Ct

A couple signed a separation agreement. The wife then died. The question was as to the effect of these events on a survivorship destination. See **Commentary** p 116.

(66) Willson v Willson
[2008] CSOH 161, 2008 GWD 40-599

We do not normally cover cases dealing with what counts as 'matrimonial property' under divorce law, but this decision may be worth noting. After the couple married, the wife disponed a property she owned to herself and her husband and the survivor. In the divorce case, the husband argued that the fact of the survivorship destination meant that the whole property was matrimonial property within the meaning of the Family Law (Scotland) Act 1985. The Lord Ordinary (Drummond Young) held that that was not so (para 16): 'The existence of the survivorship destination in respect of the pursuer's [wife's] one half share is manifestly not sufficient to convert that share into matrimonial property.' Only the half share disponed to the husband was matrimonial property.

(67) Matthews v Hunter & Robertson Ltd
[2008] CSOH 88, 2008 SLT 634, 2008 SCLR 466

A law firm was sued for having failed to deactivate a special destination. See **Commentary** p 115.

SOLICITORS, ESTATE AGENTS AND SURVEYORS

(68) Preferred Mortgages Ltd v Shanks
[2008] CSOH 23, 2008 GWD 8-144

Three individuals bought a block of flats as a buy-to-let investment. To do this they borrowed £930,000 from the pursuer, secured by standard security. The security had to be enforced, and the block sold for only £600,000. It is unclear how much was repaid by the borrowers, whether before or after the sale, but it seems that any such amounts must have been small. The lender now sued the surveyor for having, it was averred, negligently overvalued the block (the valuation had been £1,240,000), and also the solicitor – who had acted for both the lender and the borrowers – for (a) having allegedly failed to obtain an architect's certificate in respect of the block, and (b) for having allegedly failed to ensure that there was a sufficient right of access. (The access road was required by the local authority to have a bell-mouth, but that would have meant the use of land belonging to a neighbour.) In this preliminary phase of the litigation the solicitor argued that if there was any liability, it could not be joint and several. This plea was repelled by the Lord Ordinary (Drummond Young).

(69) Realstone Ltd v J & E Shepherd
[2008] CSOH 31, 2008 GWD 7-123

The pursuer was developing a housing estate in Dalbeattie. It asked its solicitors for deed plans for particular plots and the solicitors instructed architects, Andrew Ross Ltd, to prepare them. That company in turn instructed the defenders to do the work. It was averred that one of the deed plans was defective, and that as a result the pursuer had disponed too much to the buyer of one of the plots. When it had approached that buyer for return of the excess area, the buyer had held out for, and had obtained, a high price. The pursuer now sued the defenders for compensation. The question was whether, in the absence of any direct connection between the pursuer and the defenders, there could be any basis for liability. The Lord Ordinary (Hodge) **held** that, whilst in principle there could be liability, whether there was in fact any such liability would depend on the precise details of what had happened, and accordingly proof before answer was allowed.

(70) Hay v Gourley McBain
2008 SLT (Sh Ct) 101

Hay sold land to Geddes for £915,000. It turned out that title to a part of the land was bad: this part belonged to a neighbour. Geddes claimed against Hay under the warrandice clause in the disposition. This claim was settled at £30,000. Hay in turned claimed his sum from his solicitors, the defenders. His argument was that the defenders had, before the sale to Geddes, been asked to check the title to the disputed area and had negligently failed to do so. This argument persuaded the sheriff. The defenders appealed to the sheriff principal, who allowed the appeal and dismissed the action. The negligence of the defenders had not led to any loss by the pursuer. The £30,000 payment that the pursuer had had to make to Geddes was not loss. As the sheriff principal (E F Bowen QC) says (para 11):

> What the negligence of the defenders' partner caused the pursuer to do was to sell something which was not wholly his to sell. In so doing, he was paid for more than he owned. At that point the defenders' negligence had caused no loss to the pursuer. When he settled the inevitable claim at the sum of £30,000 he was on one view doing no more than refunding part of the purchase price to reflect the fact that he had sold that which was not his to sell. Unless the sum paid was such that the pursuer ended up with less than the land originally owned was worth there was no loss.

(71) McDonald-Grant v Sutherland & Co
[2008] CSOH 150

Mr Barclay owned a house at Boat of Garten. In 1993 he disponed it gratuitously to his son, reserving to himself a liferent. At that time he had a housekeeper, whom later he married. In 1998 he died. Acting through Quantum Compensation Specialists, she sued her late husband's solicitors for £350,000. Her case was that Mr Barclay's intention had been to set up an arrangement whereby she would have the house after his death. **Held**, after proof, that the solicitors had correctly implemented the late Mr Barclay's instructions, and accordingly decree of absolvitor granted. (For an earlier stage of this litigation, see [2006] CSOH 171 (*Conveyancing 2006* Case (78).)

(72) Jackson v Hughes Dowdall
[2008] CSIH 41, 2008 SCLR 650

Mr and Mrs Jackson parted, and signed a minute of agreement. She was to dispone to him the matrimonial home 'not later than three months from the date of last signature of this agreement and furthermore subject to Mr Jackson implementing all conditions contained herein'. He was to do various things in exchange, including paying off the secured loan over that house, buying another house in her name, granting her a ten-year lease of yet another property at nominal rent, and granting a liferent of yet another property to her mother. Mrs Jackson duly disponed the matrimonial home. Mr Jackson performed some of his obligations, but not all. He then became bankrupt. Moreover, it emerged that the properties to be leased and liferented did not belong to him anyway.

Mrs Jackson now sued her solicitors for £200,000 damages for negligence. (1) She argued that they should have advised her not to grant the disposition until her husband had performed his obligations. (2) She argued that they ought to have known that Mr Jackson did not own the properties to be leased and liferented. It was **held** that internal inconsistencies in the pursuer's written pleadings meant that the action fell to be dismissed on grounds of relevancy. The appeal to the Inner House is mainly concerned with points of interest to court practitioners rather than conveyancers.

(73) Marquess of Aberdeen and Temair v Turcan Connell
[2008] CSOH 183, 2009 GWD 1-18

The pursuer was fiar of certain land (the Tarves Estate) liferented by an aunt, land that had been in the family since the Middle Ages. For tax planning reasons the fee was transferred to a discretionary trust. The beneficiaries were the pursuer's children, his sister's children and his adopted cousin's children. The trustees had to exercise their discretion by a certain date. If that did not happen, then each of the discretionary beneficiaries would obtain a vested right to an equal share upon reaching 70 years of age and, in the meantime, would have a liferent in that prospective share.

In due course the pursuer had four children. He informed (as he averred) his solicitors that 'he wanted Lord Haddo [his eldest son] to take Haddo Estate and that he wanted Tarves Estate to pass to one or more of his other children [and] ... that it should only be if none of his immediate family survived him that any of his sister's children should receive the Tarves Estate and, furthermore, on no account should any of his adopted cousin's children receive it' (para 12). The decision deadline came and went without the trustees acting. The pursuer was not pleased. According to him (para 15):

> The intentions of the pursuer in his dealings with his reversionary interest in the fee of the 1965 Trust were thereby at risk of being substantially subverted, in that on the death of June, Lady Aberdeen, the Tarves Estate and associated assets would, instead of being held for the benefit of the pursuer's children or any of them, be likely to be held equally for at least nine beneficiaries, who (or whose issue) would ultimately take the capital of the trust at age 70. This would result in the break-up of a substantial part of the ancestral landholding associated with the Gordon family for hundreds of years ... in direct contradiction to the explicitly-expressed wishes of the pursuer known to the defenders and their predecessors, Messrs Dundas & Wilson, CS, for many years.

When the problem came to light a complex scheme was set up to address the problem. This scheme allegedly resulted in significant financial loss to the pursuer and his family. The pursuer sued for £700,000 in damages, averring that the defenders had been negligent in having failed to ensure that the discretion deadline was met. The defenders sought dismissal on grounds of relevancy. Proof before answer was allowed.

JUDICIAL RECTIFICATION

(74) Moncrieff v McIntosh
8 August 2007, Forfar Sheriff Court

The sellers sought rectification of a disposition under s 8(1)(a) of the Law Reform (Miscellaneous Provisions) (Scotland) Act 1985 on the basis that – as the buyer conceded – it conveyed more land on the northern boundary than was provided for by the missives. The buyer's argument was that the missives were wrong and that the parties had previously agreed the boundary as given in the disposition.

On 8 November 2006 the sheriff granted decree. The buyer appealed, but the sheriff principal (R A Dunlop QC) has now substantially upheld the sheriff's decision.

Having reviewed the authorities, the sheriff principal concluded (para 31) that they make it clear

> that there must be an antecedent agreement which the disposition was intended to give effect to coupled with proof that that disposition failed to express the common intention of the parties embodied in that antecedent agreement. In my view it is important to emphasise that the parties' common intention must be discerned from what has been expressed in the agreement between them. It is nothing to the point that one or other party had a particular intention or indeed that the parties had a common intention if that intention has not been translated into agreement between them.

In the present case there was no agreement other than the missives (para 38):

> In my view the evidence of what passed between the appellant and the first respondent prior to solicitors being involved, while instructing an agreement in general terms, not least in relation to price, does not instruct the existence of an agreement between the parties with regard to the north boundary.

(75) Malkin v Gibson
[2008] CSIH 25, 2008 SCLR 541

This was a boundary dispute between neighbours who derived title from the same common author. The pursuers sought interdict in respect of the disputed area and decree ordaining the defender to uplift various items. The defender's counterclaim sought declarator that the disputed area belonged to him and also rectification of the split-off disposition granted to the pursuers. The present stage of the litigation involved a challenge to the relevancy of the counterclaim insofar as it related to rectification. **Held:** The counterclaim for rectification was irrelevant and should not be admitted to probation. Rectification requires averments that the deed to be rectified is inaccurate, as failing to express the parties' intentions. But, since the counterclaim for rectification was not intended as an alternative to the counterclaim for ownership, the defender's case was that the disposition was properly interpreted as giving ownership to the defender – and hence that it was accurate.

DILIGENCE

(76) Park Ptrs
2008 SLT 1026

If Tom inhibits Dick after Dick has concluded missives to sell to Harry, the inhibition does not strike at the sale. Dick can dispone to Harry and Harry's title will not be subject to the inhibition. Conversely, if the inhibition comes before the missives, then the inhibition prevails, so that if Dick dispones to Harry, Harry's title is voidable. But what happens if there is a dead heat – ie the missives and the inhibition are simultaneous? This issue is now dealt with by s 149 of the Bankruptcy and Diligence etc (Scotland) Act 2007. But the story in *Park* was under the previous law.

A long lease was held by a partnership. A creditor inhibited the partnership. The effective date of the inhibition was 31 August 2007. That was also the date when the partnership concluded missives for the sale of the lease. There was no settled rule for this situation. **Held**: that the inhibition was to be considered as having taken effect at the end of the day of registration and accordingly the missives were not subject to it.

For discussion of this case, see J MacLeod, 'Chalk dust in the law of inhibition' (2009) 13 *Edinburgh Law Review* 294.

MISCELLANEOUS

(77) Blackburn v Cowie
[2008] CSIH 30, 2008 SLT 437

William Cowie was sequestrated in 1989. He owned a house in Glasgow where he lived with his wife. In 1990 the trustee in sequestration obtained the court's authorisation, under s 40 of the Bankruptcy (Scotland) Act 1985, to sell the property. Nevertheless such a sale did not happen. In 1993 Mr and Mrs Cowie divorced. Mrs Cowie continued to live in the property. She negotiated with the trustee in sequestration to buy the property. These negotiations dragged on for many years. The original trustee, who had completed title, demitted office and was replaced by another, who raised a summary cause action to gain possession of the property. The new trustee completed title, but not until after the action was raised. The main ground of defence was that the trustee had no title to sue without having had a completed title at the beginning of the action. **Held**: that the trustee had title to sue.

The defender also argued that s 40 of the Bankruptcy (Scotland) Act 1985 had not been correctly applied. That section says that a trustee in sequestration, to sell the bankrupt's home, may need the consent of the bankrupt's spouse (etc), or, absent such consent, the court's consent. The section sets forth factors that the court is to take into account. **Held**: that s 40 had been correctly applied. The case contains valuable observations on s 40.

(78) Anderson Ptr
[2008] CSOH 82

Mrs Anderson's property ('The Sea Chest') was at East Voe, Scalloway, Shetland. On neighbouring and higher ground a new housing development took place. She said that this increased the downhill discharge of water into her property, and that this caused damage. She sued both Shetland Islands Council and Scottish

Water for breach of their statutory duties, concluding both for specific implement and damages. **Held**: that no relevant basis for liability had been pled.

(79) Armstrong v G Dunlop & Sons' Judicial Factor
[2008] CSOH 174

This is the latest round in a dispute that has been running for about 20 years. Some of the rounds have been reported: *Armstrong Ptr* 1988 SLT 255; *G Dunlop & Sons' Judicial Factor v Armstrong* 1994 SLT 199; *G Dunlop & Sons' Judicial Factor v Armstrong* 1995 SLT 645; *Armstrong v G Dunlop & Sons' Judicial Factor* 2004 SLT 155 and 295 (*Conveyancing 2003* Case (39)).

Mr and Mrs Dunlop were the partners of a farming partnership in Galloway, Messrs G Dunlop & Sons. They became estranged about 1982. In 1986 Mr Dunlop petitioned for the dissolution of the partnership and for the appointment of a judicial factor to the partnership assets, and an interlocutor to that effect was pronounced in 1987. In 1988 the parties were divorced, and it was agreed between them that a part of the firm's property, namely the farmhouse, should be conveyed to Mrs Dunlop (Ms Armstrong). But the farmhouse was, like the rest of the property, subject to the judicial factory, and it seems that the judicial factor was not a party to the agreement. Another element in this long saga is that the standard security over the property, held by the Clydesdale Bank, was assigned first to Ms Armstrong's father and later to her brother.

The long conflict between Ms Armstrong and the judicial factor was essentially about the farmhouse, where she continued to live. 'A number of offers have been made over the years to settle this longstanding matter and I regret to say that it was largely the pursuer's attitude which led to matters remaining unresolved', remarks the Lord Ordinary (Lord Matthews) at para 369. In 2001 the judicial factor obtained decree ordaining Ms Armstrong to remove from the farmhouse. The present action, which has been in the Court of Session for at least five years, was an action to reduce that decree and also to ordain the judicial factor to dispone the farmhouse to her. It was **held** that the pursuer had no basis for reducing the decree. As for her claim that the judicial factor should implement the agreement that she and her former husband had come to in 1988, that the farmhouse should belong to her, it was **held** that, whilst it was arguable (as Lord Drummond Young had suggested in *Armstrong v G Dunlop & Sons' JF* 2004 SLT 155) that the judicial factor would have been so bound if the factory had still been solvent, it was now insolvent, and accordingly his duty was to realise the estate for the benefit of the creditors. Sadly, it seems that earlier on the judicial factory had been solvent, and at that time the judicial factor had been (if we understand the endless saga correctly) willing to dispone the farmhouse to Ms Armstrong, but for reasons which are unclear to us those negotiations failed. The pursuer, who was a party litigant, seems to have been under the misconception – common among non-lawyers – that because there had been a default on the standard security, the property belonged to the standard security holder (now her brother). To what extent this misunderstanding may have influenced her approach over the years is unclear. The Lord Ordinary's opinion runs to more than 55,000 words and accordingly the above is only the briefest sketch of this unhappy case.

(80) Professor the much honoured Stephen Pendaries Kerr of Ardgowan, Baron of Ardgowan Ptr
[2008] CSOH 36

Shortly before the Abolition of Feudal Tenure etc (Scotland) Act 2000 came into force, Stephen Pendaries Kerr of 3153 South Utica, Tulsa, Oklahoma, 74105, USA, petitioned the Lord Lyon for matriculation of arms in the name of 'The Much Honoured Stephen Kerr of Ardgowan, Baron of Ardgowan'. The Lord Lyon refused: 'As regards the recognition of a territorial designation, I only recognise this where there is ownership of a significant piece of land, not a superiority.' Mr Kerr judicially reviewed the decision, successfully. In essence the Lord Ordinary (Uist) **held** that a person is free to call himself what he wants.

The excellent *Scots Law News* website (www.law.ed.ac.uk/sln/) comments:

> An internet search reveals that Professor Kerr had a further swim in the by-waters of Scots law in 2004. He had a case before the Baron Court of Prestoungrange and Dolphinston in 2004, 'seeking Authorisation to Re-enact as a Bagpipe Opera [to be known as Tulsa] evidence sworn by the Very Reverend Dr Charles Kerr describing alleged miscarriages of justice concerning the Greenwood Blacks in Tulsa in 1921, which opera Professor Stephen Kerr has commissioned from Lindsay Davidson, Court Composer and Master of the Musick for the Barons Courts'.

We also have a footnote to add, albeit less exotic. The Lord Ordinary begins his opinion by noting that 'the petitioner is Professor of International Law at the Antioch School of Law'. (Presumably that was taken from Mr Kerr's pleadings.) Our researches have not succeeded in uncovering the existence of such an institution. (One of that name did exist in Washington DC from about 1972 to about 1986.)

(81) Martin Stephen James Goldstraw of Whitecairns Ptr
[2008] CSOH 34

When Mr Goldstraw acquired the superiority of Whitecairns in Aberdeenshire in 2003 he adopted the name of Martin Stephen James Goldstraw of Whitecairns, and placed an announcement in the *Edinburgh Gazette* to that effect. He applied to the Lord Lyon to have this new appendage added to his existing matriculation of arms. Lyon refused on the basis that Mr Goldstraw had a mere superiority. The judicial review of that decision was heard at the same time as the judicial review of the *Kerr of Ardgowan* case and reached the same result.

(82) Euring David Ayre of Kilmarnock, Baron of Kilmarnock
[2008] CSOH 35

The judicial review of this decision was heard at the same time as the judicial review of the *Kerr of Ardgowan* case and reached the same result. Mr David wished to have his superiority interest recognised by the addition of the words 'Ayre of Kilmarnock'.

(83) Breitenbücher v Wittke
[2008] CSOH 145

Bettina Breitenbücher, as liquidator of a German company, sued Cornelia Wittke for (a) payment of €2,913,382.97 and (b) an order to grant a standard security over the defender's property at Cragganard, Abriachan, Inverness-shire. The dispute arose out of a contract for construction works at the property. The contract, written in German, applied German law and gave the German courts exclusive jurisdiction in the event of a dispute. The defender pled that, standing the choice of law clause, the action against her in the Scottish courts fell to be dismissed. The pursuer argued that under German law the choice of law clause was invalid, because such clauses can be agreed only between parties who both have non-commercial status, and while the company had commercial status, the defender did not. The defender was domiciled in Scotland and accordingly, the pursuer argued, the court had jurisdiction. It was **held** that the defender did not have commercial status under German law, and that accordingly German law did not give the German courts exclusive jurisdiction. Since the defender was domiciled in Scotland it followed that the Scottish courts had jurisdiction.

PART II

STATUTORY DEVELOPMENTS

STATUTORY DEVELOPMENTS

Stamp duty land tax

The **Stamp Duty Land Tax (Exemption of Certain Acquisitions of Residential Property) Regulations 2008, SI 2008/2339** gives an SDLT holiday for all transfers of houses for a consideration of £175,000 or less. This lasts for a period of one year, beginning on 3 September 2008. Further changes in SDLT are made in the **Finance Act 2008 (c 9)**, for which see **Commentary** p 118.

Energy performance certificates

Every building will need an energy performance certificate (EPC). For new buildings this has been a requirement since 1 May 2007. For existing buildings, the **Energy Performance of Buildings (Scotland) Regulations 2008, SSI 2008/309**, which came into force on 4 January 2009 (oddly, a Sunday), link EPCs to sale or lease. Regulation 5(1) provides that:

> Where a building is to be sold or let the owner must make a copy of a valid energy certificate for the building available free of charge to a prospective buyer or prospective tenant.

Owners must produce an EPC within nine days of being so requested by the prospective buyer or tenant – or risk a penalty charge notice from the local authority or other enforcement authority (reg 17). So property must not be marketed for sale or lease without an EPC being already in place. But in order to accommodate an early rush for EPCs, the **Energy Performance of Buildings (Scotland) Amendment Regulations 2008, SSI 2008/389** provide that, until 1 April 2009, an owner is safe from enforcement if he (i) *requests* an energy performance certificate no later than seven days after a person becomes a prospective buyer or prospective tenant (defined in reg 3 of SSI 2008/309), and (ii) thereafter makes it available within nine days. For residential property, the EPC will in practice be produced along with the energy report, which is one component of the mandatory home report (for which see below).

The introduction of EPCs has led to minor amendments to the Building (Scotland) Act Regulations 2004, SSI 2004/406 by the **Building (Scotland) Amendment Regulations 2008, SSI 2008/310**.

The Energy Performance of Buildings (Scotland) Regulations 2008 transpose, in part, the Energy Performance of Buildings Directive (Directive 2002/91/EC), which aims at making buildings more energy-efficient. Evidently there is plenty of room for improvement: in the UK it is said that 18% of carbon emissions derive from energy used in commercial buildings and a further 27% from homes.

The form authorised for EPCs by the Scottish Building Standards Agency (on behalf of the Scottish Ministers) can be found on the SBSA website: http://www.sbsa.gov.uk/epc.htm. The content is prescribed by reg 6 of the 2008 Regulations. This provides that an EPC must express the 'asset rating' of a building, defined (in reg 2(1)) as 'a numerical indicator of the estimated amount of (a) energy consumed and (b) carbon dioxide emitted, to meet the different needs associated with a standardised use of the building'. In the EPC, this information is given in separate columns headed 'Energy Efficiency Rating' and 'Environmental Impact Rating', each graded on a scale of A–G (A being best). In addition, an EPC must look to the future by including 'cost effective recommendations for improving the energy performance of the building' (eg cavity wall insulation or draught-proof windows). EPCs can only be issued by qualified members of one of the organisations approved for the purpose by the SBSA (regs 6(1)(e), 8). Once issued, an EPC lasts for 10 years (reg 6(2)).

In an article published at p 68 of the *Journal of the Law Society of Scotland* for July 2008, Alan Simpson suggests possible effects on commercial leasing. For example, scoring well or badly in an EPC is likely to influence both capital and rental values of the buildings concerned.

Home reports

The new law

Home reports arrived on 1 December 2008. The relevant provisions of the Housing (Scotland) Act 2006 (described in *Conveyancing 2005* pp 124–130) were commenced by the **Housing (Scotland) Act 2006 (Commencement No 6 and Transitional Provision) Order 2008, SSI 2008/308**, while the contents of a home report were prescribed by the **Housing (Scotland) Act 2006 (Prescribed Documents) Regulations 2008, SSI 2008/76**. Further, practical information can be found on websites such as www.homereportsscotland.gov.uk and http://www.lawscot.org.uk/Members_Information/convey_essens/homereports.

Under the legislation, once a house is on the market, a home report must be supplied on request to all potential buyers. The home report comprises three elements:

- The *survey report* (generally referred to as 'the single survey'). This describes the condition of the property in a manner which is regarded by RICS as equivalent to a scheme 2 survey. It also identifies any problems and classifies them on a scale of 1–3 (3 being 'urgent'), gives a valuation and also the estimated reinstatement cost for insurance purposes, and finally – and this is an innovation – provides an accessibility audit covering matters such as parking, lifts, whether all door openings are greater than 75 mm and whether there is a toilet on the same level as a bedroom. The survey must be in the prescribed form.

- Under the Energy Performance of Buildings (Scotland) Regulations 2008, SSI 2008/309 (discussed above) sellers are already bound to produce an energy performance certificate ('EPC'). The *energy report* is an additional requirement, providing fuller information, including advice on measures which would improve energy efficiency. No form is prescribed for the energy report, and in practice both report and the EPC are part of a single document: see http://www.scotland.gov.uk/Resource/Doc/1125/0065332. pdf. The idea is that both can be prepared at the same time and by the same person.

- The *property questionnaire*. As its name suggests, this comprises a series of questions on the property, designed to provide information on a whole range of topics such as council tax, alterations to the building, the heating system, services, the extent of responsibility for shared maintenance, access rights and boundaries, and specialist treatments for dry rot etc.

Who prepares the report?

The survey and the energy report must be prepared by a surveyor registered with or authorised to practise by RICS (reg 5(1)). The property questionnaire is produced and signed by the seller or by a person authorised to act on the seller's behalf (reg 5(2)). The Law Society's view is that this is a matter for the client and not for the solicitor. The Law Society's Guidance on the property questionnaire is as follows:

Liability for Information Contained in Property Questionnaire

(5) Members should ensure that they have advised sellers in writing of their obligations in regard to the preparation of the property questionnaire and the importance of accurately and truthfully answering those questions, including clarifying for the client possible liability both in terms of the Property Misdescriptions Act 1991, the Housing (Scotland) Act 2006 and the Housing (Scotland) Act 2006 (Prescribed Documents) Regulations 2008.

(6) Members should make clear to selling clients completing such questionnaires that primary responsibility for the accuracy and truthfulness of those questionnaires rests with the client and that the member's only obligation in terms of compliance is to ensure that the copy which they offer members of the public who are purchasers is effectively a true copy of that form and therefore 'authentic' in terms of the legislation and regulation.

(7) The Society take the view that members do not have an obligation to check the information contained in the property questionnaire and may accept the statements therein at face value except in circumstances where they are personally aware that the statement is untrue. (For example in a situation where the member or their firm carried out the remortgage in respect of a substantial extension to the property and the questionnaire states that there are no alterations.)

Who Can Complete the Property Questionnaire?

(8) Ideally the questionnaire should be signed by at least one principal owner acting under authority from any co-proprietors.

(9) In the view of the Society 'authorised persons' (for the purposes of the regulation
     5(2)) definitely includes those acting under a Power of Attorney, Deed of Trust,
     Court Order, Solicitors and Duly Authorised Officers of a Company, but may
     include others with a similar level of formal authority. Care should be taken in cases
     where only informal authority is available. In the interests of risk management the
     Society do not recommend that solicitors sign questionnaires on behalf of clients.

No doubt the standard of questionnaires will vary considerably and, from
the buyer's point of view, they are little more than preliminary answers to issues
some of which will later require independent verification and/or be the subject of
warranties in the missives. 'Don't know' would seem to be an acceptable answer
in some circumstances, and may be a prudent one. Although the questionnaire is
not contractually binding (unless it is incorporated into the missives), it contains
representations by the seller which, if inaccurate, and hence misrepresentations,
may have legal consequences (eg allowing the buyer to rescind the missives).

A number of providers are in the market for home reports, including the Law
Society and various solicitors' property centres (see eg http://www.espc.co.uk/
HRHowCanWeHelp.html). The cost of a home report is likely to be upwards of
£500.

Elderly reports

A home report will not comply with the Regulations if it is more than 12 weeks
old at the time when the house is put on the market (reg 6(1)), and it is obviously
desirable that it should be as up-to-date as possible. From the buyer's perspective,
the Law Society's guidance is that a home report should not be relied upon if it
is more than 12 weeks old – although such a report would usually be compliant
with the Regulations. If this guidance is followed, it means that, if a house proves
hard to sell, the seller may need to update the report.

Additional mortgage valuation for the lender

Although the survey is instructed by the seller, it is provided by the **Housing
(Scotland) Act 2006 (Consequential Provisions) Order 2008, SSI 2008/1889** that
a negligent survey can give rise to liability to a buyer who has relied on it. There
is, however, no liability to a lender (ie to the buyer's bank), and lenders are likely
to continue to instruct their own mortgage valuations, at the buyer's expense. If
lenders instruct the same surveyor who prepared the single survey, then the cost
of producing a separate report in the lender's format may be absorbed into the
cost of the single survey (though it might increase that cost, thus transferring a
liability from the buyer to the seller). But, as the Council of Mortgage Lenders has
pointed out (see letter on p 8 of the *Journal of the Law Society of Scotland* for April
2008), there will inevitably be cases where the lender insists on an independent
survey – eg because the original surveyor is unacceptable to the lender or the
survey is too elderly, or because of high loan-to-value lending (in the event that
this practice ever returns to the market). If this becomes standard practice, then
it will realise some of the fears of those who opposed the single survey.

Law Society guidance

Mention was made earlier of the Law Society guidance on home reports. For completeness, it seems worth quoting the passages not already quoted or summarised above:

Making Reports Available to 'Interested Parties'

(3) Parties who have formally 'noted an interest' through solicitors or licensed conveyancers should be deemed to 'have sufficient means to buy the house' and/or be 'genuinely interested'.

(4) Members should ensure that they ask sellers if there are any persons to whom the seller would not be prepared to sell the house prior to marketing property to avoid any difficulties.

Deferred Payment Arrangements

(10) Terms of business should state or should include a separate covering document in relation to:
   (a) the price to be paid for the Home Report
   (b) a clear statement of any financial interest the selling agent has in the Home Report provider
   (c) details of any deferred payment option including any discount for early payment and charges in relation to property where the sale does not proceed or the property is withdrawn
   (d) where a mandate is to be signed for payment a clear statement of the meaning and effect of such a mandate.

Withdrawn from the market

(11) In the view of the Society a property is not 'sold' until a bargain is concluded. Property marked 'under offer' is still technically available for sale (admittedly subject to a change of agent in terms of the Society's Closing Date Gazumping and Gazundering Guidelines). Accordingly for the purposes of regulation 6(2)(b) property marked 'under offer' should not be deemed 'sold' and it should not be deemed 'withdrawn from the market' until there is a concluded bargain. On this basis it is the view of the Society that where a property is marked 'under offer' and negotiations fall through the existing Home Report could still be used in terms of regulation 6(2)(b).

Annexation of the Home Report to Offers

(12) While the Society accepts that it is a matter for individual members and their clients the Society does not recommend annexation of the Home Report to offers.

Conflict of interest

(13) In the interests of transparency where firms act for both buyer and seller in terms of the existing conflict rules they should clarify the source of the Home Report and any connection which their firm has with the supplier of the report.

(14) Where the selling solicitor is aware that multiple reports have been purchased by, or on behalf of the seller in an effort to obtain a report that portrays the property in the best light, the firm should not also represent a purchaser (notwithstanding the fact that an exemption under rule 5 of the Conflict of Interest Rules applies)

without disclosing the full circumstances due to the clear conflict of interest between the parties.

(15) Where a purchaser is to be advised to seek an additional independent report in cases where the firm already acts for the seller the firm should not represent the purchaser due to the clear conflict of interest between the parties. Exemptions under rule 5 of the Solicitors (Scotland) Practice Rules 1986 rely on the fact that the agent will not advise either party in relation to price. It is difficult to see how an additional independent report could be instructed without a discussion in relation to price.

The controversy

Opposition to the single survey element of home reports remained strong and voluble up to and beyond the last minute. On the day of introduction, Ian Ferguson, speaking on behalf of the Scottish Law Agents Society, offered the thought that:

> Today is Black Monday. It's the birth of Home Reports but, quite possibly, the death of the Scottish property market. I predict that Home Report costs will become as despised as the Poll Tax.

For a reasoned statement of the Scottish Law Agents Society's views, see http://www.slas.co.uk/media.php?mediaID=121. The Society had earlier been behind a motion which called on the Scottish Government to postpone the scheme in order to avoid inflicting further damage on an already fragile property market. The motion was carried by 2,052 votes to 52 at a SGM of the Law Society on 26 September 2008. Predictably, it made no difference.

Readers of the *Journal of the Law Society of Scotland* over the last couple of years have grown used to the arguments on both sides. Against the single survey it is argued that (i) there is no demand, as the abject failure of the pilot scheme shows; (ii) insofar as it is designed to solve the problem of multiple surveys by prospective buyers, that problem has already been solved by missives 'subject to survey'; (iii) the single survey imposes a significant, and in some cases unaffordable, burden on the seller without necessarily relieving the buyer of the burden of obtaining his own survey – either because he wants a report which is independent and up-to-date and which can be discussed with a surveyor or because his lender requires such a survey. In favour of the single survey – indeed of the home report as a whole – it is said that it will increase consumer knowledge and hence consumer choice. Prospective buyers will have more and better information at an earlier stage, and will not waste time, money and emotional energy pursuing properties which, for one reason or another, are unsuitable for them. Other anticipated benefits include more realistic upset prices and the elimination of separate surveys by multiple buyers. In the end, the difference between these positions comes down to widely different views as to the value of the single survey to potential purchasers.

Estate Agents (Redress Scheme) Order 2008, SI 2008/1712

This Order, which came into force on 1 October 2008, targets non-solicitor estate agents. It requires every person who engages in estate agency work in the United Kingdom in relation to residential property to be a member of an approved redress scheme for the purpose of dealing with complaints relating to that work. The Order is made under s 23A of the Estate Agents Act 1979, which was added to that Act by s 53(1) of the Consumers, Estate Agents and Redress Act 2007 (for which see *Conveyancing 2007* p 48). Section 53(1) was itself brought into force on 1 October 2008 by the **Consumers, Estate Agents and Redress Act 2007 (Commencement No 5 and Savings and Transitional Provisions) Order 2008, SI 2008/2550**. Estate agents who fail to register with an approved scheme face a £1,000 fixed penalty.

Register of Sites of Special Scientific Interest

This new Register, more usually known as the SSSI Register, was established by the **Register of Sites of Special Scientific Interest (Scotland) Regulations 2008, SSI 2008/221**, made under s 22(3) of the Nature Conservation (Scotland) Act 2004, and which took effect on 30 June 2008. The SSSI Register replaces and subsumes a register which was maintained by Scottish Natural Heritage.

The new Register is administered by Registers of Scotland but on the basis of data supplied by SNH. By reg 3(1), it is to be kept in electronic form only: see https://www.sssi.ros.gov.uk/ros.sssi.presentation.ui/. The Register holds the following documents on each SSSI: (i) the citation that describes the land and natural features for which SNH considers it to be of special interest, (ii) a PDF map of the boundary, and (iii) a list of operations requiring consent. The Register is searchable online by map or by entering search criteria such as a town name or postcode.

Private landlord registration

The Antisocial Behaviour etc (Scotland) Act 2004 requires private landlords of residential property to be registered (see *Conveyancing 2004* pp 92–95), with much of the detail being set out in SSIs passed the following year (see *Conveyancing 2005* pp 33–35). The **Private Landlord Registration (Information and Fees) (Scotland) Amendment Regulations 2008, SSI 2008/403** make a number of changes to the fees as originally set out in the Private Landlord Registration (Information and Fees) (Scotland) Regulations 2005, SSI 2005/558. These include exempting charities (previously they received an 80% discount) and some alterations to the discounts available for landlords with portfolios in more than one local authority. The **Private Landlord Registration (Advice and Assistance) (Scotland) Amendment Regulations 2008, SSI 2008/402** provide, succinctly, that 'where a person who is, or who is considering becoming, a tenant approaches a local authority to enquire about letting practice or landlord registration, the local authority must provide to the person general advice in relation to those matters'. This supplements the advice obligations of local authorities set out in the Private Landlord Registration (Advice and Assistance) (Scotland) Regulations 2005, SSI 2005/557.

According to figures published in July 2008, 119,438 applications for registration have been received and 96,506 (= 80.8%) approved. See www.scotland.gov.uk/News/Releases/2008/07/18141929.

Bankruptcy and Diligence etc (Scotland) Act 2007

The **Bankruptcy and Diligence etc (Scotland) Act 2007 (Commencement No 3, Savings and Transitionals) Order 2008, SSI 2008/115** brought into force, as from 1 April 2008, some of the provisions of the Bankruptcy and Diligence etc (Scotland) Act 2007. (For the Act in general, see *Conveyancing 2006* pp 131–138.) Not all the details will be mentioned here. Most of part 1 has been commenced. That includes the new rules about sequestration, including the one-year discharge period. It also includes the important provisions in s 17 aimed at protecting a grantee against the granter's sequestration. Section 17 casts further doubt on the need for a trust clause in dispositions (as to which see *Conveyancing 2004* pp 79–85). Implications of the provisions for registration practice are covered at http://www.ros.gov.uk/registration/bankruptcyupdate.html.

A commencement worth noting by commercial conveyancers is s 208 dealing with the landlord's hypothec.

Among the provisions of the Act still not in force are those about floating charges and land attachment.

New conservation bodies

Conservation bodies are bodies which are able to create and hold conservation burdens under s 38 of the Title Conditions (Scotland) Act 2003. A conservation burden is a personal real burden which preserves or protects the natural or built environment for the benefit of the public. The first list of conservation bodies, prescribed by the Title Conditions (Scotland) Act 2003 (Conservation Bodies) Order 2003, SSI 2003/453, was amended by the Title Conditions (Scotland) Act 2003 (Conservation Bodies) Amendment Order 2004, SSI 2004/400, the Title Conditions (Scotland) Act 2003 (Conservation Bodies) Amendment Order 2006, SSI 2006/110, the Title Conditions (Scotland) Act 2003 (Conservation Bodies) Amendment (No 2) Order 2006, SSI 2006/130 and the Title Conditions (Scotland) Act 2003 (Conservation Bodies) Amendment Order 2007, SSI 2007/533. The **Title Conditions (Scotland) Act 2003 (Conservation Bodies) Amendment Order 2008, SSI 2008/217** adds three further bodies: Dundee Historic Environment Trust, Inverness City Heritage Trust, and Sir Henry Wade's Pilmuir Trust.

The complete list of conservation bodies is now:

All local authorities
Aberdeen City Heritage Trust
Alba Conservation Trust
Castles of Scotland Preservation Trust
Dundee Historic Environment Trust
Edinburgh World Heritage Trust
Glasgow Building Preservation Trust
Glasgow City Heritage Trust
Highlands Buildings Preservation Trust
Inverness City Heritage Trust

Plantlife – The Wild-Plant Conservation Charity
Scottish Natural Heritage
Sir Henry Wade's Pilmuir Trust
Solway Heritage
St Vincent Crescent Preservation Trust
Stirling City Heritage Trust
Strathclyde Building Preservation Trust
Tayside Building Preservation Trust
The John Muir Trust
The National Trust for Scotland for Places of Historic Interest or Natural Beauty
The Royal Society for the Protection of Birds
The Scottish Wildlife Trust
The Trustees of the Landmark Trust
The Trustees of the New Lanark Conservation Trust
The Woodland Trust
United Kingdom Historic Building Preservation Trust

New rural housing bodies

Rural housing bodies are bodies which are able to create and hold rural housing burdens under s 43 of the Title Conditions (Scotland) Act 2003. A rural housing burden is a personal right of pre-emption. This may only be used over rural land, ie land other than 'excluded land'. 'Excluded land' has the same meaning as in the Land Reform (Scotland) Act 2003, namely settlements of over 10,000 people.

The first list of rural housing bodies was prescribed by the Title Conditions (Scotland) Act 2003 (Rural Housing Bodies) Order 2004, SSI 2004/477. More names were added by the Title Conditions (Scotland) Act 2003 (Rural Housing Bodies) Amendment Order 2006, SSI 2006/108, the Title Conditions (Scotland) Act 2003 (Rural Housing Bodies) Amendment Order 2007, SSI 2007/58, and the Title Conditions (Scotland) Act 2003 (Rural Housing Bodies) Amendment (No 2) Order 2007, SSI 2007/535. The **Title Conditions (Scotland) Act 2003 (Rural Housing Bodies) Amendment Order 2008, SSI 2008/391** adds Craignish Community Company Limited and The Highland Housing Alliance.

The complete list of rural housing bodies is now:

Albyn Housing Society Limited
Argyll Community Housing Association
Barra and Vatersay Housing Association Limited
Berneray Housing Association Limited
Buidheann Taigheadais na Meadhanan Limited
Buidheann Tigheadas Loch Aillse Agus An Eilein Sgitheanaich Limited
Cairn Housing Association Limited
Colonsay Community Development Company
Comhairle nan Eilean Siar
Community Self-Build Scotland Limited
Craignish Community Company Limited
Down to Earth Scottish Sustainable Self Build Housing Association Limited

Dumfries and Galloway Small Communities Housing Trust
Dunbritton Housing Association Limited
Ekopia Resource Exchange Limited
Fyne Homes Limited
Fyne Initiatives Limited
HIFAR Limited
Isle of Jura Development Trust
Lochaber Housing Association Limited
Muirneag Housing Association Limited
North West Mull Community Woodland Company Limited
Orkney Islands Council
Pentland Housing Association Limited
Rural Stirling Housing Association Limited
Taighean Ceann a Tuath na'Hearadh Limited
The Highland Housing Alliance
The Highlands Small Communities' Housing Trust
The Isle of Eigg Heritage Trust
The Isle of Gigha Heritage Trust
The North Harris Trust
Tighean Innse Gall Limited
West Highland Housing Association Limited
West Highland Rural Solutions Limited.

Consumer Credit Act 2006

The **Consumer Credit Act 2006 (Commencement No 4 and Transitional Provisions) Order 2008, SI 2008/831**, as amended by the **Consumer Credit Act 2006 (Commencement No 4 and Transitional Provisions) (Amendment) Order 2008, SI 2008/ 2444**, commences certain provisions of the Consumer Credit Act 2006. One effect is that the £25,000 ceiling for the applicability of consumer credit law now disappears.

This does not affect first-ranking standard securities. Section 16(6C) of the Consumer Credit Act 1974 exempts a contract if it is 'secured by a land mortgage and entering into the agreement as lender is a regulated activity for the purposes of the Financial Services and Markets Act 2000'. The 2000 Act is to be read in the light of the Financial Services and Markets Act 2001 (Regulated Activities) Order 2001, SI 2001/544, article 61, which brings within the scope of the 2000 Act cases where:

(i) a person ('the lender') provides credit to an individual or to trustees ('the borrower'); and
(ii) the obligation of the borrower to repay is secured by a first legal mortgage on land (other than timeshare accommodation) in the United Kingdom, at least 40% of which is used, or is intended to be used, as or in connection with a dwelling by the borrower or (in the case of credit provided to trustees) by an individual who is a beneficiary of the trust, or by a related person.

The expressions 'land mortgage' and 'first legal mortgage' are provided with Scottish translations.

Homelessness etc (Scotland) Act 2003

The **Homelessness etc (Scotland) Act 2003 (Commencement No 3) Order 2008, SSI 2008/313** brings into force s 11 of the Homelessness etc (Scotland) Act 2003 which provides that: 'Where a landlord raises proceedings for possession of a dwellinghouse, the landlord must give notice of the raising of the proceedings to the local authority in whose area the dwellinghouse is situated....'

New form for registration of company charges

The **Companies (Particulars of Company Charges) Regulations 2008, SI 2008/ 2996** do not change the substance of the law but mean that, as from 1 October 2009, when registering particulars of a charge at Companies House a new form must be used.

PART III
OTHER MATERIAL

OTHER MATERIAL

Right to buy: 'pressured areas'

Section 61B of the Housing (Scotland) Act 1987, as inserted by section 45 of the Housing (Scotland) Act 2001, provides that a local authority can apply to the Scottish Ministers to designate an area as a 'pressured area'. If the Ministers agree, the right to buy is then suspended in that area in respect of tenancies entered into after 30 September 2002 (as to which see Housing (Scotland) Act 2001 (Scottish Secure Tenancy etc) Amendment Order 2002, SSI 2002/415). The designation lasts for five years, but renewal is possible. The number of designated areas has been increasing. On 21 January 2008, in answer to a question in the Scottish Parliament, the Communities Minister, Stewart Maxwell MSP, published the following table:

Local authority area	Summary of areas designated	Areas designated	Period of designation
Aberdeen City	35 letting areas	Aberdeen Central, Altens, Ashgrove, Balgownie, Berryden, Bon Accord, Bridge of Don, Bucksburn, Cove, Craigiebuckler, Cults, Denmore, Dyce, Ferryhill, Fountainhall, Garthdee/ Kaimhill, George Street, Hazlehead, Hilton, Holburn, Kepplehills, Kingswells, Mannofield, Middleton, Old Aberdeen, Peterculter, Pittodrie, Rosehill, Ruthrieston, Raeden, Rosemount, Sheddocksley, Stoneywood, Union Grove and Westburn	5 Sept 2007 to 4 Sept 2012
Dumfries & Galloway	69 rural villages	Ae, Amisfield, Auchencairn, Auldgirth, Bankend, Beeswing, Boreland, Borgue, Bridge of Dee, Brydekirk, Burnhead, Cairnryan, Canonbie, Carronbridge, Carrutherstown, Carty, Chapelknowe, Closeburn, Collin, Crocketford, Crossmichael, Culquhirk, Cummertrees, Dornock, Dundrennan, Dunscore, Eskdalemuir, Gair, Gelston, Glencaple, Glenlochar, Glenstockadale, Hightae, Holywood, Isle of Whithorn, Johnstonebridge, Kelton, Kirkcolm, Kirkgunzeon, Kirkinner, Kirkmahoe, Kirkton,	5 June 2006 to 4 June 2011

Local authority area	Summary of areas designated	Areas designated	Period of designation
		Kirtlebridge, Leswalt, Lochfoot, Mochrum Park, Mouswald, Nethermill, New Luce, Old Bridge of Urr, Palnackie, Palnure, Park, Portling, Prestonmill, Rhonehouse, Rigg, Ringford, Rowanburn, Shawhead, Sibbaldbie, Sorbie, Templand, Terregles, Torthorwald, Twynholm, Westerkirk, Whauphill and Yesket	
East Renfrewshire	1 housing management area	Eastwood	7 Oct 2005 to 6 Oct 2010
Fife	2 housing management areas	St Andrew's East Neuk	8 May 2006 to 7 May 2011
Fife	13 letting areas	Aberdour, Charlestown, Crossford, Culross, Dalgety Bay, Halbeath, Kingseat, Limekilns, North Queensferry, Rosyth, Saline, Torryburn and Townhill	15 Jan 2007 to 14 Jan 2012
Highland	9 housing management areas	Badenoch and Strathspey; Easter Ross, Fort William; Nairn town and rural Nairn; Rural Inverness, Inverness Town and Culloden; Rural Lochaber (but not Kinlochleven); Skye and Lochalsh and Wester Ross (but not Aultbea)	15 Nov 2005 to 14 Nov 2010
Moray	3 housing management areas	Elgin, Forres Rural and Lossiemouth	7 March 2006 to 6 March 2011
Perth & Kinross	21 letting areas	Aberfeldy, Abernethy, Acharn, Almondbank, Balbeggie, Ballinluig, Bankfoot, Blair Atholl, Bridge of Earn, Dunkeld & Birnam, Dunning, Glencarse & St Maddoes, Guildtown, Inchture, Invergowrie, Kinloch Rannoch, Longforgan, Luncarty, Methven, Pitlochry and Scone	2 Feb 2007 to 1 Feb 2012
South Ayrshire	29 letting areas	Annbank, Annpit, Ayr Rural, Ayr South Central, Barr, Barhill, Belmont Old, Belmont South, Colmonnell, Craigie, Crosshill, Dunure, Forehill/Glencairn/Holmston, Heathfield, Kincaidston, Kirkmichael, Maidens, Monkton, Newton Green, Pinmore, Prestwick Central, Prestwick Eastfield, Prestwick East Road, Prestwick Glenburn, Prestwick Marchburn, Prestwick Moorfield, Prestwick Mossbank, Prestwick Toll and Woodfield	10 Feb 2006 to 9 Feb 2011

On 6 November 2008 it was announced that much of Aberdeenshire is to be added: www.scotland.gov.uk/News/Releases/2008/11/06094833.

Registers of Scotland

Stale application forms

The Keeper issued a practice note on 4 December 2008 (www.ros.gov.uk/ registration/form_certification.html) which reads, in part:

> Except in the case of an ARTL application, there will inevitably be a time lapse between the certification of the form and its receipt by the Keeper. Moreover, the *Registration of Title Practice Book* recommends that a prudent solicitor acting for a grantee will always adjust the terms of the application form with the granter's solicitor. However, some of the information provided on an application form could become out of date in a relatively short period of time. For instance, a company which is a party to the transaction might go into administration or liquidation. The Keeper's indemnity might be at risk if he were to rely on information which is already out of date by the time that he receives it.
>
> Solicitors are therefore asked to ensure that the information provided (whether in an application form or an ARTL application) is certified as near as possible to the date on which the Keeper receives the application. Where there is a significant time lapse (eg in excess of 5 to 10 working days, depending on the type of transaction) between the date of certification of a form and the date of receipt, the Keeper may return the application form to the solicitor to re-certify the particulars on the form.

Form 2 needed for all discharges

In a change which took effect on 5 January 2009, the discharge of a standard security now requires its own form 2 even when presented for registration at the same time as a purchaser's disposition. This removes the only case in which registration could be achieved without an application form.

Early warning of failure to apply for dual registration in respect of real burdens

On 28 July 2008 Registers of Scotland introduced a new procedure for scrutiny of deeds which purport to create real burdens. Instead of considering this issue only at a later stage, leading to the possibility of rejection of a deed weeks or even months after it was first presented for registration, RoS will now carry out a preliminary examination of all deeds that purport to constitute real burdens. The new procedure is explained in *Update 23* (available at http://www.ros.gov. uk/pdfs/update23.pdf):

> Accordingly, in the event that a deed which purports to constitute new real burdens is presented for registration in the Land Register without an accompanying application for dual registration (or Sasine recording), it will be rejected forthwith unless falling within one of the categories listed below:–

1. the deed is a disposition granted by a local authority or housing association. In such cases the burdens are likely to fall under section 53 of the 2003 Act. Here section 53(3A) of the 2003 Act modifies section 4 to remove the requirement for the nomination of, and registration against, a benefited property. It should be noted that such deeds may be rejected later in the registration process if, upon detailed examination, it emerges that section 53 is not applicable. Note: that if a deed which would otherwise fall into this category constitutes any new servitude, dual registration is necessary to comply with section 75 of the 2003 Act;

2. where either the additional information field of the registration application form, or a covering letter to the application, gives a valid reason for not presenting the application for dual registration – for example that, although the deed is not granted by a local authority or housing association, the burdens form part of a section 53 common scheme.

RoS has a useful guide on the whole topic of the registration of deeds with real burdens: see http://www.ros.gov.uk/pdfs/real_burdens_flyer.pdf.

Use of deeds of conditions to create real burdens in developments

In *Conveyancing 2007* pp 80–83 we emphasised the importance of using a deed of conditions for real burdens in developments, as opposed to putting the burdens in the individual split-off dispositions. Bruce Beveridge, the Deputy Keeper, has put a note in the *Journal* making the same recommendation: (2008) 53 *Journal of the Law Society of Scotland* Feb/17.

12% rejection rate – still

The rejection rate for applications to the Registers has remained at or around 12% for many years – despite the introduction of the option of fee-paying by direct debit. See a note by Bruce Beveridge at (2008) 53 *Journal of the Law Society of Scotland* March/17. The main causes of rejection are failure to send the fee or at least the correct amount, and defective application forms (eg unsigned, undated, information omitted).

ARTL

When first introduced in the autumn of 2007, ARTL could only be used for standard securities and their discharges. The Keeper's Direction No 1 of 2008, effective from 1 March 2008, now extends this to dispositions of the whole, assignations of leases and of standard securities, and to various minor documents such as notices of payment of improvement grants. The first full property transfer, including the processing of SDLT, took place on 17 April 2008. There have been many since, and the latest figures on the RoS website show that almost 13,000 ARTL applications (of all types) have been made since ARTL was introduced.

At present some 112 law firms, 15 lenders (including Abbey National, Royal Bank of Scotland and Halifax Bank of Scotland) and eight local authorities are signed up to use the system. For a complete list, see http://www.ros.gov.uk/artl/currentparticipants.html.

Turnaround times

These have slipped back a little for domestic first registrations, from 69.6 days in 2006/7 to 88.5 days in 2007/8 according to the RoS *Annual Report*: http://www.ros.gov.uk/pdfs/ar_0708.pdf. But they are still well within the official target of 100 days.

New form of receipt for applications

The receipt sent by RoS when an application is received no longer includes a copy of the form 4 (which, since the Land Registration (Scotland) Rules 2006, SSI 2006/485, took effect in January 2007, has ceased to be submitted in duplicate). The new receipt, which is usually sent by e-mail, states the subjects, applicants, application number, title number, parent title number (where appropriate), and – of course – the date of registration.

Deeds by foreign companies

A note by Bruce Beveridge in the *Journal of the Law Society of Scotland* for November 2008 (p 17) provides helpful guidance as to RoS practice in relation to deeds by foreign companies. As the note points out, execution should comply with para 5 of sch 2 of the Requirements of Writing (Scotland) Act 1995. In order to answer the relevant questions in the application form for registration, law agents will need to investigate the status of the company and the names of relevant officers, as well as ensuring that the company is not under any process equivalent to dissolution or insolvency. If the signatory is someone other than an officer, it will be necessary to produce evidence of authorisation (together with a certified translation if the language is not English). For further discussion of these issues, see G L Gretton and K G C Reid, *Conveyancing* (3rd edn 2004) para 25-13.

Flood Risk Management (Scotland) Bill

This reform is required because of the Floods Directive (2007/60/EC). It will modernise the law and repeal and replace the Flood Prevention (Scotland) Act 1961.

High hedges

In response to a parliamentary question by David McLetchie MSP, asking the Scottish Government whether it intends to legislate on the subject of high hedges and, if so, when, the relevant Minister, Fergus Ewing MSP, replied on 20 November 2008 as follows:

> We are in the process of investigating options – including legislative ones – for supporting a means of resolving disputes about high hedges. The findings of this work will be reported to Parliament early in 2009, alongside the findings of the review of national antisocial behaviour policy.

CML: disclosure of incentives for new-build properties

With effect from 1 September 2008 the Council of Mortgage Lenders has introduced a new policy on the disclosure of incentives in the sale of new-build properties. The required form and a list of FAQs can be found at http://www. cml.org.uk/handbook/frontpage.aspx. An account can be found on the Law Society of Scotland's website at http://www.lawscot.co.uk/Members_ Information/convey_essens/disincen/disincentives.aspx. There the following background is given: 'CML advises that the change is to help restore confidence in the new-build market. The difficulties in capturing discounts and incentives offered on new-build properties has led to price distortions and exposed lenders and the public to fraud and the risk of loss. This is now impacting upon builders and prospective purchasers due to the harder line lenders are taking to avoid hidden risks and the whole market is suffering.' Under the revised rules, solicitors must confirm that they have received a 'disclosure of incentives form' from the builder/developer of any new-build, converted or renovated property, before submitting their certificate of title. In submitting the certificate, solicitors will be deemed to confirm that the form complies with the loan instructions.

On its website (and in an article by Paul Carnan published in the *Journal of the Law Society of Scotland* in September 2008 (p 66)) the Law Society makes much of the difficulties:

> Given (a) that the Form deals with cash and non-cash incentives and is primarily a tool for the lender to use in deciding how much to lend; (b) the variety of information to be disclosed in terms of the Form; (c) the fact that each Lender may interpret the information given in the CML Disclosure of Incentives Form in a different way; and (d) that the Form will be produced prior to the Missive stage ordinarily prior to any loan instructions being issued, we fail to see how any reasonably competent solicitor, on perusal of the Form alone, could determine without specific input from the Lender whether the Form will comply with the (yet-to-be issued) loan instructions. In the ordinary case, we feel that a Solicitor has a duty of care to the Lender to prepare proper and effective security documentation, but we do not believe that a Solicitor has a duty to verify the value of the security subjects. So in all new-build cases where the purchaser will be seeking mortgage funding, our advice is that a copy of the Form should be sent to the Lender as soon as received and the Lenders' specific approval thereof sought before Missives are concluded. Failure to seek approval prior to concluding Missives on an each-and-every case basis where a loan is involved could leave the solicitor exposed to a claim in the event that the loan instructions, when issued, do not take into account the terms of the Form as delivered to the solicitor. We appreciate that not all purchasers of new-build properties will have firm offers of finance in place when they reserve a new-build property. However, if the solicitor is to ensure that the Lenders' approval of the Form as issued has been obtained prior to conclusion of Missives, then prospective purchasers will have to arrange their finance in advance of concluding Missives. Inevitably, the new disclosure requirements will result in significant delays.

CML responded with an article in the October *Journal* (p 64) dismissing these fears as alarmist. In particular, CML argues:

The form is a simple way of drawing together the information that a solicitor is already required to collect on behalf of the lender, as well as some additional information that is required for the surveyor. The intention behind the form is not to increase solicitors' workload or increase their liability, but we would hope that it would make the existing duty to report incentives in terms of the handbook easier by having all the information in one place. This is how it is being viewed in other jurisdictions. We are not, as the Society suggests, asking the solicitor acting for the purchaser to verify the information contained in the form, but the solicitor should simply confirm with the purchaser that the information provided on the form regarding the agreed sale price and incentives offered is in line with the purchaser's understanding.

Solicitors should thereafter report the incentives, as they are currently required to do, to the lender, following each lender's instructions in part 2 of the Lenders' Handbook, and contrary to Law Society of Scotland guidance should only forward the form to the lender if the lender requests this.

CML points out that surveyors also have a role to play, and that most lenders are unlikely to accept a valuation where the surveyor has not seen the disclosure of incentives form.

Low-cost initiative for first-time buyers ('LIFT')

In January 2008 the Scottish Government announced the Open Market Shared Equity Pilot, a £24 million programme in 2008/09 covering 10 local authorities. On 19 October 2008 it was announced that the scheme is to be extended to the whole of Scotland, and in 2009/10 it will have a substantially increased budget of £60 million. It will assist around 1,500 households on low incomes who want to buy a house. Under the scheme a buyer generally pays between 60% and 80% of the price, with the remainder paid for by the Scottish Government. The buyer owns the whole property, although the Government holds a security over the proportion of equity stake it has funded. If the owner sells the property, the Government will receive the value at the time of sale of the percentage equity stake funded. If, for example, the Government funds 40% of the purchase price, when the property is sold 40% of the sale value of the property will be returned to the Government. For details, see www.communitiesscotland.gov.uk/stellent/groups/public/documents/webpages/cs_021091.pdf.

Crofting

In general we do not deal with crofting. Nevertheless, two developments are noted here. The first is a prospective extension of crofting areas. The Crofters (Scotland) Act 1993 s 3A(1) (as inserted by the Crofting Reform etc Act 2007) allows Scottish Ministers to designate new areas where crofts can be created with the approval of the Crofters Commission. On 6 October 2008 the Scottish Government announced that Arran, Bute, Greater and Little Cumbrae, Moray and the parts of Highland not already within the Crofting Counties are to be designated as new crofting areas. As at the time of writing the necessary statutory instrument has not yet been made.

The other development is the Shucksmith Report (*Committee of Inquiry on Crofting: Final Report* (2008; available at http://www.croftinginquiry.org/Resource/ Doc/0/0000405.pdf)). The Scottish Government has published a response, at www.scotland.gov.uk/Publications/2008/09/25154550/1. As a taster, here are one or two recommendations that might interest conveyancers, plus Government's responses. We offer no comments.

Shucksmith	*Response*
'The Crofters Commission would … be wound up. We recommend that the regulation and enforcement function should be discharged in future by a new Federation of Crofting Boards, a single organisation consisting of 7–10 elected Local Crofting Boards.'	'The Government does not agree with this recommendation. The Crofters Commission has experience and knowledge of crofting issues and it is important that this expertise is preserved. However, it needs root and branch reform' (para 44).
'Responsibility for the Croft Register would be taken over by the Registers of Scotland.'	'The Scottish Government agrees that responsibility for establishing a definitive new Register of Crofts should be entrusted to the Registers of Scotland. The Keeper of the Registers of Scotland has welcomed the proposal' (para 69).
'The Registration of Leases (Scotland) Act 1857 should be amended to make a crofting lease registrable and hence eligible for standard securities.'	'The Scottish Government accepts the principle that crofters should be able to obtain loan finance without the necessity of decrofting. However, it may require more than amending the Registration of Leases (Scotland) Act 1857 in order to achieve this. The Government proposes to consult with the Committee of Scottish Clearing Bankers' (para 72).
'We recommend that all croft houses be tied to residency through a real burden, which would be deemed to be included in the conveyancing when next assigned or purchased. This would run with the land in perpetuity.'	'The Scottish Government recognises the problems faced by crofting communities as a result of absenteeism, neglect and speculation of croft land resulting from an external demand for second homes. However, it does not agree that the proposed burden is the best approach to addressing these problems' (para 61).
'We believe new legislation is needed to replace, simplify and clarify the accumulated laws which set the framework for crofting today.'	'New legislation will be needed to implement some of the policy proposals outlined in this Government response. The Government therefore proposes to consult in 2009 on a substantive draft Bill that will amend existing legislation.… The Government will bring forward proposals on the consolidation of crofting law when it consults on the draft amending Bill' (paras 58–59).

Landlord Accreditation Scotland

With the strapline of 'Promoting best practice in the private rented system in Scotland', Landlord Accreditation Scotland was set up in April 2008 as a voluntary system of accreditation for private-sector landlords. According to its website (www.landlordaccreditationscotland.com/):

> Landlord Accreditation Scotland (LAS) is a voluntary scheme by which landlords and letting agents can assure tenants that the tenancy arrangements they have adhere to the high standards outlined in the Scottish Core Standards for Accredited Landlords (available at http://www.landlordaccreditationscotland.com/Files/File/Core%20 Standards%2026%20Sept.pdf). Becoming a member of LAS is a way of demonstrating to landlords and tenants that your management practices are above the minimum legal requirements. The standards that have to be met prior to being awarded accredited status are reasonable and realistic; landlords who already carry out good management practices are well on their way to achieving them.

Development Management Scheme to be introduced in 2009 – perhaps

Part 6 of the Title Conditions (Scotland) Act 2003 provides for the introduction of a 'Development Management Scheme'. This is an off-the-peg (but variable) set of rules for the management and maintenance of developments, including tenements. It is thus an alternative both to the Tenement Management Scheme and also to deeds of conditions. Implementation has been delayed because the owners' association provided for under the Scheme is to be a body corporate, which is an area of law reserved to the Westminster Parliament. This means that the Scheme requires to be set out in a Westminster statutory instrument made under s 104 of the Scotland Act 1998. A parliamentary question put by Michael Matheson MSP elicited the response from the Minister for Community Safety, Fergus Ewing MSP, on 19 February 2008 that: 'My officials are in consultation with the Scotland Office and the intention is to ask UK Ministers to lay the s 104 Order in the spring.' No order was, however, laid and in response to a follow-up question from Mr Matheson, the Minister replied on 17 December 2008 that: 'The Scottish Government will ask UK Ministers to lay the Order in spring 2009.' We will see. Meanwhile no reason for the continuing delay has been given.

Property factors

In *Conveyancing 2007* pp 67–68 we reported that there was growing concern about property factoring. This has continued during the past year. Thus in December 2007 an All-Party Parliamentary Group on Land Maintenance was established at Westminster, chaired by Jim Devine MP. During 2008 it has been conducting hearings.

In June 2008 the OFT launched a market study of Scottish property managers: http://www.oft.gov.uk/news/press/2008/74-08. This will consider issues such as how much choice and information are available to homeowners, how property managers are selected, the quality and costs of the services provided, how homeowners can manage services effectively, and whether homeowners have access to redress when things go wrong. The market study follows evidence submitted to the OFT by the Scottish Consumer Council, which highlighted potential consumer harm in this area. Publication of the report is expected early in 2009.

Finally, in July 2008, the Scottish Government announced that an accreditation scheme for property managers would be set up (http://www.scotland.gov.uk/ News/Releases/2008/07/02102754). This is to be 'industry-led', ie voluntary and without public funding or status. To achieve accreditation, property managers will have to meet certain standards of service. Among other requirements, property managers will have to produce clear written contracts for every client including an explicit complaints procedure. Apparently, property managers will be expected to obtain quotations from a range of contractors and show transparent accounting and billing systems, clearly highlighting all management income being received. In an enjoyable mixture of metaphors, the Communities Minister, Stewart Maxwell MSP, said that the new scheme 'will help weed out the cowboys'.

OFT study of home buying and selling

The Office of Fair Trading is to launch a market study into home buying and selling, looking at traditional estate agency models and alternative ways of buying and selling homes: see http://www.oft.gov.uk/advice_and_resources/ resource_base/market-studies/current/buyingandselling. Ahead of this, the OFT has been writing to stakeholders to ask for their views and engage with them to discuss the scope and scale of the study, which will begin early in 2009. The OFT proposes that the market study should take a comprehensive look at home buying and selling in terms of competition on price and quality between service providers; the prospects for new entry by, in particular, internet property retailers; and the extent to which consumer interests are protected by the existing regulatory framework. The study, which is likely to include the Scottish market, may also cover the relationships between estate agents, and mortgage brokers, surveyors, solicitors and other professional advisors.

Settlement by cheque and by CHAPS transfer of funds

The following Guideline has been issued by the Professional Practice Committee of the Law Society of Scotland, effective from 1 November 2008 (and reproduced in the *Journal of the Law Society of Scotland* for November 2008 (p 31)):

> The Professional Practice Committee has seen an increasing number of requests for information or guidance on the question of whether settlement of house purchase and sale transactions should take place by cheque or electronic (CHAPS) transfer. This is also getting to be a frequently asked question by clients, and the issues are not well understood.
>
> Almost all transactions now settle by post. A solicitor can send a cheque subject to conditions but cannot attach conditions when sending a CHAPS transfer. It is perfectly proper to reach agreement with the other solicitor in advance of sending funds by

CHAPS transfer that those funds will be held as undelivered pending fulfilment of certain conditions, but if that is not agreed in advance, it is too late to impose the condition at the time the funds are sent by CHAPS transfer.

If such pre-arranged conditions are not fulfilled, the solicitor receiving the funds would risk a finding of professional misconduct if the funds are treated as delivered and paid out to clients or third parties.

An electronic transfer cannot be stopped, but if the buyer's solicitor does not receive the titles, letter of obligation, keys etc in return for a client's account cheque which has been sent to be held as undelivered he can either demand the return of a cheque or stop the cheque (in extreme circumstances). Settlement by cheque therefore protects the buyer by giving the buyer's solicitor control over the money even after the cheque has been sent. A seller's solicitor can also protect the seller by attaching conditions to deeds etc sent by post, including a condition about interest on the price if settlement has been delayed (a not infrequent problem these days).

Traditionally, when a selling solicitor received and banked another solicitor's client account cheque, he could write his own client account cheques to redeem his client's loan or settle his client's purchase on the same day. Problems are encountered very occasionally if the solicitor receiving the cheque banks at the same branch of the same bank as the solicitor sending the cheque although that is rare.

Since the introduction of the cheque clearing process known as 2-4-6 there is a risk that the cheque sent out will be presented for payment at the sender's bank before the cheque paid in has cleared. The Professional Practice department at the Society has received a number of telephone calls from solicitors affected in this way.

These problems may be surmounted by either

(1) clients arranging short term bridging loans or
(2) solicitors arranging a temporary facility with their own bank that would allow the bank to transfer sufficient funds into the client bank account to meet the presentation of an outgoing cheque where the incoming cheque has still to clear. Any interest payable could be charged to the client although that would have to be specified in the relevant Terms of Business.

If neither of these options is adopted, a third option namely

(3) settlement by CHAPS transfer is suggested to avoid the possibility of a shortfall in the client account that may in turn lead to a failure to comply with Rule 4(1)(a) of the Solicitors (Scotland) Accounts etc Rules 2001.

If a selling solicitor is also purchasing for his client on the same day and wishes the sale to be settled by CHAPS transfer the selling solicitor should put a clause in the missives requiring the sale to be settled electronically. That will be subject to agreement by the buyer, but it must be in the missives or it cannot be insisted upon.

Subject to these considerations the Professional Practice Committee remains of the view that settlement by cheque between solicitors is in both clients' interests as the cheque can be sent in advance to be held as undelivered pending delivery of relevant items and/or confirmation that the sender is in funds, and the disposition can be sent in advance subject to the seller's conditions.

Lenders and clients

The Committee agreed however that so far as settlement with the client and the lender is concerned the seller's agent should ascertain in advance whether the seller would prefer to meet the cost of a CHAPS transfer of funds or opt for the issue of a cheque in relation to (a) redemption of the loan (if the method is not prescribed by the lender), and (b) remit of the free proceeds of sale to the seller. Such instructions will of course be subject to the solicitor ensuring that there are sufficient cleared funds to meet whatever method of payment is adopted.

England and Wales

If a client is purchasing a property in England or Wales out of the proceeds of sale of a property in Scotland, it is important to ascertain the requirements for settling the purchase at the earliest possible stage. Purchase and sale transactions routinely settle by CHAPS transfer in England and Wales and the client's English or Welsh solicitor will assume that he will receive funds by CHAPS transfer. If there will not be sufficient time for a cheque to clear before funds are required in England or Wales, the selling solicitor should explain that to the client and conclude the bargain for the sale on the basis that settlement will be by CHAPS transfer or advise the client that he will need to arrange temporary bridging facilities to await cleared funds. Failure to address these issues at an early stage is likely to lead to a dissatisfied client and a possible complaint to the Scottish Legal Complaints Commission.

Decisions by the Scottish Information Commissioner

In *Conveyancing 2007* pp 62–64 we noted several cases in which the Scottish Information Commissioner, acting on the basis of the freedom of information legislation, had ordered local authorities to release details of statutory notices within their area to organisations such as Miller & Bryce. In 2008 a local authority tried out a different statutory ground in order to resist a request by Miller & Bryce for a copy of all notices or orders made, served, discharged or released, and those which remain extant (ie works and/or monies still outstanding to the Council) during the period 18 January 2008 to 9 July 2008, under or pursuant to s 108 of the Housing (Scotland) Act 1987. See Decision 161/2008, available at http://www.itspublicknowledge.info/ApplicationsandDecisions/Decisions/Decisions.php.

The Council – North Lanarkshire Council – argued that, as failure to comply with such notices might result in a court action by the Council to recover the cost of carrying out the works, the information requested was exempt under s 34(4) of the Freedom of Information (Scotland) Act 2002. This exemption applies to information obtained for the purposes of civil proceedings arising out of investigations which involve the obtaining of information from confidential sources. It was held by the Information Commissioner (i) that the purpose of the statutory notices was not to raise civil proceedings (though that might sometimes be a consequence) but rather was 'for the purposes of instructing those persons having control of houses in serious disrepair to carry out specified works to put right certain defects and to bring the houses up to a reasonable standard of repair', and (ii) that in any event there was no question of obtaining information from confidential sources. Hence the Council was ordered to provide the information requested.

PSG offer to sell investment property

The most recent style produced by the Property Standardisation Group (www.psglegal.co.uk) is an offer to sell an investment property (ie a property which is subject to one or more leases). Iain Macniven introduces the new style in the *Journal of the Law Society of Scotland* for October 2008 (p 62).

House sales down 41%

Figures from Registers of Scotland show that in the third quarter of 2008 (July–September), sales transactions showed a decrease of 41.1% compared to the same quarter in 2007. They were also down 19.4% on the immediately preceding quarter. See http://www.ros.gov.uk/pdfs/2008_11_release.pdf. The actual prices remained, on average, more or less the same as a year ago.

Subcontracting the work: Solicitors Conveyancing Services

In what is no doubt a sign of the times, Your Conveyancer (www.yourconveyancer.co.uk) is offering to do conveyancing work on behalf of law firms in return for a share of the fee. A claimed advantage is that firms will not then 'have to retain, manage and pay for a conveyancing department during periods of economic uncertainty'. Apparently, much of the work is to be done online.

Money laundering

We noted the Money Laundering Regulations 2007, SI 2007/2157, in *Conveyancing 2007* pp 48–49. James Ness has since issued a useful list of FAQs: see (2008) 53 *Journal of the Law Society of Scotland* Feb/30.

Vacant and derelict land

Local government and the Scottish Government produce an annual *Scottish Vacant and Derelict Land Survey*. 'Vacant land' is land which is unused for the purposes for which it is held and is viewed as an appropriate site for development. This land must either have had prior development on it or preparatory work has taken place in anticipation of future development. 'Derelict land' (and buildings) is land which has been so damaged by development that it is incapable of development for beneficial use without rehabilitation. In addition the land must currently not be used for the purpose for which it is held or a use acceptable in the local plan.

The most recent survey, for 2007, is available at http://www.scotland.gov.uk/Publications/2008/01/24150145/0. It discloses that:

- There were 10,240 hectares of derelict and urban vacant land, of which 2,660 hectares (26%) were urban vacant and 7,580 hectares were derelict (74%).
- Since 2002, there has been a decrease of 448 hectares in the total amount of derelict and urban vacant land recorded in the survey, from 10,687 hectares in 2002 to 10,240 hectares in 2007. This is attributable to land being brought back into productive use or being removed due to naturalisation.

- Since 2002, an average of 616 hectares of derelict and urban vacant land was brought back into use each year. The 2007 survey recorded 642 hectares of derelict and urban vacant land being re-used since 2006.
- The local authority with the highest amount of recorded derelict and urban vacant land is North Lanarkshire, containing 1,399 hectares (14% of Scotland total). Glasgow City has the second highest amount with 1,268 hectares (12% of Scotland total). Highland is third with 1,044 hectares (10%).
- 27% of Scotland's population is estimated to live within 500m of a derelict site. The local authorities with the highest proportion of their population living within 500m of derelict land are West Dunbartonshire (59%), Glasgow City (59%) and North Lanarkshire (50%).

Community right to buy

The 100th application to buy was made recently under part 2 of the Land Reform (Scotland) Act 2003 (as to which see *Conveyancing 2003* pp 135–140). Details can be found at www.scotland.gov.uk/News/Releases/2008/12/31101355. Of these 100 applications, 74 have been approved by Ministers but, by the nature of things, most are now waiting until the land in question comes up for sale. Only seven purchases have been completed under the Act while a further two were completed without using the Act. Successful purchases include:

- Silverburn Community Company (Midlothian): the old Chisholm Tank owned by Scottish Water, bought to provide a split-level community hall and green space for the community;
- Neilston Development Trust: the former Clydesdale Bank in Neilston, Renfrewshire, bought to provide opportunities for self-development, training and employment of the community;
- Comrie Development Trust: five parcels of land forming the disused MOD Cultybraggan Camp, at Comrie, Perthshire. The land and buildings are being used for a range of community facilities including low-cost business units and sports facilities.

Barony titles

Two long-running actions against the Lord Lyon were settled in November 2008. These were *Hamilton Ptr* (*Conveyancing 2006* Case (87)) and *Lindberg Ptr* (*Conveyancing 2007* Case (57)). The basis of settlement can be found in an announcement on the Lyon Court website (http://www.lyon-court.com/lordlyon/536.html).

Hamilton Ptr was the culmination of a heated dispute as to the status of barony titles following their severance from the land by s 63 of the Abolition of Feudal Tenure etc (Scotland) Act 2000. Since the 1930s it had been Lyon's practice, in granting coats of arms to barons, to include certain baronial additaments, notably a helmet, red chapeau and mantle. In *Hamilton Ptr*, decided on 15 May 2006, Lyon refused to grant the additaments on the basis that these reflected the heritable jurisdiction of barons and ceased to be appropriate once that jurisdiction was abolished. Further, the practice of granting additaments had arisen at a time when barony titles were associated with a major estate of land, but after the 2000 Act there had ceased to be a connection with the land. Lyon was unmoved by the argument that s 63(1) had preserved a 'right' to additaments. The petitioner, Mrs Hamilton, sought judicial review of Lyon's decision and it is this action which has now been settled. The result is a compromise: barons are to receive one of the additaments, the helmet, but not the others. The full statement by Lyon is as follows:

> In respect of future Petitions for Grants of Arms by persons owning a dignity of baron which has been acquired post the appointed day (that is, 28 November 2004), provided that the Lord Lyon determines that the dignity of baron exists, that the petitioner is a virtuous and well deserving person and determines to exercise his discretion in their favour to grant arms the Lord Lyon will, (1) if so required, officially recognise the petitioner as 'Baron of [the barony]' and (2) grant them ensigns armorial with a helmet befitting their degree, namely the helmet assigned to the barons.

In the second case, *Lindberg Ptr*, decided on 2 April 2007, Lyon declined jurisdiction in a petition for arms on the basis that the petitioner's only connection with Scotland was his barony title, which, after the 2000 Act, no longer attached to land. The settlement terms are that Lyon will, after all, accept jurisdiction in cases such as this. Lyon's statement reads:

> When a petitioner has no connection with Scotland that otherwise brings the petitioner within the jurisdiction of the Lord Lyon, Lyon accepts that subject to other relevant considerations he will accept the ownership of a dignity of a barony as sufficient to bring the petitioner within his discretionary jurisdiction to grant arms to that person as a person who will require to bear arms in Scotland by reason of his ownership of the dignity.

Books

Ross Gilbert Anderson, *Assignation* (Edinburgh Legal Education Trust 2008; ISBN 9780955633201)

Ann Faulds, Trudi Craggs and John Saunders, *Scottish Roads Law*, 2nd edn (Tottel Publishing Ltd 2008; ISBN 9781845927806)

George L Gretton and Andrew J M Steven, *Property, Trusts and Succession* (Tottel Publishing Ltd 2009; ISBN 9781845921538)

Kenneth G C Reid and George L Gretton, *Conveyancing 2007* (Avizandum Publishing Ltd 2008; ISBN 9781904968252)

Robert Rennie (ed), *The Promised Land: Property Law Reform* (W Green & Son Ltd 2008; ISBN 9780414016989)

Robert Rennie and Stewart Brymer, *Conveyancing in the Electronic Age* (W Green & Son Ltd 2008; ISBN 9780414017214)

Articles

(Unattributed) 'Keeping a clean sheet' (2008) 53 *Journal of the Law Society of Scotland* Nov/58 (discussing the treatment of defective titles under the Land Registration (Scotland) Act 1979)

Donna Brown and Ross McDowall, 'Landmark contaminated land case in the House of Lords' (2007) 90 *Greens Property Law Bulletin* 1

Stewart Brymer, 'What next for missives?' (2007) 91 *Greens Property Law Bulletin* 1

Stewart Brymer, 'Linking faces, spaces and places' (2008) 93 *Greens Property Law Bulletin* 5

Stewart Brymer, 'National Gazetteer for Scotland' (2008) 97 *Greens Property Law Bulletin* 1

Tim Bunker, 'Demystifying commercial rent reviews' (2008) 96 *Greens Property Law Bulletin* 5

Jim Burberry, 'VAT and property: new rules for opting to tax' (2008) 96 *Greens Property Law Bulletin* 1

Paul Carnan, 'Another hoop to jump' (2008) 53 *Journal of the Law Society of Scotland* Sept/66 (considering the CML's new disclosure of incentives form)

George B Clark, 'Home reports' (2008) 92 *Greens Property Law Bulletin* 4

Malcolm M Combe, 'No place like home: access rights over "gardens"' (2008) 12 *Edinburgh Law Review* 463

Alistair Duncan, 'The right to roam' (2007) 91 *Greens Property Law Bulletin* 6

Kennedy Foster, 'CML Handbook: why the fuss?' (2008) 53 *Journal of the Law Society of Scotland* Oct/64

Alasdair G Fox, 'Always in the Land Court?' (2008) 53 *Journal of the Law Society of Scotland* March/41

Alasdair G Fox, 'Diverse guidance' (2008) 53 *Journal of the Law Society of Scotland* Sept/56 (considering cases on the provisions in the Agricultural Holdings (Scotland) Act 2003 regarding diversification by the tenant)

Alasdair G Fox and Douglas Reid, 'The power of agreement' (2008) 53 *Journal of the Law Society of Scotland* Dec/54

Len Freedman and Robert Rennie, 'An idea whose time has gone' (2008) 53 *Journal of the Law Society of Scotland* Sept/68 (questioning the 20-year limit for residential leases)

Emma Fursman, 'Repairing the standard' (2008) 53 *Journal of the Law Society of Scotland* Feb/48 (commenting on the new repairing obligations on private landlords introduced by the Housing (Scotland) Act 2005: for a summary see *Conveyancing 2005* pp 26–28)

William M Gordon, 'The struggle for recognition of new servitudes' (2009) 13 *Edinburgh Law Review* 139 (considering *Romano v Standard Commercial Property Securities Ltd* 2008 SLT 859)

George L Gretton, 'Private law and human rights' (2008) 12 *Edinburgh Law Review* 109 (considering *J A Pye (Oxford) Ltd v UK* (2008) 46 EHRR 45)

Hilary Hiram, 'Bequests of residue and crofting tenancies: *Gardner v Curran*' (2009) 13 *Edinburgh Law Review* 143

Martin Hogg, 'Contract formation in the electronic age' (2009) 13 *Edinburgh Law Review* 121 (considering *Carmarthen Developments Ltd v Pennington* [2008] CSOH 139)

Gordon Junor, 'Defining good and tenantable repair – how far can it be done?' (2008) 95 *Greens Property Law Bulletin* 4

Peter Martin, 'Time to face facts: EPCs for non-domestic buildings in Scotland' (2008) 96 *Greens Property Law Bulletin* 3

Stewart Maxwell, 'A better buy' (2008) 53 *Journal of the Law Society of Scotland* May/60 (responding to Graeme McCormick's article)

Graeme McCormick, 'Home reports critique' (2008) 53 *Journal of the Law Society of Scotland* April/60

Alan McMillan and David McArdle, 'Experts and arbiters: ne'er the twain shall meet?' 2008 *Juridical Review* 273

Kirsty Nicholson, 'Leasing by example' (2008) 53 *Journal of the Law Society of Scotland* Aug/68 (on 'green leases')

Peter Nicholson, 'Home reports' (2008) 53 *Journal of the Law Society of Scotland* March/10 and Nov/10

Roddy Paisley, '*Ben Cleuch Estates Ltd*: justice done' (2008) 92 *Greens Property Law Bulletin* 2

Kyle Peddie et al, 'Property and financial markets' (2008) 53 *Journal of the Law Society of Scotland* Oct/10

Tom Quail, 'Family law for conveyancers' (2008) 53 *Journal of the Law Society of Scotland* March/50 (considering the position where parties contribute unequally to a purchase; on this issue see also *Conveyancing 2004* pp 66–71)

Sandra Quinn, 'Making CHAPS work for you' (2007) 90 *Greens Property Law Bulletin* 4

Chris Rae, 'Upwards-only rent review' (2007) 91 *Greens Property Law Bulletin* 4

Kenneth G C Reid, 'Accessory rights in servitudes' (2008) 12 *Edinburgh Law Review* 455 (considering *Moncrieff v Jamieson* 2008 SC (HL) 1)

Robert Rennie, '*Barker v Lewis* on appeal' 2008 SLT (News) 77

Jill J Robbie, 'Short-term benefit and the Lands Tribunal' (2008) 12 *Edinburgh Law Review* 114

Kenneth Ross, 'There may be trouble ahead' (2008) 53 *Journal of the Law Society of Scotland* Jan/48 (commenting on the vagueness of descriptions of common parts in housing developments)

Kenneth Ross, 'Old lessons hold good' (2008) 53 *Journal of the Law Society of Scotland* Oct/60 (discussing insolvency conveyancing)

Alistair Sim, 'Lender claims' (2008) 53 *Journal of the Law Society of Scotland* July/52 (giving examples of possible claims by lenders against solicitors)

Alistair Sim, 'Checking out checklists' (2008) 53 *Journal of the Law Society of Scotland* Nov/44 (discussing risk management and conveyancing)

Laura Smith, 'Battening down in buy-to-let' (2008) 53 *Journal of the Law Society of Scotland* Nov/63

Adrian Stalker, 'Houses in multiple occupancy' 2008 SCOLAG 260

Andrew J M Steven and David A Massaro, 'Standard securities and variations to the standard securities' 2008 SLT (News) 271

Ken Swinton, 'What does a reservation reserve?' (2008) 76 *Scottish Law Gazette* 40 (discussing *McDougall v Heritage Hotels Ltd* 2008 SLT 494)

Ken Swinton, 'Enforcing real burdens – *Barker v Lewis*' (2008) 76 *Scottish Law Gazette* 67

I S Thornton-Kemsley, 'Mobile mast sites for lawyers' (2008) 94 *Greens Property Law Bulletin* 1

Andrew Todd, 'The community infrastructure levy' (2008) 93 *Greens Property Law Bulletin* 4

Andrew Todd, 'Is the price right? A lender's duty to obtain the best price' (2008) 95 *Greens Property Law Bulletin* 3

Andrew Vennard, 'Dually registered or duly registered?: The Title Conditions (Scotland) Act 2003' 2008 SLT (News) 265

Alistair Watt, 'Future access rights: *res merae facultatis*' (2008) 92 *Greens Property Law Bulletin* 1 (discussing *Peart v Legge* 2007 SLT 982)

Lu Xu, 'Problems in the law of the tenement' 2008 *Juridical Review* 131

PART IV
COMMENTARY

COMMENTARY

MISSIVES OF SALE

Buying a new-build property

Buying a new-build house can be a slow business. If the house is bought off plan, or when far from ready, there may be a substantial interval of time between paying the initial deposit and the day when the builder finally announces that the house is ready and entry can be taken. During that time the value of the house may change. If it goes up – as until recently it usually did – the builder may regret having sold so cheaply and look for ways of escaping from the bargain. But if it goes down, it will be the buyer who will be looking for a way out.

Value going up

McDougall v Heritage Hotels Ltd[1] dates from the happy times when house prices seemed always to go up. Heritage Hotels Ltd built a development of residential properties in North Berwick known as 'West Links'. Ms McDougall was interested in buying apartment 8W. The selling price was £360,000. The selling agents, Stewart Saunders, gave her a copy of a leaflet which set out the 'reservation procedure' which, so far as relevant, was as follows:

> Thank you for your interest in West Links Suites, North Berwick. If you wish to purchase a property, the following procedure applies:–
>
> 1. You will be asked to fill out a Reservation Form. A cheque for £500 made payable to Boyds Solicitors will be required to secure the reservation and should be handed to the Selling Agents when completing the reservation form, a copy of which will be issued to you as a receipt. This ensures reservation of your chosen property for a period of fourteen days (no refund of the deposit will be made should you subsequently decide to withdraw).
> 2. The solicitors to the development, Boyds Solicitors, will then send the Missives to your solicitors, and you shall be asked to sign them. During the fourteen day Reservation Period you may organise the relevant valuations/survey reports, as

---

1 [2008] CSOH 54, 2008 SLT 494. For a discussion, see K Swinton, 'What does a reservation reserve?' (2008) 76 *Scottish Law Gazette* 40.

required. Assuming you are satisfied, you will then instruct your solicitors to accept the offer. When Missives are concluded you become bound to purchase the property.

On 20 July 2006 Ms McDougall duly completed the form and paid the £500 deposit, but the 'missives' provided for in the leaflet were never issued. Instead, on 5 October the money was repaid with interest under explanation that 'we have decided to retain Property 8W until further notice'.[1]

Was the builder entitled to do this? That depended on the legal effect of the reservation procedure. The first issue was whether there was a contract between the parties at all. The builder, after all, had not signed anything, and in any event the reservation form included the following unpromising statement:

This form does not create a contract between the developer and the purchaser. The purchaser will be required to enter into missives with the solicitors of the developer within 14 days, failing which the reservation fee may be retained and the property sold to another party.

Although the issue is not closely focused, the court seems to have accepted that there was, or at least might be, a contract between the parties. This conclusion can easily be defended. As the contract would not amount to one for the transfer of land, there was no statutory requirement of writing.[2] And, having regard to its second sentence, the contractual disclaimer just quoted can be read as referring to missives and therefore as not excluding the possibility of a preliminary contract.

But if there was a contract, its terms were far from clear, for it is not easy to make sense of the reservation leaflet. In the action Ms McDougall's first conclusion was for declarator that Heritage Hotels was under a contractual obligation 'to make a formal offer to sell to the pursuer Apartment 8W'. In failing to make such an offer, it was suggested, the defender was in breach of contract. The Lord Ordinary (Lord Clarke) disagreed:[3]

While I am prepared to acknowledge that the language of the documents issued by the first defenders in relation to the reservation procedure, and the terms of certain of the correspondence coming from their agents, might have raised certain expectations in the mind of a lay person reading them,[4] the issue is what legal rights, if any, were created thereby which are now enforceable by the pursuer. In my judgment, the only right she obtained in return for paying £500 was that, during a period of fourteen days after signing the reservation form and paying the £500, the first defenders were not to contract with any other potential purchaser in relation to the property or to sell it to any such person.[5]

---

1 We have no information as to the reason.
2 Requirements of Writing (Scotland) Act 1995 s 1(1)(a)(i). This point was made by counsel for the pursuer: see para 19.
3 Paragraph 22.
4 In fact the documentation was indeed intended to be read, and acted on, by lay persons.
5 The expression 'contract ... or sell' is slightly unhappy. To sell is to contract. Perhaps for 'sell' read 'convey'.

In other words, this is no more than an exclusivity agreement.[1]

The reservation leaflet can certainly be read as supporting such a construction. Admittedly, clause 2 begins by saying that the selling solicitors 'will then send the Missives[2] to your solicitors', but it can be argued that 'will' is being used as a verb of the future rather than as a verb of obligation, for later in the same clause it is stated that 'you will then instruct your solicitors to accept the offer', which was plainly not meant to impose an obligation on the buyer. If that is right, then only clause 1 remains, with its bland statement that payment 'ensures reservation of your chosen property for a period of fourteen days'.

The outcome, however, is hardly satisfactory. In what sense can the buyer be said to have 'reserved' the property? For a period of 14 days the builder was unable to negotiate with anyone else, but there was no obligation to negotiate with the person who made the reservation, still less to send out to that person an offer. And after 14 days the builder could do as it pleased. That is poor value for £500.[3]

One other aspect of the case may be briefly mentioned. On 16 October 2006 Heritage Hotels had disponed the whole development to another company, M H Apartments Ltd, and Ms McDougall argued that it, too, was bound by the contract, on the basis of the 'offside goals' rule.[4] Given the court's view of the effect of the contract, this was plainly a hopeless argument. But even if the contract had been regarded as imposing an obligation to sell, and so as conferring an option on the buyer, it does not follow that such an option would trigger the offside goals rule. The issues are complex and it is not necessary to go into them here.[5] The only cases to have reached the courts have come to opposite results: *Davidson v Zani*[6] and, more recently, *Advice Centre for Mortgages v McNicoll*.[7] In *McDougall* Lord Clarke expressed the *obiter* view that 'it does seem to me that the criticisms made by the Lord Ordinary in the *Advice Centre for Mortgages* case of the sheriff principal's decision in the *Davidson* case appear to have some foundation'. But the question remains an open one.[8]

Value going down

In the current economic climate the value of a new-build house is more likely to go down than up. In most cases there is nothing that can then be done. The buyer

1 An example of such an agreement can be found in another case from 2008, *Aisling Developments Ltd v Persimmon Homes Ltd* [2008] CSOH 140, 2008 GWD 36-542 at paras 12, 13.
2 A strange turn of phrase that suggests that the drafter did not understand the term 'missives'.
3 As already mentioned, the money was repaid, but in fact it is not clear that the buyer was entitled to its return.
4 For the offside goals rule, see K G C Reid, *The Law of Property in Scotland* (1996) paras 695–700; D A Brand, A J M Steven and S Wortley, *Professor McDonald's Conveyancing Manual* (7th edn 2004) paras 32.52–32.62.
5 See A J M Steven, 'Options to purchase and successor landlords' (2006) 10 *Edinburgh Law Review* 432.
6 1992 SCLR 1001.
7 [2006] CSOH 58, 2006 SLT 591.
8 A new decision which touches on this subject, *Gibson v Royal Bank of Scotland* [2009] CSOH 14, will be covered in next year's volume.

is tied into the contract and, when settlement finally happens, must hand over the money in the unhappy knowledge that it is more than the property is now worth. But it is possible that the position is different if there has been serious delay on the developer's part. Suppose for example that missives were concluded back in 2007. Entry is to be 10 days after the house is certified as habitable. Promises as to completion are made but not kept. Months pass and then years. The house is still not ready. Must the buyers wait for ever, their whole life on hold until the builder deigns to finish a house which it may not even have started? Common sense suggests not. Although the contract is unlikely to allow rescission by the buyer for delay, such a right can probably be implied in the event that the house is not completed within a 'reasonable' time.[1] Of course, the difficulty then remains of determining the point at which delay ceases to be reasonable.

Some builders' missives have an express provision on delay, for example exculpating the builder from liability. That may be enough to prevent a 'reasonable time' clause from being implied, on the basis that an express term can sometimes exclude an implied term on the same topic.[2] If so, a possible way round this difficulty is to argue that the express clause is an unfair term – and so invalid – under the Unfair Terms in Consumer Contracts Regulations 1999.[3] In a sense this is not news. The 1999 Regulations transpose an EU Directive from 1993.[4] But while it has always been clear that the Regulations apply to the sale and supply of moveable property – regulation 6 refers to 'goods' – there was doubt as to whether they also apply to land and to buildings on land. That doubt was removed for England by the decision of the Court of Appeal in *R (Khatun and Others) v Newham Borough Council*[5] which held that the Regulations do indeed apply to land. It is improbable that a Scottish court would reach a different conclusion.[6]

The 1999 Regulations are restricted to contracts between a seller or supplier, acting for purposes related to his trade, business or profession, and a 'consumer', defined as a natural person acting outside his trade, business or profession.[7] In consequence, the Regulations would not normally affect 'ordinary' missives of sale, but they can apply to builders' missives unless the buyer is acting in the course of business or is a company or other juristic person. A term can be challenged as unfair only if it has not been 'individually negotiated'.[8] It is further provided that 'a term shall always be regarded as not having been individually negotiated where it has been drafted in advance and the consumer has therefore not been able to influence the substance of the term'.[9] Where the buyers consult

---

1 We owe this suggestion to Professor Robert Rennie. For an example of an implication of 'reasonable' time, in the context of the purifying of suspensive conditions, see *T Bolland & Co v Dundas's Trs* 1975 SLT (Notes) 80.
2 W W McBryde, *The Law of Contract in Scotland* (3rd edn 2007) para 9–10.
3 SI 1999/2083. See eg W C H Ervine, *Consumer Law in Scotland* (4th edn 2008).
4 Council Directive 93/13/EEC, OJ 1993 L95/29.
5 [2005] QB 37.
6 See also Case C-237/02 *Freiburger Kommunalbauten GmbH Baugesellschaft & Co KG v Hofstetter* [2004] ECR I-03403, a decision of the European Court of Justice which takes for granted that Directive 93/13/EEC applies to land.
7 SI 1999/2083 regs 3(1), 4(1).
8 Regulation 5(1).
9 Regulation 5(2).

their solicitors on the terms before missives are concluded the developer might perhaps be able to argue that the terms are to be regarded as having been 'individually negotiated'. Such an argument will not be an easy one, however, for two reasons. In the first place, the burden of proof lies on the builder.[1] Secondly, the fact that *some* of the terms might be individually negotiated is unlikely to affect those which are not, for it is provided that 'notwithstanding that a specific term or certain aspects of it in a contract has been individually negotiated, these Regulations shall apply to the rest of a contract if an overall assessment of it indicates that it is a pre-formulated standard contract'.[2] In cases where the Regulations apply, the result is an important new set of rights for house buyers faced with standard-form contracts containing unpalatable terms.

The Regulations provide that a contractual term 'shall not be binding on the consumer' if it is 'unfair', that is to say, if 'contrary to the requirement of good faith, it causes a significant imbalance in the parties' rights and obligations arising under the contract, to the detriment of the consumer'.[3] Although authority is lacking, and much will depend on the wording of the contract in question, it is easy to see how a term allowing a builder to delay completion indefinitely and without financial penalty might be unfair under this test. Equally, other terms commonly found in builders' missives might be vulnerable to challenge – for example, unreasonable provisions as to payment of the price and the running of interest, or provisions allowing the builder to change the design of the house or the shape of the plot.[4] There is, however, a specific exemption for adequacy of the price,[5] so that a consumer who has made what turns out to be a bad bargain cannot have the price struck down or altered as 'unfair'.

'Would' is not 'could'

In *Connell v Hart*[6] missives of sale of a house set in five acres of land near Shotts provided that:

> We [the sellers' agents] shall obtain a Coal Mining Report and you will have a period of ten days from receipt of same in which to satisfy yourselves [the buyers' agents] in relation to the terms of same. In the event that the report contains anything which in the opinion of the Chartered Surveyor appointed by your clients to inspect the subjects would adversely affect the mineral stability of the subjects then your clients will be entitled but not bound to resile from the bargain.

In the event, the coal mining report warned that 'the property is within the likely zone of influence on the surface from workings in 4 seams of coal at

---

1 Regulation 5(4).
2 Regulation 5(3).
3 Regulations 5(1), 8(1). For further guidance on the meaning of 'unfair', see regs 5(5), 6(1) and sch 2.
4 For example, in another decision from 2008, *Gray v Welsh* [2008] CSIH 11, 2008 GWD 5-84, builders' missives provided that the layout plan 'may be varied by you [ie the builder] as circumstances require'.
5 SI 1999/2083 reg 6(2)(b).
6 [2008] CSIH 67, 2009 GWD 1-12.

shallow to 60m depth, the last date of working being 1938'. It further disclosed the presence of a former mine entry on the site and within 20 metres of the house itself. The report added that 'we have no record of what steps, if any, have been taken to treat the mine entry for possible instability' and suggested a further report might be necessary.

In order to comply with the 10-day period, the buyers' agents immediately sent the report to their clients' surveyor who, it turned out, had been engaged to carry out a mortgage valuation and was not a mining surveyor. Perhaps unsurprisingly, his letter in response was equivocal:

> We note the contents of the report and accordingly recommend the points raised are brought to the attention of the property insurers. An additional report to determine the status of the mine entry will be required before a full assessment can be made by the underwriters.
>
> Should it be determined that the mine entry has not been treated, then this may well have an adverse bearing on the mineral stability of the subjects. Consolidation works would then be necessary to render the entry shaft safe....
>
> We are unable to provide any assurance that the future stability of the property will not be adversely affected by the presence of the mine entry, notwithstanding satisfactory execution of works necessary to stabilise the shaft, should they be required.

On the strength of this letter the buyers purported to resile. The question before the court was whether they were entitled to do so.

The answer turned on the proper meaning of the provision in the missives. This was perhaps in an unusual form. It is common for missives to allow the buyers to resile if the *buyers* are not satisfied as to certain things. But here, doubtless to protect the sellers, there was an attempt at objectivity by requiring that the decision as to whether the report was satisfactory was to be left to a *professional*, namely the buyers' surveyor. In the event, the surveyor had expressed doubt as to the property's future stability. But was doubt enough?

The wording of the relevant clause was reasonably clear. The buyers could resile if and only if, on the basis of the report, their surveyor concluded that there was something which 'would' adversely affect the mineral stability of the property.[1] The surveyor, however, had not gone so far. Partly, perhaps, because of a lack of relevant expertise, he had expressed himself with a degree of caution. If untreated, the mine entry 'may well' give rise to problems, and in any event there could be no 'assurance that the future stability of the property will not be adversely affected by the presence of the mine entry'. In other words, the information disclosed in the report could result in future instability. But as 'could' is not the same thing as 'would', it appeared that the surveyor's letter did not entitle the buyers to resile.

Faced with missives provisions which do not say what one wants, two possible gambits are available. One is to seek to change the words, by means

---

1 Actually the missive clause is slightly odd. A literalist might wonder how anything in the report could 'adversely affect the mineral stability of the subjects'. Words in a report cannot undermine buildings.

of an application for judicial rectification under section 8 of the Law Reform (Miscellaneous Provisions) (Scotland) Act 1985. The other is to leave the words alone but to seek to interpret them in a manner that suits the party. For this purpose the well-known speech of Lord Hoffmann in *Investors Compensation Scheme Ltd v West Bromwich Building Society*[1] provides useful ammunition. In articulating five principles of interpretation, Lord Hoffmann lays particular stress on interpreting words in the context – by reference to the factual matrix – in which they were used. In this way, words may not mean what they seem, for they must be read with regard to the views of 'a reasonable person having all the background knowledge which would reasonably have been available to the parties in the situation in which they were at the time of the contract'.[2] And there is virtually no limit to such background knowledge, which in principle 'includes absolutely anything which would have affected the way in which the language of the document would have been understood by a reasonable man'.[3] Armed with these *dicta*, the buyers sought to prove, by reference to the background circumstances, that 'would' meant 'could', and that accordingly they were entitled to resile on the basis of the surveyor's letter.

Lord Hoffmann's views have been controversial, and in Scotland they have won only qualified approval.[4] In *Glasgow City Council v Caststop Ltd*,[5] the Lord Ordinary, Lord Macfadyen, re-emphasised the importance of the words actually used:

> On the one hand, the approach adopted by the Lord President in *Bank of Scotland v Dunedin Property Investment Co Ltd*[6] involved first inquiring as to the ordinary meaning of the words used, then, having reached a conclusion on that matter, considering the surrounding circumstances in which the contract was entered into to see whether they affected the result of the original inquiry. On the other hand, the approach advocated by Lord Hoffmann in *Investors Compensation Scheme Ltd* runs those two stages together, by regarding the task of construction as the ascertainment of the meaning which the document would convey to a reasonable person having all the background knowledge reasonably available to the parties in the situation in which they were at the time of the contract. Whichever of these approaches is adopted … the result should be the same. The language of the contract is of paramount importance. As Lord Mustill said in *Charter Reinsurance Co Ltd v Fagan*,[7] in a passage quoted with approval by the Lord President in *Bank of Scotland v Dunedin Property Investment Co Ltd* at 661G: 'the inquiry will start, and usually finish, by asking what is the ordinary meaning of the words used'.

This passage by Lord Macfadyen was approved by the Inner House in *Caststop*[8] and has now been approved again in the Inner House in *Connell v Hart*.[9] On the

---

1 [1998] 1 WLR 896.
2 [1998] 1 WLR 896 at 912.
3 At 912–913.
4 See eg Lord Bingham of Cornhill, 'A new thing under the sun? The interpretation of contract and the *ICS* decision' (2008) 12 *Edinburgh Law Review* 374.
5 2002 SLT 47 at para 33.
6 1998 SC 657.
7 [1997] AC 313 at 384B.
8 *Glasgow City Council v Caststop Ltd* 2003 SLT 526 at para 21 *per* Lord Kirkwood.
9 [2008] CSIH 67 at para 27 *per* Lord Carloway.

basis that the words were to be given their ordinary meaning, the court concluded, without difficulty, that 'would' meant 'would' and not 'could'. Accordingly, the buyers were not entitled to resile.

One final thought. Had the missives been left open until the coal mining report was available, the story would presumably have ended quite differently.

Don't collect the mail

Giving notice on behalf of clients is a part of everyday life. But when does such a notice take effect? That was the question at issue in *Carmarthen Developments Ltd v Pennington.*[1]

The facts were remarkable. Missives were concluded for the sale of two plots of land, subject to suspensive conditions in respect of matters such as planning permission. The conditions could be purified only by 'expressly intimating the same in writing to the seller or to the seller's solicitors', and a notice could be sent by post, by hand or by fax. In the event that the conditions were neither purified nor waived by the buyer, either party was entitled to resile at any time after two years. The two-year period ended on 19 October 2007 without purification having been intimated. The following day – a Saturday – the seller's solicitors, who were based in Jedburgh, faxed a letter resiling from the contract. In terms of the missives this did not take effect until 9 am on the next working day, Monday 22 October. But the buyer's solicitors, anticipating this response, prepared and signed a letter declaring the conditions to be purified. That was on the previous day, Friday 19 October. Due to an oversight, the letter was not sent by fax but it was sent by first-class post on the Friday. On the evidence, the Lord Ordinary (Lord Hodge) decided that it did not reach the seller's solicitors until the Monday post.

There were thus two competing letters in transit over the weekend and due to arrive, in a legal sense, on the Monday. As already mentioned, the seller's letter resiling from the bargain would take effect at 9 am on Monday. The question for the court was whether the buyer's letter purifying the condition was served before 9 am. If so, the contract remained in force; if not, the seller was free of the bargain.

Rather than rely on a Post Office delivery, the seller's solicitors usually collected the mail from the local sorting office. The events of the Monday morning are described by Lord Hodge in this way:[2]

> On the morning of Monday, 22 October 2007, Mr Soeder, as was his normal practice, travelled by car with his two daughters from his home to the centre of Jedburgh, where he picked up the firm's mail bag from the sorting office of the Post Office at about 8.50am. Normally he deposited the mail bag in the firm's office nearby before driving for about five minutes to deliver his daughters to their school on the outskirts of Jedburgh just before 9 am. On this occasion, however, his eldest daughter was

---

1 [2008] CSOH 139, 2008 GWD 33-494. For a discussion, see M Hogg, 'Contract formation in the electronic age' (2009) 13 *Edinburgh Law Review* 121.
2 Paragraph 9.

anxious to arrive at school slightly earlier than normal. So Mr Soeder placed the firm's mail bag in his car and drove to the school before returning to the centre of Jedburgh, parking his car and entering his firm's office at about 9.03 am.

It was not seriously argued that the seller's solicitors had actually to *open* the letter (and the mail bag) before notice could be said to have been given. As Lord Hodge put it, 'It is the task of the recipients of mail to arrange for its prompt handling and the sender of a notice cannot be prejudiced by internal delays in so doing.'[1] But if they did not have to open the letter, they at least had to receive it. When did this occur? At 8.50 when the mail bag was collected, or at 9.03 when it reached the office? In those 13 minutes lay the difference between a contract and no contract.

Reasonably enough, Lord Hodge decided that the letter was received when the mail bag was collected. Unluckily for the seller's solicitors, the very act of collecting the mail, slightly ahead of normal office hours, had the effect of defeating their own faxed letter withdrawing from the contract. Collection might not always have this effect. Relying on remarks by Lord Wilberforce in *Brinkibon Ltd v Stahag Stahl GmbH*,[2] Lord Hodge said that questions of when messages were communicated were to be resolved by having regard to the intention of the parties, sound business practice and, in some cases, by a judgment of where the risks should lie.[3] For example, 'different considerations might apply if at the weekend a member of staff of the defender's solicitors happened to be in the Post Office and chose to pick up a mail bag and leave it in the firm's office for consideration on the next working day'.[4] But collection on a working day was a different matter.

Another argument for the buyer had been that notice was given as soon as the letter was *posted*, on the previous Friday. But, surely correctly, Lord Hodge said that the so-called postal rule was confined to the acceptance of offers, and that the exercise of an option, such as an option to declare conditions purified, 'is not the acceptance of an offer but the exercise of a contractual right conferred by the option agreement'.[5]

REAL BURDENS

Economic development burdens

A novelty of the post-feudal world is the 'personal real burden', distinguished from ordinary real burdens by the absence of a benefited property. A personal real burden is thus a burden on a piece of land (the burdened property) in favour, not of another piece of land but of a person. Hence the name. Unlike ordinary real burdens, personal real burdens are available only in strictly limited circumstances

---

1 Paragraph 31.
2 [1983] 2 AC 34 at 42C–D.
3 Paragraph 33.
4 Paragraph 33.
5 Paragraph 14. A brief but helpful analysis of the legal characterisation of options is given in para 15.

and so are uncommon. The Title Conditions (Scotland) Act 2003 allows eight types of personal real burden, classified both by content and by the person in whose favour they may be granted.[1] These are: conservation burdens, rural housing burdens, maritime burdens, economic development burdens, health care burdens, manager burdens, personal pre-emption burdens and personal redemption burdens.[2] Such burdens tend to make two appearances in legislation. In the first place, provision is made for the creation of such burdens for the future (other than pre-emptions and redemptions which may not be so created).[3] Secondly, real burdens imposed under the feudal system which had the characteristics of some (but not all) of the personal real burdens could be converted into such burdens, usually by service and registration by the superior of a notice before the appointed day (28 November 2004).[4] In *Teague Developments Ltd v City of Edinburgh Council*[5] these legislative provisions are considered for the first time by a court, with some unexpected results.

Teague Developments considers economic development burdens, one of the most intriguing and mysterious of the personal real burdens. In its Report on *Real Burdens*, the Scottish Law Commission had opposed the use of personal real burdens for clawback of planning gain and other similar purposes.[6] Nonetheless, an Executive amendment to the Title Conditions Bill during its parliamentary passage resulted in the introduction of the economic development burden. From the start its specification was vague. Section 45(1) of the Title Conditions Act provides that it is 'competent to create a real burden in favour of a local authority, or of the Scottish Ministers, for the purpose of promoting economic development'. What is meant by 'economic development' remains unexplained, beyond the statement in subsection (3) that 'an economic development burden may comprise an obligation to pay a sum of money', presumably by way of clawback. It will be evident that these rather vague provisions leave plenty of scope for doubt and for judicial interpretation.

Teague Developments concerned a burden which had been imposed by the City of Edinburgh District Council in feu dispositions of two plots of land at Salamander Place in Leith granted in 1987 and 1990. Both burdens were similar in substance, and only the 1987 burden need be quoted:

> (EIGHTH) The feu and all buildings to be erected on the feu and any buildings erected in substitution therefor shall be used for general industrial purposes including the feuars' business of agricultural merchants only (provided that for the period from the said date of entry to completion of the development as aforesaid only the feu may also be used for the purposes of car parking in connection with the feuar's business) and

---

1 See further R Paisley, 'Personal real burdens' 2005 *Juridical Review* 377.
2 Title Conditions (Scotland) Act 2003 s 1(3).
3 Title Conditions (Scotland) Act 2003 part 3.
4 Abolition of Feudal Tenure etc (Scotland) Act 2000 ss 18A, 18B, 18C, 27, 60.
5 27 February 2008, Lands Tribunal, available at http://www.lands-tribunal-scotland.org.uk/ decisions/LTS.AFT44.2007.02.rub.html. The Tribunal comprised J N Wright QC and I M Darling FRICS.
6 Scottish Law Commission, Report on *Real Burdens* (Scot Law Com No 181 (2000), available at www.scotlawcom.gov.uk) para 9.34.

no part of the feu or the buildings thereon shall be used at any time for the purpose of brewing, distilling or chemical works or for the purpose of keeping a public house or tavern or clubhouse licensed for the sale of excisable liquors or for the purpose of trading in, selling or keeping for sale spirits, wines or malt liquors; Further, in no circumstances shall anything be done upon any part of the feu which shall be deemed a nuisance or which may occasion disturbance or annoyance to the Superiors or any of the neighbouring feuars or proprietors or their tenants or may injure the amenity of the neighbourhood and the Superiors shall be the sole judge of what constitutes a nuisance, annoyance, disturbance or injury to amenity; Further, no business nameplate or sign or advertisement of any kind shall be affixed or displayed anywhere on the feu without the prior consent in writing of the Superiors.

Wishing to preserve the burdens, Edinburgh Council served and registered the appropriate notice under section 18B of the Abolition of Feudal Tenure Act – one of only 31 such notices to be registered.[1] The owner of the land challenged the notice before the Lands Tribunal.[2]

The main issue for the Tribunal was whether the burdens qualified as economic development burdens – whether, in other words, they were imposed 'for the purpose of promoting economic development'. An initial difficulty, the Tribunal acknowledged, was presented by the negative character of the burdens: 'we accept that the negative, restrictive expression is not a very good starting point in the search for a purpose of "promoting"'.[3] But while it was true that the restrictive language prevented certain types of economic activity – brewing and distilling for example – it also prevented all *non*-economic use, and its broad effect was to restrict the land to uses which were industrial and so conducive to economic development. Extrinsic evident reinforced this impression. Council employees testified to the existence, at the time, of an elaborate Leith Project, involving Edinburgh Council, the SDA and Lothian Regional Council. One of its aims was to clear sites and make them available for manufacturing firms. The preparation and sale of the sites at Salamander Place could readily be presented as part of this Project. Accordingly, the Tribunal concluded, the burdens met the test of promoting economic development.

Two points in particular can be taken from this decision. First, in deciding whether a burden has the purpose of promoting economic activity, it is competent – indeed often necessary – to consider evidence as to the parties' intentions. The implications, however, are unsettling. Being potentially perpetual, real burdens may often have to be read and understood long after they were created. That is why the content of burdens must be discoverable within the four corners of the deed.[4] But admirable as this self-denying rule is, it loses much of its point if the actual validity of the burden relies on extrinsic evidence of the events surrounding its birth. Yet that would seem to be the position with economic

---

1 For the numbers of notices registered, see *Conveyancing 2004* pp 95–96.
2 For jurisdiction, see Abolition of Feudal Tenure etc (Scotland) Act 2000 s 44.
3 Paragraph 39. See also K G C Reid, *The Abolition of Feudal Tenure in Scotland* para 4.12 (quoted at para 46 of the Tribunal's opinion).
4 Title Conditions (Scotland) Act 2003 s 4(2)(a). Puzzlingly, the Tribunal referred (para 35) to the four *walls* of the deed.

development burdens, and perhaps with other similar types of personal real burden (such as conservation burdens and health care burdens) as well. If that result is to be avoided in practice, it will be important for the burdens themselves to contain information as to the economic development which they are intended to promote.

Secondly, it is not necessary that economic development be the only purpose of a burden so long as it is 'a material and important purpose'.[1] Other purposes can then be carried along on its coat tails. In the burdens considered in *Teague Developments*, the Tribunal discerned as additional purposes the interests of good estate management and the requirements of public accountability, and to these can be added the purpose of preventing disturbance to neighbours. None of this matters. As long as the test of promoting economic development is satisfied, a burden can also include provisions which have nothing to do with such development.[2] Whether so accommodating a view is good law does, however, seem open to doubt.

Interest to enforce

Ordinary real burdens

To enforce a real burden there must be interest as well as title, and one of the innovations of the Title Conditions (Scotland) Act 2003 is that interest is now the subject of a statutory definition, in section 8. Thus, at least in the normal case, a person has such interest if and only if

> in the circumstances of any case, failure to comply with the real burden is resulting in, or will result in, material detriment to the value or enjoyment of the person's ownership of, or right in, the benefited property.

This provision allows for two alternatives: there must be material detriment either to the *value* of the benefited property, or to its *enjoyment*. And in both cases the guardian against inappropriate enforcement is the word 'material'. Only detriment which is 'material' will justify enforcement. Anything less must be endured with the fortitude which is to be expected of a good neighbour.

The first case on the meaning of section 8, *Barker v Lewis*[3] – a decision of Sheriff G J Evans at Cupar Sheriff Court – was discussed in last year's volume.[4] Since then an appeal has been heard by the sheriff principal.[5] The dispute concerned a modern development of five houses at Cauldside Farm Steadings, about two miles from St Andrews. Access was by a private road. The development was regulated by a deed of conditions which, among other restrictions, limited the use

---

1 Paragraph 41.
2 At para 49 the Tribunal commented that each of the other purposes in the burden 'takes its content from the industrial use provision – nuisance or annoyance would no doubt be gauged in the context of industrial use'.
3 2007 SLT (Sh Ct) 48.
4 *Conveyancing 2007* pp 73–77.
5 2008 SLT (Sh Ct) 17.

of each house to 'a domestic dwellinghouse with relative offices only and for use by one family only and for no other purpose whatsoever'. The 'tranquil location' promised by the developer's brochure appeared under threat when one of the owners began to use her house for a bed-and-breakfast business.[1] Eventually, the owners of three of the other houses sought interdict. At first instance the sheriff accepted that the business was in breach of the burden in the deed of conditions, and that there was title to enforce.[2] The question of interest, however, was seen as more difficult. It was true that life for the pursuers had been made less pleasant. The defender's business attracted around 250 visitors a year, leading to more traffic, increased noise from late arrivals and early departures, some inappropriate parking, and a general loss of privacy and peace. The disturbance was increased by the secluded nature of the development, and the fact that the houses were close together. Nevertheless, the sheriff concluded that the pursuers had failed to show interest to enforce, and interdict was refused. There was detriment to the pursuers' enjoyment of their properties, no doubt, but such detriment was not 'material' in the manner required by section 8.

This decision was not only surprising; it was alarming. It seemed to strike at the very foundations of the system of real burdens. Consider the facts. The defender bought her property in the full knowledge of the restrictions in her title. These she deliberately disregarded, causing continuing upset and disruption to her neighbours.[3] Yet the neighbours could not enforce the conditions to which all parties had voluntarily agreed. If a deed of conditions could not be made to work in a small and isolated community such as Cauldside Farm Steadings, how could it be made to work in the urban housing estates where it was more commonly found? If the sheriff's decision was correct, deeds of conditions would be little more than pious exhortations, about as legally binding as New Year's resolutions.

The sheriff's decision was founded on an expansive reading of 'material detriment'. 'Material', said the sheriff, meant 'substantial'; furthermore, in seeking to understand its scope it was helpful to look at the standards applied in the law of nuisance. Both propositions, however, could be challenged, as one of us pointed out in an article which was relied on in the appeal.[4] 'Material' could not mean 'substantial' because 'substantial' was used elsewhere in the Title Conditions Act and must presumably mean something else. And there was no basis for using the common law of nuisance to interpret a statutory test of interest to enforce. In the event the respondents did not seek to support the sheriff's approach on these

---

1 See www.millhouse-standrews.com/.

2 On this point the sheriff's judgment contains an interesting discussion (at 54–55) of the extent to which *Low v Scottish Amicable Building Society* 1940 SLT 295 is consistent with the decision of the First Division in *Colquhoun's Curator Bonis v Glen's Tr* 1920 SC 737.

3 In fairness, she had obtained a letter from the developer's solicitors, at the time of purchase, to the effect that 'notwithstanding the terms of the Deed of Conditions etc ... our clients consent to the use by your client ... of the subjects ... as a bed and breakfast establishment'. But it was the neighbours, not the developer, who had continuing enforcement rights.

4 K G C Reid, 'Interest to enforce real burdens: how material is "material"?' (2007) 11 *Edinburgh Law Review* 440. The arguments are summarised in *Conveyancing 2007* pp 74–76.

two points. In the words of the sheriff principal,[1] what the sheriff had done was to 'set the threshold too high'.[2]

The question then remained as to what the proper threshold might be? In other words, how 'material' must detriment be before neighbours are able to show an interest to enforce? On this question the sheriff principal was reluctant to be drawn. Whether the detriment is material, he said, 'will depend on the particular circumstances of the case'.[3] The sheriff principal continued:[4]

> If one has to resort to synonyms at all, in my view a better reflection of the true meaning of 'material' in this context would be found in words such as 'significant', 'of consequence' or 'important', although in relation to the latter word it might be thought to carry an inappropriate connotation of subjectivity which it is necessary to remove. Even these words however are no less imprecise than the word 'material' itself. While this imprecision might be seen as a weakness in the legislation, it might equally be inferred that there is a deliberate intention to leave the identification of an interest to enforce to the judgement of the court on the basis of a common sense and practical approach in light of the particular circumstances presented to it. Much will depend on the nature of the burden and its breach, the nature of the neighbourhood, including issues of proximity of burdened and benefited properties, and no doubt other circumstances particular to the case under consideration – the question being whether in those circumstances the detriment, viewed objectively, is of sufficient significance or import to persuade the court that it is proper to allow the benefited proprietor to enforce the burden. If that leaves an element of uncertainty for burdened and benefited proprietors that is simply the consequence of the general and imprecise terms in which the Scottish Parliament has chosen to legislate.

This test is less exacting than that originally suggested by the sheriff but, as Professor Rennie has pointed out,[5] more exacting than under the previous common law.[6] Until there is further case law it not possible to be more precise. In the meantime the sheriff principal's decision is to be welcomed as restoring purpose and content to the law of real burdens.

In the event the appeal was refused. Having won on the law, the appellants were deemed to lose on the facts, for the sheriff principal was not prepared to disturb the sheriff's view that the evidence disclosed 'only infrequent minor irritations'.[7] 'Even on a lowered threshold of detriment', therefore, 'the appellants have not demonstrated that the incidents founded on constitute "material detriment" to the enjoyment of their ownership of their respective properties'.[8]

1　R A Dunlop QC.
2　Paragraph 25.
3　Paragraph 23.
4　Paragraph 27.
5　R Rennie, '*Barker v Lewis* on appeal' 2008 SLT (News) 77 at 79.
6　Ken Swinton suggests that 'in a far wider range of cases than might have commonly been envisaged, neighbouring proprietors may not be able to prove material detriment and therefore have no interest to enforce'. See 'Enforcing real burdens – *Barker v Lewis*' (2008) 67 *Scottish Law Gazette* 67 at 68.
7　Paragraph 30.
8　Paragraph 32.

No doubt that is a reasonable approach. Yet one wonders whether the sheriff's initial evaluation would have been so benign if he had applied the correct test of material detriment.

Personal real burdens

The definition in section 8 of interest to enforce does not apply to personal real burdens.[1] This is because, by section 47, 'the holder of a personal real burden is presumed to have an interest to enforce the burden'. In *Teague Developments Ltd v City of Edinburgh Council*,[2] discussed earlier, the presumption in section 47 was taken by the Lands Tribunal to be irrebuttable, so that a holder would always have an interest to enforce. Among the reasons given for adopting this view was the fact that 'burdened proprietors who can demonstrate lack of interest have, under the statutory scheme, a recognised means of ridding themselves of the burden',[3] namely by applying to the Lands Tribunal for discharge on the basis of factor (b) of section 100 (the extent to which the condition confers benefit on the benefited property/the public). The argument is perhaps a strange one. On the one hand, it acknowledges that the holder of a personal real burden might not have interest to enforce. On the other hand, it proposes that the fact that lack of interest can be pled *indirectly*, in a Lands Tribunal application, is an indication that it cannot be pled *directly* – despite the fact that the indirect remedy is equally available in the case of ordinary real burdens.

In fact there is nothing in the language of section 47 to suggest that the presumption is irrebuttable. After all, if that had been the intention, then – as was indeed argued by the appellants in *Teague Developments* – it would have been easy to say so expressly. As it happens, the actual intention is made perfectly clear in the report of the Scottish Law Commission which led to the legislation:[4]

> In the absence of a benefited property, praedial interest cannot be required, and we suggest that interest be presumed but capable of rebuttal, for example on the ground that the restriction is trivial or inappropriate.

There is nothing surprising in this approach. Personal real burdens are replacements for feudal burdens where the rule, likewise, was that the interest to enforce of the holder – the feudal superior – was presumed but could be rebutted.[5]

---

1 Title Conditions (Scotland) Act 2003 s 8(6).
2 27 February 2008, Lands Tribunal, available at http://www.lands-tribunal-scotland.org.uk/ decisions/LTS.AFT44.2007.02.rub.html. The Tribunal comprised J N Wright QC and I M Darling FRICS.
3 Paragraph 54.
4 Scottish Law Commission, Report on *Real Burdens* (Scot Law Com No 181 (2000)) para 9.21. This passage does not seem to have been drawn to the attention of the Lands Tribunal in *Teague Developments*.
5 For a full discussion, see R Rennie, 'Interest to enforce real burdens', in R Rennie (ed), *The Promised Land: Property Law Reform* (2008).

One-family restrictions and HMOs

Ballantyne Property Services Trs v Lawrence[1] is the first occasion on which the Lands Tribunal has been asked to vary a one-family-only burden in order to allow multiple occupancy. And whereas applications before the Tribunal are usually successful,[2] this decision is notable for the fact that the application failed. The decision is thus bad news for buy-to-let landlords, but good news for those who want to stop the house next door from being rented out to students.

The case concerned the Inveresk Gardens estate in Musselburgh, where 467 houses are governed by a single deed of conditions recorded in 1988. The applicants were the trustees for a firm which specialised in buy-to-let properties. They had recently bought one of the houses in the estate – the semi-detached house, 7 Denholm Drive – with the intention of letting it to five students from nearby Queen Margaret University. When neighbours spotted the advertisements they called on them to comply with the title conditions. These included a requirement that 'none of said houses shall ever in any way be sub-divided or occupied by more than one family at a time'. The current application was for variation of that requirement to the extent of allowing multiple occupancy. It was opposed by a number of neighbours, while many others signed a *pro forma* letter of objection.

Where an application is opposed, the Tribunal must determine whether it is reasonable to grant it in the light of the 10 factors set out in section 100 of the Title Conditions Act.[3] As often, the Tribunal began its consideration with factor (f) (the purpose of the condition). In the Tribunal's view, the purpose of the condition in question, and indeed of other conditions in the deed of conditions, was 'to create and then preserve, so far as it is possible to do so, full residential amenity in a modern family-oriented housing estate'.[4] That purpose could still be fulfilled today. Furthermore, it conferred obvious benefit on the respondents (factor (b)). No doubt it was an exaggeration to say that the presence of students would mean 'noisy parties and more, noisier and faster cars, threatening the peace of the neighbourhood and the safety of young children'.[5] Apart from anything else, 'from its statistical profile produced to us, this university appears to us to be inclined towards vocational higher education which may not attract rowdier elements of the student population' (perhaps an optimistic assessment).[6] And the HMO licensing system imposed a further element of control. Nonetheless, the Tribunal accepted that the application, if successful, would lead to more traffic and more noise, and if (as seemed likely) there were more such applications, this would begin to change the character of the estate and perhaps lead to a decline in property values.

Against factor (b) must be set factor (c) (impeding enjoyment of burdened property). But the applicants bought the property with their eyes open. Even with the title condition, it could still be used profitably for renting – although the rent

---

1 31 October 2008, Lands Tribunal, available at http://www.lands-tribunal-scotland.org.uk/decisions/LTS.TC.2008.18.html. The Tribunal comprised J N Wright QC and K M Barclay FRICS.
2 *Conveyancing 2007* pp 87–89. And see pp 155–58 below.
3 Title Conditions (Scotland) Act 2003 s 98.
4 Paragraph 23.
5 Paragraph 27.
6 Paragraph 29.

from five students was likely to be higher (c £1500 a month rather than £900 a month for a family house). Or it could be occupied by the owners.

The Tribunal summarised its views as follows:[1]

> Weighing all the matters up, we first remind ourselves that we are considering a particular application in relation to a particular house, although it is accepted that it would be likely to have a wider implication for the estate. The factors in the applicants' favour would appear to be the loss of the rental value increase and the more general consideration of the reasonableness of meeting a new demand for accommodation in the area. Set against this, we think that this is a title condition which contributes substantially to achieving the purpose of preserving residential amenity. We note the scale of this application – not just two or three unrelated persons but five in one house, with the clear indication that other such cases would be likely to follow. That persuades us that there would be a substantial risk of at least gradual deterioration in the amenity. The condition is of substantial benefit to the benefited proprietors. The newness of the estate – residents in this part have not been there any more than 10 years – influences us: this is not a title condition introduced in and for a different era, and it can still achieve its original purpose. We are not persuaded that the arrival of the university is a change which reasonably requires these house owners to give up an important protection in their titles. While the public interest in the provision of accommodation is a factor, the interest in maintaining residential amenity at this estate is also a community interest and is entirely legitimate. Although they are of course fully entitled to apply to have the title condition lifted, the applicants were well aware of the condition and should have been in no doubt that their proposal fell foul of it. In all the circumstances, we have reached the view that it would not be reasonable to grant this application.

This is an important decision, suggesting a reluctance to vary one-family-only provisions for the benefit of students. But its limitations should be noted. It relates to a modern housing estate and not to the more individualised Victorian tenements often colonised by students. It relates to a relatively large group of students and so may not be a reliable guide to the Tribunal's attitude to a smaller group. And, while it saves the burden, it leaves open the question, discussed above, as to whether there would necessarily be interest to enforce in the event that the student let went ahead – especially if the occupants, being vocational students, were as quiet and sober as the Tribunal seems to have envisaged.

LEASES

A new clause for commercial leases?

In the *Possfund* case[2] the pursuer was the landlord and the defender the tenant of commercial property at Falcon Road West, Edinburgh. The landlord wished to send in contractors to test the ground under the building to see if fuel kept on

---

1 Paragraph 42.
2 *Possfund Custodial Trustee Ltd v Kwik-Fit Properties Ltd* [2008] CSOH 79, revd [2008] CSIH 65, 2009 SLT 133, 2008 Hous LR 82. In the Inner House the opinion of the court was delivered by Lord Reed.

site had caused contamination. The works would take several days and would include the drilling of test boreholes. The tenant refused permission, whereupon the landlord raised this action to have it declared that it was entitled to carry out the work. The lease had no provision expressly dealing with such an issue. At first instance it was held that the lease, reasonably interpreted, gave the landlord this right. The tenant reclaimed. The Inner House held that the lease, reasonably interpreted, did not give the landlord this right.

The Inner House's starting point seems to have been that 'since a lease is essentially a grant of possession of the subjects of the lease for the period of the lease, it is implicit, if not expressed, that the landlord is precluded from any action which encroaches materially upon the tenant's possession of those subjects during that period'.[1] A clear basis in the lease would therefore have been needed to allow the landlord to carry out such works.

We draw attention to this decision because it may be that solicitors acting for landlords in new leases should consider the possibility of adding a clause giving the landlord the sort of right claimed in this case. Obviously this, like everything else, is a matter for negotiation and agreement between the parties.

Irritancy

The story

The background to *Tawne Overseas Holdings Ltd v The firm of Newmiln Farms*[2] can be found in a report published in the *Daily Telegraph* on 22 April 2005:

> A couple who transformed a run-down mansion into a luxurious hotel frequented by A-list celebrities are facing eviction by the ruling family of the Gulf state of Qatar. Newmiln House Hotel in Perthshire is owned by Prince Abdul Aziz al-Thani, the brother of the Emir of Qatar, and has been used as a bolthole by the actors Jude Law and Liam Neeson and the model Kate Moss. It offers its guests some of the best shooting and fishing in Britain, which has attracted country sports enthusiasts such as the cricketer Ian Botham and the footballer Paul Gascoigne. A three-day break costs £2,500 and guests are welcomed by a piper to the 18th century property set in 700 acres.

Actually the owner was not Abdul Aziz al-Thani, but Tawne Overseas Holdings Ltd, a British Virgin Islands company: seemingly Prince Abdul Aziz al-Thani was the company's principal shareholder. Newmiln House Hotel was leased to Mr and Mrs McFarlane as individuals. There was also a farm, and that was leased to a firm called Newmilns Farm, of which Mr and Mrs McFarlane were the partners. The aggregate annual rent for the two leases was £115,000. When the McFarlanes had difficulty paying, a new agreement was entered into, reducing the aggregate rent to £85,000 (£20,000 for the house, and £65,000 for the farm). Various other changes to the terms of the leases were made at the same

---

1 Paragraph 13.
2 [2008] CSOH 12, 2008 Hous LR 18.

time. Clause 7 of the new agreement said:

> In the event that the McFarlanes fail hereinafter to make any payment of rent under the house lease or the agricultural lease within one month of the due date of payment, then Tawne shall, without prejudice to any other remedy available to them, be entitled to immediately claim ... the amount which they would have been entitled to collect by way of rent in terms of the house lease and the agricultural lease, had the aggregate rental of both leases remained at £115,000 per annum.

Despite the renegotiated terms the McFarlanes still had difficulties with paying the rent. A further agreement reduced the aggregate rent to £70,000 (£20,000 for the house and £50,000 for the farm), but the McFarlanes still had problems, and by July 2004 £35,000 was overdue (£10,000 on the house lease and £25,000 on the farm lease). On 26 July 2004 Tawne served pre-irritancy notices. The McFarlanes made partial payment and no irritancy notices were served. In October 2004 Tawne invoked clause 7 (above) and demanded rent at the original level. The McFarlanes tendered payment at the lower rate but this payment was rejected by Tawne. On 25 October 2004 Tawne served another pre-irritancy notice. The McFarlanes continued to tender full payment of the lower rent but this continued to be rejected. Notices dated 30 November 2004 from Tawne were served on the McFarlanes irritating the two leases. The McFarlanes refused to flit. Tawne then raised an action of declarator of irritancy plus a removing and a second action for payment of unpaid rent (as calculated under clause 7) in respect of each lease – four actions altogether. All four failed.

The first ground: the pre-irritancy notice was invalid

The first ground of decision was that the pre-irritancy procedure required by section 4 of the Law Reform (Miscellaneous Provisions) (Scotland) Act 1985 had not been properly complied with. That section says that the pre-irritancy notice must give the tenant at least 14 days from the date of the *service* of the notice. But the pre-irritancy notices served by Tawne had required payment within 14 days from the date of the notice itself. Tawne admitted the error, but sought to argue that strict compliance was not necessary. Not surprisingly, the Lord Ordinary[1] was unimpressed. He held the pre-irritancy notice to be ineffectual. Therefore the irritancy had not been incurred.

Section 7 of the 1985 Act says that section 4 does not apply to agricultural tenancies.[2] Hence the first ground of the decision could apply only to the house lease, not to the farm lease. Moreover, the decision that the pre-irritancy notice was invalid in point of form could not affect Tawne's action for payment of rent at the original high rate. In other words, the first ground of decision applied only to one of the four actions – irritancy of the house lease.

---

1 Lord Malcolm.
2 The Scottish Law Commission has recommended that statutory control of irritancy should be extended to agricultural tenancies: see Report on *Irritancy in Leases of Land* (Scot Law Com No 191 (2003)) para 3.17; and see also paras 1.18–1.23.

The second ground: clause 7 was void

Section 48 of the Agricultural Holdings (Scotland) Act 1991 provides:

> Notwithstanding any provision to the contrary in a lease of an agricultural holding, the landlord shall not be entitled to recover any sum, by way of higher rent, liquidated damages or otherwise, in consequence of any breach or non-fulfilment of a term or condition of the lease, which is in excess of the damage actually suffered by him in consequence of the breach or non-fulfilment.

The defenders invoked this in relation to the farm lease. It was held that the provision applied and that accordingly the higher rent was not due in respect of the farm rent.

What about clause 7 in relation to the house lease? The Lord Ordinary held that section 48 of the 1991 Act 'broadly reflects the common law'[1] and had no difficulty in striking down clause 7 for the house lease too, as a penalty clause. It is not often that the courts strike down a clause as a penalty clause. It is apparent that the Lord Ordinary considered this a clear case. Tawne argued that clause 7 was merely part of a pro-tenant package and so could not be considered unfair but the Lord Ordinary did not agree:[2]

> Various terms of the original agreements were changed, some to the benefit of the defenders, some to the benefit of the pursuers. Had the only change been a reduction of the rent, then it would have been easier to accept the pursuers' position, though even then, I would have expected it to be made plain that the change was being made without prejudice to the original agreements and purely by way of a concession to the defenders. As it is, the original agreements were altered in various material respects.

The third ground: irritancy therefore never incurred

Given that the rent never did revert to the original level, there could be no basis for the two actions seeking recovery of unpaid rent, for the tenants had either paid or tendered payment of the reduced rent, and if Tawne had refused to accept the tendered rent, that was its problem. As for the irritancy actions, they necessarily failed too, because they were in respect of non-payment of rent that in fact was not due.

SERVITUDES

Possession 'as of right'

Good possession and bad

In order for possession to found positive prescription, it must be possession *of the right kind*. The point is easily overlooked. Yet a person who possesses in the wrong way gains nothing, even if the possession is for 20 years.

---

1 Paragraph 17.
2 Paragraph 16.

When is possession of the right kind? The Prescription Act gives some help: if a person is to acquire a servitude by prescription he must possess 'openly, peaceably and without judicial interruption'[1] – a series of ideas which recalls, no doubt intentionally, the Roman law expression, possession *nec vi nec clam nec precario*.[2] Missing from the Prescription Act is *nec precario* (not by permission), yet this too is an indispensable requirement for prescription. Today it is usually expressed by saying that the possession must be 'as of right', and hence not by mere permission or on some other basis. In Scotland this idea is, however, a modern one. It is absent from the institutional writers. Perhaps more surprisingly, it is absent too from Mark Napier's celebrated *Commentaries on the Law of Prescription in Scotland*, which was published, in two parts, in 1839 and 1854. It can first be found in cases decided in the last quarter of the nineteenth century,[3] and by the end of that century it was an established part of the law. The idea is not unique to Scotland. It is found in English law, as one might expect,[4] but also in French law[5] and in the law of other Continental systems.[6]

In Scotland, 'regular' prescription – prescription in respect of ownership and most other real rights – requires a registered title as well as possession, and the main requirement for possession is that it be on the basis of the title – 'founded on' the title, as the Prescription Act puts it.[7] But with servitudes, and also public rights of way, no registered title is necessary, only possession;[8] and it is in those two areas, where possession is all, that the idea of possession 'as of right' has been mainly developed. Although the point has sometimes been disputed,[9] it is now well established that, in this respect at least, there is a uniform doctrine as between servitudes and public rights of way, and that the cases can be used interchangeably.[10]

Although the law has sometimes seemed to be otherwise,[11] the accepted test today is that a person possesses 'as of right' where he possesses *as if* he had the

---

1 Prescription and Limitation (Scotland) Act 1973 s 3(2).
2 D 8.5.10 pr (Ulpian). The context is *aquaeductus*.
3 *Purdie v Steil* (1749) Mor 14511 is sometimes classified as an example (see eg D J Cusine and R R M Paisley, *Servitudes and Rights of Way* (1998) para 10.19), but no reason for the decision is given, and Napier (*Prescription* p 349) may be correct in classifying it as an example of failure of *animus possidendi*.
4 See eg K Gray and S F Gray, *Elements of Land Law* (5th edn 2009) paras 5.2.62 ff.
5 Code Civil art 2232.
6 For a brief discussion, see L van Vliet, 'Acquisition of a servitude by prescription in Dutch law', in S van Erp and B Akkermans (eds), *Towards a Unified System of Land Burdens?* (2006) pp 58–60.
7 Prescription and Limitation (Scotland) Act 1973 s 1(1).
8 Although with servitudes it is also possible to acquire by prescription on the basis of a title: see Prescription and Limitation (Scotland) Act 1973 s 3(1). This provision is rarely relied on.
9 *Nationwide Building Society v Walter D Allan Ltd* 2004 GWD 25-539 at para 39 *per* Lady Smith.
10 *McGregor v Crieff Co-operative Society Ltd* 1915 SC (HL) 93 at 103–104 *per* Lord Dunedin; *Aberdeen City Council v Wanchoo* [2006] CSOH 196, 2007 SLT 289 at para 31 *per* Lord Glennie; *Neumann v Hutchison* 2008 GWD 16-297 at para 42 *per* Sheriff Principal R A Dunlop QC.
11 In *Nationwide Building Society v Walter D Allan Ltd* 2004 GWD 25-539 at para 15, Lady Smith seemed to revive a view, associated with Lord Young but long since abandoned, that prescriptive possession did not *constitute* a right but rather *proved* that such a right had been granted at some unknown time in the past. For Lord Young's view, see *Grierson v School Board of Sandsting and Aithsting* (1882) 9 R 437 at 442–443; *Macnab v Munro Ferguson* (1890) 17 R 397 at 402; *Duke of Athole v McInroy's Trs* (1890) 17 R 456 at 463.

right or, in another formulation, in *assertion* of the right. 'As if of right' would thus be a more accurate formulation than 'as of right'. The test is an objective one: as Lord Mackay said in *Marquis of Bute v McKirdy & McMillan*,[1] 'in selecting between tolerance on the one hand and user as of right on the other, it is not what the parties thought or said in their private minds, it is what they did'.[2] If the volume and nature of the possession is such as might be taken by a person who already holds a servitude right, that is sufficient for the purposes of establishing such a right by prescription. Whether either party *thought* that the right existed is irrelevant. Apart from anything else, the Scottish law of prescription makes no requirement of good faith.

The essentials of the doctrine of possession 'as of right' are well-settled, therefore, and have been for many years. Yet it continues to give trouble. It is as if the very imprecision of the words 'as of right' provides a standing temptation for courts to go astray. In our 2006 volume we discussed two cases – *Neumann v Hutchison*[3] and *Aberdeen City Council v Wanchoo*[4] – in which, or so it seemed to us, the courts had indeed gone astray. Both decisions have since been appealed, in part on the back of our comments. In *Neumann* the sheriff principal has undone the damage which was done by the trial judge.[5] In *Wanchoo*, however, an Extra Division of the Court of Session has affirmed the original decision.[6] These cases can now be considered in turn.

Neumann v Hutchison

If possession is not 'as of right' it is usually because it is by permission or, as it is sometimes called, by tolerance – although there are other possibilities as well, as will be seen later. This means that disputes about the quality of possession tend to resolve into disputes about whether the possession is by tolerance or as of right. *Neumann v Hutchison*[7] was such a dispute. The facts were that, since 1976, the pursuer had owned a mid-terrace house, 146 Main Street, Callander, and more or less from the start he had taken access by car to the rear of the house by means of a private road and yard at one end of the terrace. The road and yard were part of what was originally a bus depot belonging to Walter Alexander & Son Ltd. The bus depot closed in 1992 and today, after one intermediate owner, it is a vehicle service and repair workshop known as MAC Burnside Garage and owned by the defenders.

In 2004 the defenders applied for planning permission to build flats in the yard. Under the plans the area directly in front of the pursuer's access would be either garden ground or parking spaces. Either way access to the pursuer's property

---

1 1939 SC 93 at 99.
2 See also *Aberdeen City Council v Wanchoo* 2008 SC 278 at para 18 *per* Lord Eassie; *Neumann v Hutchison* 2008 GWD 16-297 at paras 54–57 *per* Sheriff Principal R A Dunlop QC.
3 2006 GWD 28-628, discussed in *Conveyancing 2006* pp 124–128.
4 [2006] CSOH 196, 2007 SLT 289, discussed in *Conveyancing 2006* pp 122–124.
5 2008 GWD 16-297.
6 [2008] CSIH 6, 2008 SC 278, 2008 SLT 106.
7 2008 GWD 16-297.

would cease to be possible from the yard. At about the same time the defenders began to park vehicles in the yard in such a way as to block the pursuer's access. The pursuer responded by raising this action, in which he sought to establish a servitude by prescription over the yard and to interdict the defenders from interfering with it.

After a proof the sheriff was satisfied that there had been possession for 20 years, and that its volume was sufficient for the purposes of prescription. Admittedly, the use in the early years – at which time the pursuer's property was tenanted – was limited to access for occasional deliveries and for visits by friends. But in later years possession was regular and sustained, with the pursuer adding hard standing (which encroached on the yard) in 1984, and building a carport 10 years later. Whether that possession was by tolerance or 'as of right' was, however, a different matter.

Possession is by tolerance if it is founded on permission. The equivalent of *precarium* in Roman law, it requires 'a positive act of granting the use of the property, as opposed to mere acquiescence in its use'.[1] Of course, the granting of permission can be done informally or even by implication, as Lord Dunedin emphasised,[2] but it must amount to more than the passive accepting of a neighbour's intrusion.[3] In practice, of course, there is often no clear evidence one way or the other, and in this respect the facts of *Neumann* were typical. Thus there had been no express permission on the part of the owner of the yard, but equally – one isolated incident apart – there had been no active opposition. For as long as the yard was still a bus depot, the response of the bus drivers, and presumably of their employers, was one of indifference. On the evidence, the next person to own the yard – who also lived in the end-terrace house – was more obviously supportive of the access needs of his neighbour and at one stage even helped him to build the carport. The final owner, the defenders, were initially indifferent and ultimately hostile. But until the current dispute, none of the owners appeared to have given expression to their views.

What is one to conclude from evidence like this? The sheriff's view had been robust but unworkable.[4] In order, said the sheriff, to establish a servitude by prescription, the onus was on the pursuer to show, not merely 20 years' possession, but also that the possession could not be explained by tolerance. The pursuer, in other words, must prove a negative. And if the evidence was scanty or equivocal – if it was not possible to know whether the owner had given permission or not – the pursuer must fail. This approach derived from an *obiter dictum* of Lady Smith which in turn derived from a case decided in England.[5] If it was the law in

---

1 *R (Beresford) v Sunderland City Council* [2003] UKHL 60, [2004] 1 AC 889 at paras 57, 65 *per* Lord Rodger. For *precarium* in Scots law, see K G C Reid, *The Law of Property in Scotland* (1996) para 128.

2 *McGregor v Crieff Co-operative Society Ltd* 1915 SC (HL) 93 at 103.

3 In *Neumann v Hutchison* 2008 GWD 16-297 the sheriff principal concluded (at paras 51–52) that the sheriff had misunderstood the law on this point.

4 2006 GWD 28-628.

5 *Nationwide Building Society v Walter D Allan Ltd* 2004 GWD 25-539 at para 31. The English case is *Patel v W H Smith (Eziot) Ltd* [1987] 1 WLR 853.

Scotland it would present a formidable obstacle to the establishment of servitudes by prescription.

Fortunately, there was clear contrary authority. In *Grierson v School Board of Sandsting and Aithsting*,[1] Lord Rutherfurd Clark put matters like this:

> [I]t is said that the use which has existed is to be attributed to mere tolerance. But I would rather draw the inference that it was due to right. A long sustained and uninterrupted use is, I think, to be presumed to be in the exercise of a right, unless there is something either in its origin or otherwise to shew that it must be ascribed to tolerance.

The idea that, once a sufficient degree of possession had been established, the onus passed to the defender to show possession by tolerance, if he could, appears again a few years later in a passage by Lord Selborne in the context of public rights of way:[2]

> Now, when you have the fact of user of a road of this description in the manner and to the extent which would be the natural consequence of its being a matter of public right, that fact proved by a sufficient amount of evidence, how is that to be met? According to the well-known text of the civil law a claim of right of this kind will be repelled if it is shewn to have been enjoyed either *vi* ... or *clam* or *precario*.

Or again in *McGregor v Crieff Co-operative Society*[3] Lord Sumner expressed the view that: 'Open unqualified user in ordinary course may well be deemed to be in fact adverse user as of right, *when no more appears*.'

With the benefit of these unanimous voices, the task of the sheriff principal in *Neumann* was relatively straightforward. There were two propositions. In the first place, said the sheriff principal, whether possession could be regarded as 'as of right' depended mainly on its quantity and extent. Significant use of a 'servitude' indicated exercise as of right – except where the contrary could be shown. The same view can be found in the recent opinion of the Extra Division in *Aberdeen City Council v Wanchoo*, discussed below.[4] Secondly, the onus of showing the contrary rested, not on the owner of the putative dominant tenement – as the sheriff had held – but on the owner of the putative servient.[5] That meant that if the evidence was equivocal, the servitude would be held to be established. The sheriff principal put it in this way:[6]

1 (1882) 9 R 437 at 441.

2 *Macpherson v Scottish Rights of Way and Recreational Society Ltd* (1888) 15 R (HL) 68 at 70.

3 1915 SC (HL) 93 at 108. See also *Marquis of Bute v McKirdy & McMillan* 1937 SC 93 at 104 *per* Lord Mackay.

4 2008 SC 278 at para 18. In reaching the view, the court had particular regard to D J Cusine and R R M Paisley, *Servitudes and Rights of Way* (1998) para 10.19 and W M Gordon, *Scottish Land Law* (2nd edn 1999) para 24–49.

5 See D Johnston, *Prescription and Limitation* (1999) para 17.24: 'In general, once the use is established, an owner who wishes to argue that it has been only by his tolerance rather than as of right will bear the burden of demonstrating that.'

6 Paragraph 46.

[I]f the user is of such amount and of such a character as would reasonably be regarded as being an assertion of right it will readily be inferred that the use was as of right unless that inference can be displaced by evidence of permission or tolerance as those words are properly to be understood. But if there is no such evidence, or if the evidence is of insufficient weight, there is in my view no justification for refusing to hold that the use was as of right simply because the pursuer has failed to exclude the speculative possibility that the use might be attributable to permission.

Applying these principles to the facts, the sheriff principal had no difficulty in deciding that, contrary to the view taken by the sheriff, a servitude had been created by prescription.

The decision in *Neumann v Hutchison* is to be welcomed as providing a particularly clear statement of the law in an area where there have been difficulties in the past. What the decision shows is that whether a servitude is established by prescription is largely a matter of the amount of the possession. That is a welcome clarification of the law.

Aberdeen City Council v Wanchoo

The Extra Division's approach in *Aberdeen City Council v Wanchoo*[1] was strikingly similar to that of the sheriff principal in *Neumann v Hutchison*,[2] and the result arrived at was the same. Yet in one crucial respect the facts were different, for in *Wanchoo* the possession appears to have been taken on the basis of a contract.

In *Wanchoo* a warehouse had been the subject of substantial alterations to allow lorries to be loaded and unloaded. But this work presupposed that access could be taken over certain land which belonged to Aberdeen Council. On the evidence, the Lord Ordinary found that the parties had reached an agreement in principle in respect of access and, while the nature of that agreement was not fully explored, the court seems to have viewed it as a personal right and not a real right (notably a servitude). As the agreement was not committed to formal writing, there was a difficulty as to form, which was met by the *rei interventus* brought about by the owner's actings in carrying out the alterations.[3] Thereafter, and on the basis of this agreement, the warehouse owner took access for more than 20 years. The Lord Ordinary held that a servitude had been created by prescription,[4] and this view has now been upheld by the Extra Division.

At one level the decision is straightforward. As in *Neumann*, there was sufficient possession to suggest that the access was being exercised as of right:[5]

In this case the Council and their local government statutory successors knowingly allowed access to be taken over their property for a period in excess of the prescriptive period and so, unless it can properly be said that the access so taken could not be 'of

---

1 [2008] CSIH 6, 2008 SC 278, 2008 SLT 106. The opinion of the court was delivered by Lord Eassie.
2 2008 GWD 16-297, discussed above.
3 The events occurred before the Requirements of Writing (Scotland) Act 1995, and so the rules of the common law applied.
4 [2006] CSOH 196, 2007 SLT 289.
5 Paragraph 17.

right' but could only be by mere 'toleration', the servitude right for which the defender contends is established or constituted.

But, said the Extra Division, there was no 'toleration' because it was not possible to characterise the agreement with the Council as 'one which contemplated only the precarious use of the site for access at the whim of the Council'.[1] It followed, therefore, that a servitude had been created by prescription.

This argument, however, goes too far too fast. It assumes that, unless the agreement with the Council amounted to tolerance (ie to a *precarium*), it had no bearing on the running of prescription at all. '[W]ith the passage of time and the expiry of the prescriptive period a personal right of access may become a real right of servitude by user.'[2] But such a view is hardly compatible with the proposition advanced by the appellant, and accepted by the court as uncontroversial, that 'possession as of right must be unequivocally referable to the putative servitude right and not some other basis such as contract, lease or mere toleration'.[3] In *Wanchoo* – unlike in *Neumann* – the possession *was* referable to 'some other basis'. Admittedly, as the court pointed out, that basis was not 'toleration'. Instead it was a 'contract' between the parties allowing access to be taken. But the difference between possession by 'toleration' and possession by 'contract' is slight.[4] It is merely that, in the first case but not (usually) the second,[5] the landowner can bring the arrangement to an end as and when he wants. For present purposes it is the similarities that are more important. In both cases the possession is by agreement with the owner, and in both cases that agreement amounts to a (personal) right to possess.

Possession taken on the basis of one right cannot be used to establish, by prescription, a right of a different kind. If the Council cedes possession on one basis, it cannot be met by a claim, 20 years down the line, that the possession was all along being taken on a different basis.[6] The reason is obvious. If a right is to be established against a person by prescription, that person must be given notice and hence the opportunity to interrupt the possession. As Lord Watson put it, in a passage quoted with approval in *Wanchoo*:[7]

> I do not doubt that, in order to found a prescriptive right of servitude according to Scots law, acts of possession must be overt, in the sense that they must in themselves

---

1 Paragraph 16.
2 Paragraph 17.
3 Paragraph 11.
4 K G C Reid, *The Law of Property in Scotland* (1996) para 128. Indeed *precarium* is itself a contract.
5 Although it will depend on the terms of the contract.
6 See eg D Johnston, *Prescription and Limitation* (1999) paras 16.26 and 16.27. If this point was put to the court, as appears to have been the case (see para 11), it seems to have been misunderstood. At para 17 the court says: 'We reject the submission advanced by counsel for the pursuers and reclaimers that the right of access upon which the prescriptive claim is founded has to be a real right of servitude. If it were a real right of servitude there would be no need to invoke the positive prescription.' The point here of course is that the 'right' to which the possession relates must indeed be a servitude – but no such servitude will actually exist until 20 years' possession has taken place.
7 Paragraph 18. Lord Watson's *dictum* can be found in *McInroy v Duke of Athole* (1891) 18 R (HL) 46 at 48.

be of such a character or be done in such circumstances as to indicate unequivocally to the proprietor of the servient tenement the fact that a right is asserted, and the nature of the right.

Possession taken on the basis of contract neither indicates that a different type of right is being asserted nor does it indicate the nature of that right.

The mistake in *Wanchoo* was the assumption that only tolerance could prevent prescription. The truth is that tolerance is a species of a larger genus – the genus of rights to possess, both real and personal. If the Council had granted Mr Wanchoo a liferent over the land, or a lease, no one would imagine that his possession as liferenter or tenant could count for the purposes of the prescriptive acquisition of a different right.[1] Indeed the contrary is the subject of express decision.[2] The position is no different if, for these real rights, there is substituted a personal right to possess.

Maintaining the fixed list

The idea that Scots law has virtually a fixed list of servitudes can be traced back at least as far as the *Principles* of George Joseph Bell, written in the 1830s.[3] While, Bell notes, '[m]any servitudes are enumerated at great length in the books of the civilians', '[o]ur servitudes are few and well known',[4] being 'limited to such uses or restraints as are well established and defined, leaving others as mere personal agreements'.[5] The reason for this would today be called the 'publicity principle': because real rights affect third parties, their constitution should be attended with publicity, and, in the case of land, publicity tends to mean registration. Servitudes, however, need not be registered. Therefore 'a prudent principle developed whereby, in order to be constituted, they had to be of a known type'.[6] As Bell notes:[7]

> What shall be deemed servitudes of a regular and definite kind is a secondary question, as to which the only description that can be given seems to be, that it shall be such a use or restraint as by law or custom is known to be likely and incident to the property in question, and to which the attention of a prudent purchaser will, in the circumstances, naturally be called.

Servitudes which would escape the attention of Bell's 'prudent purchaser' are not allowed. Admittedly, this principle has been departed from by section 76 of the Title Conditions (Scotland) Act 2003 in respect of servitudes created by

---

1 At one stage, indeed, it was argued that possession was on the basis of a lease – and so ineligible for the purposes of prescription – but this had been dropped by the time of the hearing in the appeal court: see para 21.

2 *Houstoun v Barr* 1911 SC 134.

3 The passages in question do not appear until the 3rd edition, which was published in 1833.

4 Bell, *Principles* § 1000.

5 Bell, *Principles* § 979.

6 *Romano v Standard Commercial Property Securities Ltd* [2008] CSOH 105, 2008 SLT 859 at para 23 *per* Lord Carloway.

7 Bell, *Principles* § 979 (note).

registration on or after 28 November 2004. But section 76 is not retrospective; nor does it apply to servitudes created by prescription. So for all pre-2004 servitudes as well as for post-2004 servitudes created other than by registration, the fixed list remains in place.

A question which has never been entirely settled is: how 'fixed' is the list? Although there are *dicta* to the effect that the category of servitudes 'must alter and expand with the changes that take place in the circumstances of mankind',[1] the law has in practice been most reluctant to admit new servitudes. An important exception is the recent decision in *Moncrieff v Jamieson*,[2] where the House of Lords recognised the servitude of parking. And in addition, *Moncrieff* offered up an enticing *dictum* by Lord Scott:[3]

> I can see no reason in principle, subject to a few qualifications, why *any* right of limited use of the land of a neighbour that is of its nature of benefit to the dominant land and its owners from time to time should not be capable of being created as a servitudal right *in rem* appurtenant to the dominant land (see Gale, *Easements*, para 1.35).

If that were an accurate statement of Scots law, it would be tantamount to the abandonment of the fixed list – a remarkable and unexpected development. But as the reference to Gale on *Easements* might suggest, this is English law and not Scots.[4] Whether it might have any future in Scotland will depend on how it is received in subsequent case law. *Romano v Standard Commercial Property Securities Ltd*[5] is the first case.

Romano concerned two adjacent tenements in Buchanan Street in Glasgow, numbers 203–205 and 209–213, both of which were subject to the same deed of conditions. The pursuer, who owned the basement flat at 209–213, sought declarator that he had 'a heritable and irredeemable right to attach to the subjects known as the ground or upper ground floor of the tenement 209 Buchanan Street, Glasgow ... a shop front, including fascia'.[6] This claim had two foundations. In the first place, there was a disposition of 1962 which, in splitting the basement flat from the flat on the ground floor, granted 'the servitude right and privilege' to attach to the front wall of the ground flat 'a shop front including fascia'. In the second place, there were averments of prescriptive possession since 1962. These were needed because the front elevation was the common property of all the owners in the two tenements, and the 1962 servitude was therefore *a non domino* in respect that it was only granted by one of the *pro indiviso* owners.

1 *Dyce v Hay* (1852) 1 Macq 304 at 313–314 *per* Lord St Leonard LC. For references, see D J Cusine and R R M Paisley, *Servitudes and Rights of Way* (1998) para 2.87.
2 2008 SC (HL) 1. See on this point *Conveyancing 2007* pp 108–111.
3 Paragraph 47 (our emphasis).
4 It is hardly acceptable that, in a Scottish appeal, a judge should treat English law as automatically applying in Scotland.
5 [2008] CSOH 105, 2008 SLT 859.
6 In fact, the tenements were the subject of a compulsory purchase order, and the purpose in establishing the servitude seemed to be related to the amount of compensation which the pursuer would receive.

The opinion on the Scottish Courts website contains alluring photographs of the shop front at different times.[1] After the division in 1962, the basement became an Italian restaurant – the Sorrento Restaurant – which had a substantial shop front 'including a faux tiled roof projection in the image of an Italian taverna'.[2] Later there was 'a false multiple archway design, which had been created below the ground floor windows in another attempt to create an Italian ambience'.[3] Despite these attractions the restaurant closed in 1976, and the premises later came to be used as an amusement centre with appropriately gaudy signage.

For present purposes the important question was whether Scots law recognises a servitude of signage. In Lord Carloway's view, such cases as touched on the topic – and there were not many – did not support the idea of a servitude. That of course would not matter if Lord Scott's *dictum* could be accepted as accurate. Rather than challenge its accuracy, however, Lord Carloway sought to explain it away. Lord Scott had used the expression 'a servitudal right *in rem*'. That meant, said Lord Carloway, that he was not talking about servitudes in the strict sense:[4]

> In what must be assumed to be a careful use of language, he was, presumably, not saying that any such use could thereby become a 'servitude', as that term has hitherto been known in Scots law, distinct from an ordinary real burden or condition. *Moncrieff v Jamieson* (supra) is certainly not authority for such a wide proposition.

It followed that the pursuer must fail. We understand that the decision has been appealed.

Lord Carloway's analysis of Lord Scott's *dictum* is charitable but not convincing. A 'right of limited use' of the kind discussed by Lord Scott cannot be constituted as a real burden.[5] On the contrary, the only type of title condition which is available is a servitude. By using 'servitudal right *in rem*' Lord Scott was, no doubt, revealing a lack of familiarity with Scottish legal terminology, but he cannot have meant anything other than a servitude. If Lord Carloway's reasoning is suspect, however, the outcome is satisfactory. Lord Scott's *dictum* does not represent the law of Scotland.

If the fixed list is to remain, however, it should not be interpreted so strictly as sometimes in the past. In *Moncrieff v Jamieson*,[6] Lord Rodger commented that:

> Certainly, the mere fact that a right equivalent to parking was not recognised as a praedial servitude by Roman law would not, of itself, prevent Scots law from recognising such a servitude, just as it has recognised, for instance, a praedial servitude to take coal and a praedial servitude of fuel, feal and divot, neither of which was recognised by Roman law.

---

1 See http://www.scotcourts.gov.uk/opinions/CSOH105.html.
2 2008 SLT 859 at para 5.
3 Paragraph 7.
4 Paragraph 28.
5 Except as an ancillary burden: see Title Conditions (Scotland) Act 2003 s 2.
6 2008 SC (HL) 1 at para 73.

Apart from anything else, the apparent omission of a particular servitude 'may just be due to an accident of the compilers' work in reducing the jurists' writings for inclusion in the *Digest*'. Lord Rodger continued:[1]

> Even though parking is not a new phenomenon, I would not regard the apparent silence on the matter of the traditional sources of Scots law on servitudes as an indication that such a servitude would be fundamentally alien to Scots law. Ultimately, as with any proposed development of the law, the position must be determined by applying the relevant principles to the situation in Scotland today.[2]

As Professor W M Gordon put it in a recent article commenting on *Romano*, 'the question is not simply what servitudes are recognised but what servitudes should be recognised'.[3] And since an intruding shop sign is both visible and obvious, a rigid adherence to the fixed list can hardly be justified on grounds of lack of publicity. Professor Gordon's solution to *Romano* is an elegant one. Both Roman law and the later civil law recognised a servitude of projecting part of one's building over the property of a neighbour, the *jus projiciendi vel protegendi*. If recognised in Scotland, such a servitude would readily encompass the signage of the Sorrento Restaurant.[4]

Three other points about *Romano* seem worth making. First, the court appears to have assumed that, if the front elevation is declared to be common property in a deed of conditions, this has the effect of creating common property.[5] It does not. A deed of conditions can create real burdens but it cannot create common property. Only a registered conveyance can do that. Thus, in order for common property to be created, it would be necessary for the split-off[6] dispositions of the individual flats to repeat the grant of common property or to incorporate the relevant part of the deed of conditions by reference. We have no information as to whether this was done in this case.

Secondly, even if everything had been otherwise in order, it seems improbable that a servitude over the wall could be granted in favour of one of its *pro indiviso* owners. In *Clydesdale Bank plc v Davidson*[7] it was held by the House of Lords that a lease cannot be granted in favour of a *pro indiviso* owner. This was because the doctrine of confusion prevents an owner from holding a subordinate real right in

---

1 Paragraph 74.

2 This may be contrasted with the view of Sheriff I A Poole in *Mendelssohn v The Wee Pub Co* 1991 GWD 26-1518. In rejecting a servitude of signage, she said that: 'Shop signs would seem to have been known in classical times. They were certainly known in the Old Town of Edinburgh where [the close] is situated and are, I think, no new response to the needs of a changing society. I have concluded that had such a servitude right existed, as is claimed by the defenders in this case, it would have been recognised by the authorities centuries ago.' This passage was approved by Lord Carloway in *Romano* at para 26.

3 W M Gordon, 'The struggle for recognition of new servitudes' (2009) 13 *Edinburgh Law Review* 139 at 142.

4 Indeed Professor Gordon argues that this servitude is the best explanation of the decision in *McArly v French's Trs* (1883) 10 R 574. For a full discussion, see D J Cusine and R R M Paisley, *Servitudes and Rights of Way* (1998) para 3.22.

5 2008 SLT 859 at para 2.

6 If the grant was contained in a *later* disposition, it would be ineffective as *a non domino*.

7 1998 SC (HL) 51.

the same property: the lesser right would become absorbed into the greater.[1] If that is correct, it is hard to see why the same logic would not apply to a servitude.[2]

Thirdly, as the 1962 disposition contained an express grant of servitude, it seems likely that, on first registration of the basement flat, the servitude was included in the A Section of the title sheet. In that case (but subject to the previous points), the deficiency in the granter's title would cease to matter.[3]

Ancillary rights 1967-style

Chalmers Property Investment Co Ltd v Robson, decided by the Outer House in 1965,[4] is a leading authority on the creation of servitudes by acquiescence.[5] What was not known until recently[6] was that the Lord Ordinary's decision was appealed, and not once but twice – to the Inner House and again to the House of Lords. Until 2008 neither appellate decision had been reported. This has now been put right.[7] The reason for the sudden if belated interest in *Chalmers* is that the decision was relied on by Lord Rodger in the House of Lords in *Moncrieff v Jamieson*.[8] The context was the implication of ancillary rights into servitudes, and it is for this topic and not for acquiescence – which faded away as an issue[9] – that the appellate stages of *Chalmers* are of significance.

The servitude in *Chalmers* was contained in a split-off feu disposition of land in Mull granted in 1943. It read:

> together also with the right to my said disponee and her foresaids to draw water for domestic purposes from the spring or well situated some ninety-five yards or thereby to the north east side of the said subjects but without any guarantee as to the sufficiency, purity or suitability for the purpose aforesaid of the water supply; and for the above purpose to lay and maintain at the expense of my said disponee and her foresaids adequate water pipes for the purpose of withdrawing water for the purposes aforesaid.

It will be seen from the wording that the servitude – the familiar servitude of *aquaehaustus* – was already furnished with an ancillary right, itself another servitude (*aquaeductus*), namely the right to install and use pipes for carrying the water. But the owner of the dominant tenement had done more. She had installed

---

1 See Lord Hope at 56.
2 Indeed that is taken for granted in *Grierson v School Board of Sandsting and Aithsting* (1882) 9 R 437, where the servitude was allowed only because the dominant and servient tenements were owned by the same persons in different capacities. See Lord Rutherfurd Clark at 441.
3 Land Registration (Scotland) Act 1979 s 3(1)(a). See further *Conveyancing 2007* pp 123–124.
4 1965 SLT 381.
5 This, however, was only a secondary argument in the case, and in the event the Lord Ordinary (Kissen) decided that the servitude had been created by express grant, without the need for recourse to acquiescence.
6 Except by Lord Rodger of Earlsferry, who had gone to the trouble of seeking out copies of the judgments.
7 2008 SLT 1069.
8 [2007] UKHL 42, 2008 SC (HL) 1. For a full discussion of that case, see *Conveyancing 2007* pp 106–117.
9 It was discussed only by Lord President Clyde: see 2008 SLT 1069 at 1072.

a small dam in order to collect sufficient water to enter the pipes, and she had added a settling tank. The servient proprietor disputed her right to do so.

Could ancillary rights be implied to cover this work? According to Lord Reid, a dominant owner could construct on the servient tenement 'such works as were essential to make the servitude effective',[1] while for Lord Guest, relying on Ferguson on *Water Rights*,[2] an ancillary right would be implied where it was 'essential to the carrying out of the purpose for which the original servitude was granted'.[3] Although Lord Rodger was to adopt these views,[4] the balance of opinion in *Moncrieff v Jamieson* favoured a more accommodating test, namely that of reasonable necessity.[5] It follows that, at the precise moment of its rediscovery, *Chalmers* can no longer be regarded as good law on this point. But the case remains of value as showing the kind of rights which can be implied.

Two difficulties stood in the way of implying the rights disputed in *Chalmers*. One was the rather exacting formulation of the test favoured by Lords Reid and Guest just mentioned. The other was the fact that one ancillary right (the right to lay pipes) was already *expressly* granted, which might be taken as an exhaustive statement of such rights. In the event, neither the First Division nor the House of Lords had any difficulty in implying the necessary rights. As the dam had actually been built by a company associated with the servient proprietor, that proprietor did not, at the end of the day, insist on its removal. And as for the tank, the court was satisfied that, without it, the pipes would become clogged with silt.[6]

ACCESS RIGHTS AND THE PRIVACY EXEMPTION

Not all land is available for the statutory access rights conferred by part 1 of the Land Reform (Scotland) Act 2003, for the Act contains a number of exemptions. Among the most important is the exemption for the privacy of dwellinghouses, set out in section 6(1)(b)(iv):[7]

> The land in respect of which access rights are not exercisable is land which comprises in relation to a house sufficient adjacent land to enable persons living there to have reasonable measures of privacy in that house and to ensure that their enjoyment of the house is not unreasonably disturbed.

This exemption has already been litigated, in the celebrated and controversial case involving Kinfauns Castle and Ann Gloag: *Gloag v Perth & Kinross Council*.[8]

---

1 2008 SLT 1069 at para 10.
2 J Ferguson, *The Law of Water and Water Rights in Scotland* (1907) p 264.
3 2008 SLT 1069 at para 15.
4 2008 SC (HL) 1 at paras 77–82.
5 See eg para 110 *per* Lord Neuberger.
6 2008 SLT 1069 at para 15 *per* Lord Guest.
7 For ease of understanding we have removed the words which apply only to caravans and other like places.
8 2007 SCLR 530. For commentary on this case, see *Conveyancing 2007* pp 127–139; T Guthrie, 'Access rights', in R Rennie (ed), *The Promised Land: Property Law Reform* (2008) p 125.

There Mrs Gloag sought and obtained a declaration that a part of her estate – amounting to some 14 acres out of a total of 23 – was exempt from access rights. A new case, *Snowie v Stirling Council*,[1] now makes that claim look rather modest.

Mr and Mrs Snowie own Boquhan House and grounds extending to 70 acres and lying to the south of the A811 Drymen to Stirling road. Access is by a driveway leading from each of two gates, one on the west and the other on the east. In the past, members of the public routinely took access over the estate on foot and by bicycle. In 2003 the Snowies restored and mechanised the gates, and at the same time locked the pedestrian gate on the west. Although the locked gate did not prevent access altogether – the east gate remained open, and access even from the west remained possible by other means, such as squeezing through a hedge – it had the practical effect of discouraging members of the public. Following complaints, Stirling Council served a notice under section 14 of the 2003 Act calling on the Snowies to re-open the gate. The Snowies appealed that notice, and at the same asked for a declaration under section 28(1)(a) of the Act that the *whole* 70 acres, including the driveway, were exempt from public access rights. Later they restricted their claim to 40 acres.

After a proof and a site inspection, the sheriff[2] declined to exempt even the reduced area of 40 acres. He accepted that the Snowies should have privacy in the immediate vicinity of their house. In his view, the exemption included (i) a substantial portion to the front of the house (ii) the rear garden and (iii) certain other garden areas, including the tennis courts and a riding area. But it did not include the driveway, which was too distant to be needed for privacy. Furthermore, there seemed no good reason for locking the pedestrian gate, especially in view of the fact that other access points were available.

Following *Gloag,* the sheriff emphasised that reasonableness was to be viewed objectively:[3]

> It seems to me that the court is obliged, in interpreting this part of s 6, to determine what a reasonable person living in a property of the type under consideration would require to have to enjoy reasonable measures of privacy and to ensure enjoyment of the house was not unreasonably disturbed. That is an objective test.... In my opinion, if the test were subjective, that would lead to the possibility of repeated applications being made depending on the particular views, concerns, family circumstances and even prejudices of any particular proprietor, which cannot be the purpose of the Act. I regard the test as an objective one, which factors in the particular characteristics of the property.

But, as with *Gloag,* there was a tendency to confuse what a reasonable owner would *like* with what the privacy exemption actually allows:[4]

---

1 2008 SLT (Sh Ct) 61. A related application, relating to the West Lodge owned by Professor and Dr Ross, was heard at the same time and resulted in a judgment which was more or less identical: see *Ross v Stirling Council* 23 April 2008, Stirling Sheriff Court. For commentary, see M M Combe, 'No place like home: access rights over "gardens"' (2008) 12 *Edinburgh Law Review* 463.
2 Sheriff A M Cubie.
3 Paragraphs 51 and 53.
4 Paragraph 55. For criticism of the same tendency in *Gloag,* see *Conveyancing 2007* pp 131–132.

Again I agree with Sheriff Fletcher in that anyone contemplating the purchase of a house such as Kinfauns Castle or in this case Boquhan House would not consider doing so if the house itself and its grounds (and by that I mean a material area around the house) were not able to be used by them privately. The reasonable person would consider that reasonable measures of privacy for that house ... would require a reasonably substantial area of ground.

In the present case the Snowies, quite naturally, would have liked to exclude the public from the whole estate. For better or for worse, the law was less accommodating.

At least at an intuitive level, the result in *Snowie* seems broadly satisfactory. The public get to use the driveway but the Snowies are undisturbed in their gardens and tennis courts. Formally speaking, the decision was a defeat for the Snowies, and this was reflected in the award of expenses.[1] No doubt this is why the decision has escaped the opprobrium which attached to *Gloag*. Yet the Snowies did hardly less well than Mrs Gloag. They secured 12.6 acres of exempt land to Mrs Gloag's 14.5, and the two areas were roughly proportionate to the sizes of the houses.[2]

On the law the decision disappoints. Reasonably enough, it relies heavily on *Gloag*, but there is little attempt at independent analysis and none at probing beneath the surface of what remains a difficult and obscure provision.[3] What is the relevance of past usage by members of the public? Did it make a difference that there was a public right of way on one of the boundaries? Does the size of the house matter, and if so why? Is there a difference of meaning, in section 6(1)(b)(iv), between privacy and disturbance of enjoyment? Without further judicial analysis it will remain difficult to advise clients or to predict the outcome of individual cases.

SPECIAL DESTINATIONS

Two cases in 2008 were on that tricky subject of the evacuation of special destinations: *Matthews v Hunter & Robertson Ltd*[4] and *Lavery v Lavery*.[5] The background to both is *Gardner's Exrs v Raeburn*,[6] so we begin with a few words about that case. A husband and wife bought a house together, with a survivorship destination. When they parted, the husband bought out the wife's share, and she accordingly disponed to him her half share, including her 'whole right, title and

---

1 2008 GWD 27-427.
2 See the comments by George Menzies at http://www.scotways.com/news/detail.php?newsid=121.
3 There also seems to be an inconsistency. At para 55 the sheriff says, correctly, that 'The purpose of excluding the ground from the rights of access contained in the Act would not be to secure the enjoyment of the "policies" for the occupants of the house, but to secure the enjoyment of the house itself.' But at para 58 he allows privacy 'for persons in the house when visiting the garden area, tennis court or changing room'.
4 [2008] CSOH 88, 2008 SLT 634, 2008 SCLR 466.
5 2008 Fam LR 46, 2008 GWD 11-205.
6 1996 SLT 745.

interest, present and future in and to the said subjects'. Later he died, still owning the house. It was held that his *original* half share was, at his death, still subject to an unevacuated destination in his wife's favour, and accordingly passed to her. This is the '*Raeburn* trap'. Though there is no decision confirming the point, it is the general view of conveyancers (and we would agree with that view) that if the disposition had been by both in favour of the husband alone then that would have washed the title clean of all destinations.[1]

Destinations and negligence

Much the same happened in *Matthews v Hunter & Robertson Ltd*.[2] Robert and Isabella Urquhart owned a house in Paisley. The title contained a survivorship destination. In 1975 they parted, and Robert disponed his half share to Isabella. In 2005 Isabella died, still owning the house, and survived by Robert. Her will left the bulk of her estate to charity. But her original one half share passed to Robert by virtue of the original destination. Her executor now sued the successor of the law firm that had acted in the preparation of the 1975 disposition for having failed to deactivate the destination.

One difficulty faced by the executor was that, even if the deceased had had any cause of action against the law firm, it would probably have prescribed negatively, given that the conveyancing had happened back in 1975. An even greater difficulty was that it was difficult or impossible to identify any loss that the deceased could be said to have suffered from the law firm's alleged negligence. The executor therefore took a different tack. In such cases as *Holmes v Bank of Scotland*[3] it has been held that a solicitor preparing a will owes a duty to the intended beneficiaries to draft the will promptly and correctly. The executor argued that a similar duty existed in these circumstances: in having failed to deactivate the destination the law firm had failed in a duty of care to the client's future executor. The Lord Ordinary (Brodie) was not prepared to accept this argument, and he dismissed the action. There was no authority on either side of the border which would take the duty of care so far. As he commented:[4]

> What is posited is a relationship between a solicitor instructed in respect of a specific transaction and a yet-to-be-appointed executor of the solicitor's client in respect of an interest that the client could never have. I do not regard that as proximate. I regard that as remote.

To this sensible decision we have one or two comments to add. In the first place, it will be noted that in such cases as *Holmes* the duty is to the beneficiaries, and thus in such cases it is the disappointed beneficiaries who sue. Here the beneficiaries did not sue. Presumably the result would have been the same if they had sued.

---

1 For evacuation of special destinations, see *Conveyancing 2005* pp 74–78.
2 [2008] CSOH 88, 2008 SLT 634, 2008 SCLR 466.
3 2002 SLT 544. *Matthews* was not the only 2008 case to distinguish *Holmes*: see *Fraser v McArthur Stewart* [2008] CSOH 159, 2009 SLT 31.
4 Paragraph 42.

Secondly, the action was against the (successor of the) firm that prepared the original 1975 disposition. It was not against the firm that prepared the deceased's will, which was executed in 2003.[1] Might the executor, or more plausibly the disappointed beneficiaries, have a claim against that firm? When preparing a will, does a law firm have a duty to check the title to the client's heritable property? We do not know the answer to that question.

Thirdly, the conveyancing was done in 1975 and at that time the *Raeburn* trap was little-known. Indeed, it was not until *Gardner's Exrs v Raeburn* was decided in 1995 that it was finally established that there *was* a trap. Hence it is arguable that in 1975 it could not have been negligent to overlook it. But this argument does not seem to have been advanced.

The pursuer averred that it was both parties' intention that the deceased should become the sole owner of the subjects and that Robert Urquhart should retain no rights in it.[2] That was an important point because, unless that was so, the law firm could not have been at fault. Had the case proceeded to proof, it may be that that could have been proved. But if it could have been proved then that would open up another vista, for if a deed fails to implement the mutual intentions of the parties, it can be judicially rectified.[3] This line of reasoning was not, it seems, advanced by the defender, but it would have been interesting to see how the Lord Ordinary would have dealt with it. The argument would be that if there was a problem, the remedy lay in the executor's hands: rectify the disposition. At most the law firm would have been liable for modest damages by way of expenses incurred. Of course, rectifying a formal deed is seldom easy because it has to be proved that the parties had agreed terms that were not reflected in the deed. But what is sauce for the goose is sauce for the gander: either a mutual intention to deactivate the destination existed or it did not exist. If proof would have failed in a rectification action against the former husband then it would equally have failed in this negligence action against the law firm. It is true that the 1975 deed pre-dated the statutory rules about the rectification of documents, but it seems that those rules apply to existing documents as well as new ones.[4] It may however be that the disposition could no longer be rectified, because of prescription. The interaction of the law of prescription with the law of judicial rectification is obscure.

The *Raeburn* trap distinguished

In *Lavery v Lavery*[5] Mr and Mrs Lavery were the owners of a house in Bridge of Don. The title had a survivorship destination. They parted and signed a separation agreement. One of its provisions was this: 'Mr Lavery shall convey to Mrs Lavery his whole right, title and interest in and to the former matrimonial home at 7 Centre Point, Bridge of Don, Aberdeen.' A disposition was duly drawn up in

---

1 Here we assume that it was professionally prepared and not a home-made will.
2 See para 2 of the Lord Ordinary's opinion.
3 Law Reform (Miscellaneous Provisions) (Scotland) Act 1985 s 8.
4 *Bank of Scotland v Graham's Tr* 1992 SC 79.
5 2008 Fam LR 46, 2008 GWD 11-205.

which both parties were disponers and Mrs Lavery was the disponee. Although Mr Lavery signed, Mrs Lavery died leaving the deed unsigned. Had she lived a few days longer, she would have been the sole owner. As it was, Mr Lavery was the sole owner: he was the undivested owner of his original half share, and he had acquired the other half share when his wife died. Mrs Lavery's executrix, her daughter Louise Lavery, now called on Mr Lavery to dispone to her (*qua* executrix) the whole property, pursuant to his obligations in the separation agreement. He accepted that he continued to be bound to dispone his *original* half share, but he argued that Mrs Lavery's share, that he had acquired on her death, was not covered by the separation agreement and that accordingly he was entitled to keep it. The executor raised this action for him to be ordained to convey both half shares. Not surprisingly, the defender relied on *Gardner's Exrs v Raeburn*.[1]

The pursuer was successful before the sheriff. The defender appealed to the sheriff principal, but the appeal was refused. The key question was whether the defender's obligation to convey included not only his original one half share but also his right under the destination in respect of Mrs Lavery's half share. In *Gardner's Exrs v Raeburn* the disposition of the half share had included the disponer's 'whole right, title and interest, present and future in and to *the said subjects*' and 'the said subjects' meant not the whole property but the half share. By contrast, in *Lavery* the obligation was to convey 'his whole right, title and interest in and to *the former matrimonial home*'. Thus *Gardner's Exrs v Raeburn* could be distinguished. The question was then whether a right under a destination fell within the meaning of the phrase 'whole right, title and interest'. It was held that it did. Admittedly a right under a destination is not in itself a real right, but the quoted expression was considered to be a broad one and not necessarily limited to real rights. Moreover, the phrase occurred not in a deed but in a contract and so was more open to purposive interpretation.

It was common ground that when Mrs Lavery died, her half share passed to Mr Lavery. One might put together a counter-argument. Clause 11 of the separation agreement provided:

> Both parties hereby renounce and discharge for all time coming his or her legal right of *jus relictae* or *jus relicti* and also any prior rights and such other rights of succession which may arise on the death of the other party under the Succession (Scotland) Act 1964 or any amendment thereof *or at common law*.

A right under a destination is a right of succession, albeit of an unusual type,[2] and so there must be an argument that this clause constituted a renunciation by Mr Lavery of his rights under the destination. Whilst clause 11 was not itself brought into focus, there was some discussion of the possibility that the separation agreement as a whole might amount to an evacuation, and it seems to have been a matter of concession that it did not, the main reason lying in *dicta* in *Fleming's Tr v Fleming*[3] to the effect that a destination can be evacuated only by a registered

---

1 1996 SLT 745.
2 Thus a person who takes under a special destination is a type of heir (*haeres provisione hominis*).
3 2000 SC 206.

deed, except in those cases where testamentary evacuation is competent. However, those *dicta* do not deal with evacuation *by the substitute*, ie by renunciation of the benefit of the destination. Clause 11 is a renunciation. While there may be scope for debate, we incline to think that it was effective in relation to the destination. Whether its effect was real or personal may be arguable,[1] though this distinction would not have mattered much on the facts of the case.

SDLT AND VAT[2]

Stamp duty land tax

The change in stamp duty land tax with the widest effects this year derived not from the Budget or Finance Act, nor even from the Pre-Budget Report. Instead, in a move with similarities to putting a sticking plaster on a burst artery, the Government reacted to the early stages of the credit crunch by increasing the zero rate threshold for residential property from £125,000 to £175,000. This took effect for transactions with an effective date on or after 3 September 2008; and is scheduled to end on 3 September 2009.[3] As an SDLT holiday it is more akin to a wet weekend at Butlins than a Caribbean cruise – the tax remains a cliff-edge levy, which means that once a threshold is crossed, the whole consideration is chargeable at the relevant rate. This change has at least temporarily removed any advantage from being in a so-called disadvantaged area (threshold £150,000). The extension of the threshold to £175,000 does not apply to premiums on new residential leases or to assignations of residential leases, but this exclusion is unlikely to be of much relevance in Scotland; nor (because of the limitations on the length and hence the value of residential leases in Scotland) are the complications brought in to deal with the SDLT due on the rent under new residential leases.

The most important changes in the Finance Act 2008 itself were administrative. Form SDLT 60, which allowed for self-certification in a variety of circumstances where SDLT was not due, has been withdrawn, although not before publication of a strange Budget statement that such self-certificates could in future be signed by agents. In some circumstances, it will remain a matter of practical necessity to explain to Registers of Scotland why a transaction with apparently significant consideration does not attract SDLT, doing the job formerly done by the SDLT 60.

In relation to notification more generally, for transactions on or after 12 March 2008 (Budget day), the threshold for notification of transactions other than leases is raised from a chargeable consideration of £1,000 to one of £40,000. For transactions involving leases for a term of seven years or more, notification is only required where any chargeable consideration other than rent is £40,000

---

1 See *Conveyancing 2005* p 76 for discussion.
2 This part is contributed by Alan Barr of the University of Edinburgh.
3 See the Stamp Duty Land Tax (Exemption of Certain Acquisitions of Residential Property) Regulations 2008, SI 2008/2339.

or more or where the annual rent is £1,000 or more. The provisions dealing with notification are also re-cast.[1]

There is an SDLT exemption on the first acquisition of zero-carbon homes, where the consideration is £500,000 or less.[2] This has not been a great success. Due to a drafting error, the exemption was restricted to whole dwellinghouses and an amendment with retrospective effect was needed to extend it to flats as well as complete buildings.

The special rules that apply for SDLT on lease premiums are changed, so that they apply where the annual rent is £1,000 or more (formerly £600); and the lease is of non-residential property only. In such cases (now thus more limited), the nil rate band for SDLT is disapplied and the whole premium is chargeable to SDLT at 1% at least.[3]

The group relief clawback rules are tightened. Previously, group relief was withdrawn if the transferee company left the group within three years of the intra-group transfer. There was no clawback if there was a change in the group relationship by the vendor leaving the group. Under new rules, there could be a clawback if the vendor leaves the group and there is a subsequent change of control of the purchaser.[4] As with many pieces of anti-avoidance legislation, this is capable of catching relatively innocent transactions within company reorganisations, although there were assurances in relation to certain transactions during the Finance Bill debates.

Of all the unsatisfactory parts of the constantly evolving legislation dealing with stamp duty land tax, probably the least satisfactory and least understood (even by HMRC) is that relating to partnerships.[5] This has been altered in every Finance Act since its introduction. A welcome alteration this time round is a restriction on charges on changes of partnership share to what are termed 'property investment partnerships'. The Finance Act 2007 brought in rules which meant that a charge could arise in such partnerships even where no consideration had passed. This is now relaxed, by providing that various categories of transfer will not be of 'relevant partnership property', on the value of which the SDLT charge could arise.[6] There is also provision for an election to be made which changes, irrevocably, the basis on which SDLT is or has been charged on the transfer of land into a partnership, which election might enable advantage to be taken of the new relaxation in the rules on transfer of partnership interests.[7]

Anti-avoidance is also to the fore in relation to two other measures. First, the rules proving SDLT relief for 'alternative property finance' (Islamic mortgage) transactions are removed where they involve arrangements to obtain control of

---

1 See Finance Act 2003 ss 77, 77A, substituted by Finance Act 2008 s 94(2).
2 Finance Act 2003 ss 58B, 58C; Stamp Duty Land Tax (Zero-Carbon Homes Relief) Regulations 2007, SI 2007/3437.
3 See Finance Act 2003 sch 5 para 9A, inserted by Finance Act 2008 s 95(3).
4 Finance Act 2003 sch 7 para 4ZA, inserted by Finance Act 2008 s 96(4).
5 Finance Act 2003 sch 15.
6 Finance Act 2008 s 97, sch 31 part 1.
7 Finance Act 2008 s 97, sch 31 part 2.

a relevant financial institution.[1] This is to prevent an avoidance scheme under which companies were set up by lenders to take advantage of the new rules and to facilitate onward sales without payment of SDLT. Presumably such blatant exploitation of tax avoidance schemes may be less likely now that many lenders are under the effective control of Government.

The second measure, on which details are not yet available, will extend the disclosure regime for SDLT avoidance schemes[2] to include residential property of a value in excess of £1 million. Prior to this, the disclosure regime was restricted to commercial property.

Finally in relation to SDLT, 1 December 2008 marked its fifth birthday. Quite apart from the boundless celebration this undoubtedly engendered, the anniversary also marked the first date on which a number of provisions took effect. These included the rules on abnormal rent increases; and it is absolutely typical of the whole short history of SDLT that new rules on such increases seem certain to be introduced in Finance Act 2009.

Value added tax

This survey does not normally deal with value added tax, but it is worth mentioning changes in relation to 'option to tax' (election to waive exemption, although that expression is no longer to be used). The change involves the complete substitution of schedule 10 of the Value Added Tax Act 1994 with effect from 1 June 2008.[3] There is also a new version of the VAT Notice 742A, some of which has the force of law. Space does not permit the changes to be dealt with in full, but the following changes are highlighted in the new VAT Notice:

- new rules providing that an option to tax affects land and buildings on the same site, with transitional rules, and ability to exclude new buildings from the scope of an option to tax;
- a new certificate for buildings to be converted to dwellings etc and new ability for intermediaries to disapply the option to tax;
- a new certificate for land sold to housing associations;
- new rules for ceasing to be a relevant associate of an opter;
- an extension to the 'cooling off' period for revoking an option to tax (which is now six months);
- the introduction of automatic revocation of the option to tax where no interest has been held for six years;
- the introduction of rules governing the revocation of an option to tax after 20 years;
- a revised definition of occupation for the anti-avoidance test including a new exclusion for automatic teller machines;

---

1 Finance Act 2003 s 73AB, inserted by Finance Act 2008 s 155(3).
2 See Finance Act 2004 s 306; Stamp Duty Land Tax Avoidance Schemes (Prescribed Description of Arrangements) Regulations 2005, SI 2005/1868.
3 By the Value Added Tax (Buildings and Land) Order 2008, SI 2008/1146.

- the introduction of a new way to opt to tax (a real estate election, which covers all relevant land owned or acquired after the real estate election).

OF TITLES AND TOMBS

John Livingston's tomb

Chamberlain Road, Edinburgh, leads off Holy Corner. At one end there is a tiny park, too small even to put a house on. At the point where it reaches the road there is a small planted area with a bench on it. Going further in one comes to a walled enclosure. The walls date from the seventeenth century and enclose the tomb of John Livingston, who lived here and died here. On the grave slab one can still read, notwithstanding the best efforts of three and a half centuries of Scottish weather:

> This saint whos corps lyes buried heir
> Let all posterities admoir
> For upright lif in godly feir
> When judgements did this land surround
> He with God was walking found
> From which from midst of feirs he's cround
> Heir to be interred. Both he
> And friends by providence agrie
> No age shall los his memorie

> His age 53 Died 1645

We have read better poetry, but sepulchral verse must always impress a reader, if only with thoughts of mortality. And the 'memorie' of John Livingston has yet to be lost in this part of Edinburgh. The micro-park attracts visitors, and sometimes people sit on the bench in the garden area and watch the world go by. Locally it is a well-known spot. Recently, however, it has become best known because of a conveyancing dispute which ended in a litigation: *McCoach v Keeper of the Registers of Scotland*.[1]

Overview

The conveyancing story is complex, so it may help to start with an outline. The micro-park was owned by Edinburgh City Council on a Sasine title.[2] The adjacent property, 1 Chamberlain Road, was also owned on a Sasine title. In 2003/2004 it was sold, thereby triggering a first registration. The Sasine title, though not plan-based, unambiguously excluded the micro-park.[3] Yet the buyers ended up

---

1 19 December 2008, Lands Tribunal, available at http://www.lands-tribunal-scotland.org.uk/decisions/LTS.LR.2006.03.html. The Tribunal comprised J N Wright QC and K M Barclay FRICS.
2 As is explained below, the Council's title was based on an *a non domino* disposition recorded in 1989.
3 The 'discrepancy between the foundation title [the 1938 disposition] and the title submitted for registration' is described by the Tribunal as 'glaring': transcript p 48.

with a registered title not only to 1 Chamberlain Road but to the micro-park as well. There was no exclusion of indemnity. The new owners removed the public bench, took down the information plaque, put in metal fencing to exclude the public, raised an action of interdict against the City Council to exclude their park maintenance workers,[1] and declined to agree to the rectification of the Register. When the Keeper nevertheless went ahead and rectified the inaccuracy by removing the micro-park from the title, they appealed to the Lands Tribunal to have their title restored to the Register.[2] The City Council came into the case as an 'interested party'. The Council itself might have raised an action against the Keeper to require rectification, but it had not done so by the time that the Keeper decided to rectify without being ordered to do so.

The Tribunal's opinion runs to more than 60 pages and is rich in factual detail about how this extraordinary conveyancing mess happened, and also rich in discussion of the legal issues involved. A 'proprietor in possession' is protected against rectification of an inaccuracy unless, in the words of section 9(3)(a)(iii) of the Land Registration (Scotland) Act 1979, 'the inaccuracy has been caused wholly or substantially by the fraud or carelessness of the proprietor in possession'. Were the buyers of 1 Chamberlain Road in possession of the micro-park? Had the City Council been in possession? Here there were difficult issues of both fact and law for the Tribunal to decide. And if the buyers were in possession, had there been 'carelessness' and if so had that carelessness been a 'substantial' cause of the inaccuracy? What duties are owed to the Keeper in applying for registration? What is the nature of a property definition report and when is a buyer entitled to rely on one? The Tribunal's decision, upholding the Keeper's decision to rectify, is one of major importance for land registration law and practice, and also for the law of prescription.

The competing titles

The City Council

When, in the mid-1980s, there was concern about the tomb's physical condition, Edinburgh Council made enquiries as to ownership, but no owner could be identified. The Council decided that it would take over the upkeep and seek to acquire a title by prescription. An *a non domino* disposition was recorded in the Register of Sasines in 1989. The tomb was renovated and over the years the Council maintained the micro-park. In 1999 a large plaque was added, which mentioned, among other things, that the micro-park was owned by the Council. A good deal of the Tribunal's opinion is devoted to the question of whether the Council had acquired a valid prescriptive title. Evidence was led of restoration work done to the tomb and of visits by maintenance workers. The Tribunal felt able to conclude that there had been sufficient possession, commenting, no doubt correctly, that 'the nature of the subjects was such that one could not reasonably

---

1 We do not know what happened in that action other than that an attempt to obtain interim interdict failed.
2 Land Registration (Scotland) Act 1979 s 25.

expect any different or higher degree of possession'.[1] It is noteworthy, however, that the use of the micro-park by members of the public was not regarded by the Tribunal as possession by the Council.[2]

Strictly speaking, the question of whether the Council had acquired a good title before the neighbouring property was sold was irrelevant, for whoever owned the micro-park, it was not the owner of 1 Chamberlain Road. When, therefore, the Keeper included the micro-park within the title sheet for 1 Chamberlain Road, the result was an inaccuracy in the Register. So even if the Tribunal had come to the conclusion that the Council had not obtained a good prescriptive title, the final outcome of the case would presumably have been the same: deletion of the micro-park from the 1 Chamberlain Road title sheet.

The Council's prescriptive title was completed in 1999. During the 10 years from 1989 to 1999 the micro-park was not yet in the Land Register. That is important because there is some uncertainty as to whether prescription can run on a title in the Sasine Register where the land is registered in the name of someone else in the Land Register. On the facts the issue did not arise, but the Tribunal expressed a tentative view that had the issue arisen it would have held that prescription cannot run.[3] The Scottish Law Commission has taken a different view.[4]

The owners of 1 Chamberlain Road

Before the sale in 2003/2004, the property next to the micro-park, 1 Chamberlain Road, was held on a Sasine title. Originally a large private house, it had become a nursing home. The descriptive writ was a 1938 disposition. This contained neither a plan nor a full bounding description, but it did state that the length of the property along the street front was 92 feet. That was a correct measurement of the property's frontage, *excluding the micro-park*. In other words, the measurement made it clear that the frontage of the micro-park could not be part of the frontage of 1 Chamberlain Road. In short, the micro-park was excluded. Moreover, the property was said to be 'bounded ... partly by the walls of the old tomb'. As the two expert witnesses said,[5] and we would respectfully agree, the presumptive meaning of that phrase was that the tomb was excluded.

The sale of 1 Chamberlain Road

Before settlement

The question of the micro-park was raised by the buyers at an early stage. For example, before offering they wrote to their solicitors: 'What is the position with regard to the grave to the right of the house? Does Edinburgh Council own it

---

1 Transcript p 24.
2 Transcript p 24.
3 Transcript p 23.
4 Scottish Law Commission, Discussion Paper on *Void and Voidable Titles* (Scot Law Com DP 125 (2004); available at www.scotlawcom.gov.uk) para 5.12.
5 Robert Rennie and Donald Reid: see transcript p 49.

outright?'[1] And a note at about this time on the buying solicitor's file said that the buyers were 'both keen to have the boundaries[2] especially with regard to the grave which is understood to be excluded from the sale'.[3]

The seller's solicitor obtained a property definition report from a private firm. The PDR plan included the micro-park. The Tribunal was unable to discover how this came about. A PDR maps the boundaries in the GRS title onto the OS map. This PDR did not do that. Why it was erroneous we do not know. The PDR was obtained before conclusion of missives. It is unclear how the missives (which were concluded on 17 September 2003) described the subjects of sale. Probably they did so by reference to the PDR plan, ie as including the micro-park.[4] The price was reported in the media as having been £855,000.

What about the examination of title? This was done by a paralegal at the buyers' solicitors, who, in her notes on title, wrote 'very old common law description and extremely vague'. Here is one of the innumerable puzzles of this case. The 1938 description was hardly 'very old', and, despite the lack of a plan, to call it 'extremely vague' seems to go too far.

A form 10 report was instructed and obtained, but it described the subjects by reference to the title of 1 Chamberlain Road. The report disclosed all the relevant deeds affecting that title. Naturally it did not disclose anything about the title to the micro-park.[5]

Settlement and registration

The transaction settled on 17 March 2004. The disposition contained a deed plan which showed the micro-park as part of the property. The disposition was of:

> All and whole that dwellinghouse number 1 Chamberlain Road Edinburgh in the County of Midlothian together with the garden ground pertaining thereto being the subjects described in and disponed by Disposition by Isabella Day McNeill or Botting in favour of Janet Williamson or White dated sixteenth and eighteenth and recorded in the Division of the General Register of Sasines applicable to the County of Edinburgh (now Midlothian) on nineteenth all April 1938; all as the subjects hereby disponed are shown delineated and coloured blue on the plan annexed and signed as relative hereto.

On 7 April 2004 the application for registration in the Land Register was lodged with the Keeper. On the form 1, question 3, which is about whether a third party

---

1 Transcript p 14.
2 Presumably a word such as 'clarified' is absent here – ironically, for absence of clarity is a theme of the case.
3 Transcript p 15.
4 We infer this because on 30 March 2004 (after settlement but before registration) the buyers seem to have been advised by their solicitors that, if it turned out that the seller had no title to the micro-park, then 'the seller's continuing contractual obligation would cover that situation' (transcript p 19). We have not seen the whole of the disposition so do not know whether absolute warrandice was granted in relation to the micro-park.
5 This intrinsic limitation on searches in the Sasine Register is all too easy to overlook. The Sasine Register is not map-based.

has possession of any part of the property, was answered in the negative. So was question 14, which is the 'is there anything else you should tell us?' question.[1] The buyers were duly registered as owners of the plan area – ie 1 Chamberlain Road plus the micro-park – without exclusion of indemnity.

How did it all go so badly wrong?

The Tribunal comments: 'Surprisingly, neither the appellants[2] nor apparently anyone else employed on either side of the conveyancing transaction[3] nor the Keeper, checked the measurements' in the GRS descriptive writ.[4] Later in its opinion the Tribunal justifies that word 'surprisingly' with a long and convincing list of reasons why the title to the micro-park called for investigation.[5]

Even though a great amount of evidence was put before the Tribunal, much about this extraordinary story remains obscure. More than once the Tribunal itself hints at a certain sense of frustration. For example: 'Unfortunately ... we did not hear from any of Ms Readie,[6] Mr Clark,[7] Mr Johnson,[8] the searcher in Ross Lornie or the individual or individuals within the Keeper's office who processed this application.'[9] Or: 'Unfortunately, there is no record of what, if any, view Brodies took.'[10] This is the story of a conveyancing disaster, and ultimately it is unclear precisely how and why it happened, though evidently the erroneous PDR was central.

It is also difficult to reconstruct how matters appeared to the buyers. It seems that at the pre-missives stage they had understood that the micro-park was not included in the sale and indeed knew that it might be owned by the City Council. They informed their solicitors to that effect and asked that the matter be looked into. What the response was is unclear. Assuming that the missives expressly included the micro-park (see above), then by that stage the buyers knew that they would either get the micro-park or damages in lieu, but whether they actually believed the title would be good is unclear. It seems most improbable that their solicitors could have advised them that the title would be definitely good.[11]

Among the many puzzles of this case is the price. The offer was made on 23 July 2003.[12] We do not know how the property was described but at that stage it seems that neither side considered that the micro-park was included in the sale.

---

1 'Are there any facts and circumstances material to the right or title of the applicant which have not already been disclosed in this application or its accompanying documents?'
2 The buyers.
3 We take it that this includes the seller's solicitors, the buyers' solicitors and the private firm that produced the PDR.
4 Transcript p 1.
5 Transcript pp 47–48.
6 The paralegal at the buyers' solicitors.
7 The partner at the buyers' solicitors who was responsible for the transaction in its earlier phase.
8 The partner at the seller's law firm.
9 Transcript p 42. We understand that the searchers were Ross Lornie & Co (Searchers) Ltd and not Ross Lornie & Co Ltd.
10 Transcript p 50.
11 The Tribunal considers this issue (p 53 of the transcript) but leaves it open.
12 Transcript p 14.

It seems only to have been on 11 September, shortly before conclusion of missives, that the seller's solicitor first asserted title.[1] Was the price upped as a result? We do not know.

After settlement

After settlement the buyers 'embarked on a major scheme of alterations and renovation'.[2] As already mentioned, they removed the public bench,[3] removed the large plaque that mentioned the Council's ownership,[4] and put high metal fencing across the frontage of the micro-park so that the public could no longer enter.[5] Uproar ensued. There was a good deal of media attention. The buyers at some stage raised an action of interdict against the Council. In that action an attempt to obtain interim interdict was refused: what has subsequently happened we do not know. The buyers would not agree to a rectification of the Register. In the end the Keeper decided that, even without such agreement, he would rectify, and he did so in July 2006, by removing the micro-park from the buyers' title sheet. Their response was to appeal to the Lands Tribunal.

Inaccuracy and rectification

Inaccuracy

The first question was whether the Land Register had been inaccurate in showing the buyers as proprietors of the micro-park. The answer was obviously yes. Whoever owned the micro-park, it was clearly not part of the 1 Chamberlain Road title and so should not have been registered in the name of the buyers. Ultimately the buyers themselves conceded that the Register had been inaccurate.[6] They nevertheless argued that the Keeper's rectification had been unlawful.

Rectification

If the Keeper rectifies the Land Register, a person adversely affected can seek indemnity under section 12(1)(a) of the 1979 Act, or alternatively can appeal against the decision under section 25 of the Act.[7] There are two possible grounds of appeal. One is that there was never any inaccuracy.[8] The other, invoked by the buyers, was that the inaccuracy could not be rectified because they were proprietors in possession.[9] In effect, the buyers were asking the Keeper to make the Register inaccurate once more.

---

1 Transcript p 16. And see transcript p 47.
2 Transcript p 20.
3 Transcript p 36.
4 Transcript p 21.
5 Transcript p 21.
6 Transcript p 2.
7 At least, that is what happened here, and the Tribunal held the procedure to be competent. But see the discussion of remedies below.
8 Land Registration (Scotland) Act 1979 s 9(1).
9 LR(S)A 1979 s 9(3)(a).

The idea that in certain types of case the Land Register *ought to remain inaccurate* is remarkable. But such indeed is the law.[1] So the buyers had to show that, at the time of rectification, (a) they were proprietors of the micro-park, and (b) they were in possession. But that was not enough. The rule that a proprietor in possession is protected from rectification is subject to one or two qualifications. The qualification relevant here was that the protection does not apply where 'the inaccuracy has been caused *wholly or substantially* by the fraud or *carelessness* of the proprietor in possession'.[2] To take away the protection, it has to be shown both (c) that the inaccuracy arose from the proprietor's carelessness, and (d) that that carelessness was *wholly or substantially* the cause of the inaccuracy.

All four points – (a), (b), (c) and (d) – were fought over. The buyers won (a) and (b). To be home and dry they needed to win only *one* of (c) and (d). But they lost both, and with it the appeal.

Point (a): were the buyers 'proprietors' of the micro-park?

At the time of the rectification, were the buyers the 'proprietors' of the micro-park? The answer given by the Tribunal is that they were, and this conclusion is clearly correct. Of course, had this been a Sasine transaction, the answer would have equally obviously been negative. In the Sasine Register, the common law principle applies that a person who does not have a right cannot transfer it.[3] But in the Land Register that principle does not apply, or at least it does not apply as such. If the Keeper knows that the application is based on an invalid deed, he will normally reject it. But if he does accept it, then the grantee acquires the right in question, however wrongfully.[4] Why? Because of section 3 of the 1979 Act, which says: 'Registration shall have the effect of ... vesting in the person registered as entitled to the registered interest in land a real right in and to the interest.' This has been described as the Keeper's Midas touch: everything the Keeper touches turns to gold.[5] The buyers had been registered as owners of the micro-park. Therefore they were the owners of the micro-park.

Point (b): were the buyers 'in possession' of the micro-park?

The question of whether the buyers had sufficient possession of the micro-park was considered at length, with the Tribunal concluding 'not without difficulty

---

1 The authors, as successive Scottish Law Commissioners, consider this aspect of the law of registration to be unsatisfactory, and that any inaccuracy should in principle be rectifiable. The Keeper ought to be in the business of keeping a register that is as accurate as possible, and not one that is knowingly inaccurate. See Scottish Law Commission, Discussion Paper on *Registration, Rectification and Indemnity* (Scot Law Com DP No 128 (2005)) para 6.32: 'Where the Register is inaccurate, rectification should be available without restriction.'

2 Land Registration (Scotland) Act 1979 s 9(3)(a)(iii).

3 *Nemo plus juris ad alium transferre potest quam ipse haberet* (D 50.17.54), or, more snappily if less accurately, *nemo dat quod non habet.*

4 There are one or two qualifications to this statement. For one of them see pp 141–42.

5 Scottish Law Commission, Discussion Paper on *Void and Voidable Titles* (Scot Law Com DP 125 (2004)) para 5.34. As in the case of King Midas, the Keeper's magic touch has benefits but also disadvantages. Even if the Keeper registers someone with exclusion of indemnity (which of course did not happen in the present case) the Midas touch still takes effect.

that the appellants did just enough to establish that they were in possession'.[1] Whilst this conclusion seems a reasonable one on the basis of the evidence before the Tribunal, it does once again show that the law is less than satisfactory in this area, because it places too much weight on who happens to be in possession.[2]

Point (c): was there 'carelessness'?

Were the buyers careless? It was a matter of concession, surely rightly, that for the purposes of the legislation any carelessness on the part of their solicitors would be attributable to the buyers. Expert conveyancing evidence was led as to whether the buyers' solicitors had been careless. Donald Reid gave evidence favourable to the buyers, while Professor Robert Rennie gave evidence to the contrary effect. The Tribunal gave no preference to either view. Its approach was that, whatever may be the position in more typical transactions, in this transaction the buyers' solicitors had acted without due care:[3]

> In cases which can be described as routine, particularly where the existing title was plan-based, the amount of thought required about the extent of the title will be minimal and it *may* be acceptable, following a quick glance at the title, simply to go through the process of obtaining the normal searches, in effect relying on the property definition reporters.... However we do not think that was sufficient by the standards of the reasonably competent solicitor in the circumstances of this case.

There were simply too many factors indicating that the title to the micro-park needed careful investigation.[4]

At this point a few words may be apposite about property definition reports. The function of a PDR is to map a GRS bounding description (which may be a purely verbal bounding description or a plan-based bounding description) onto the OS. The purpose of a PDR is 'to compare a plan and/or a bounding description with the ordnance map and to disclose any discrepancy'.[5] The Tribunal says the same.[6] Since the descriptive deed (the 1938 disposition) did not have a bounding description (its measurements were limited to the street frontage) then a PDR was logically impossible. Put in other words, the purported PDR was not a PDR.

In its opinion, the Tribunal seems to divide the carelessness into two elements.[7] The first was the failure to investigate properly the title to the micro-park. The second was that, after settlement but before the application for registration was lodged, the buyers yet again contacted their solicitors about the micro-park as a result of 'some communication [to the buyers] from the Greenhill Community

---

1 Transcript p 36.
2 See eg *Kaur v Singh* 1999 SC 180.
3 Transcript p 54 (emphasis added).
4 The Tribunal lists these factors at pp 47–48 of the transcript.
5 *Registration of Title Practice Book* (2nd edn 2000) para 4.8. As this statement implies, there could also be a PDR where there is a split-off disposition from a GRS property. In that case the PDR would be mapping the plan in the split-off deed with the OS.
6 Transcript pp 44, 48 and 52.
7 These are, we think, the 'two episodes of carelessness' mentioned at p 60 of the transcript.

Association'.[1] The letter from the buyers to the solicitors was dated 28 March 2004, ie about 10 days after settlement. In it the buyers informed their solicitors of the plaque stating that the area was owned by the City Council. The application for registration was on 7 April. The Tribunal accepted that the buyers had not noticed this plaque at an earlier stage,[2] but they had noticed it now and the Council took the view that this was something that should have been drawn to the Keeper's attention in the form 1. However, the Tribunal held that the negative answer to question 3 in the form 1[3] was, though untrue, not careless.[4]

Point (d): causation

To open the door to rectification, it is not enough for there to have been carelessness. The carelessness must have caused the inaccuracy. In the words of section 9 of the 1979 Act, it is necessary that 'the inaccuracy has been caused wholly or substantially by the fraud or carelessness of the proprietor in possession'. The buyers pointed to the words 'wholly or substantially'. *Esto* the solicitors had been careless, there was also carelessness on the Keeper's part. If the solicitors had failed to notice that the micro-park was not part of the title to 1 Chamberlain Road, so had the Keeper. The Tribunal agreed that the Keeper had been careless. But it nevertheless held that the 'wholly or substantially' test had been satisfied:[5]

> In our opinion, 'substantial' in this provision does not mean 'principal' or 'main'. It means a real cause of substance as opposed to something which had no, negligible or only slight causative effect. We do not accept that, since the Keeper's checking is the last, essential stage, earlier carelessness ... may not have a causative effect.

The Tribunal expressly accepted that there might be cases where the Keeper's carelessness so exceeded that of the applicant that the latter was to be disregarded.[6] But this was not such a case. With respect, this seems to us a sound interpretation of section 9.

Onus probandi

The Tribunal took the view that if the issue of fraud or carelessness is raised, the burden of proof lies on the person who asserts that there has been fraud or carelessness. Thus it was not for the buyers to show that they had not been careless: it was for the Keeper to show that they had been. That seems right: *omnia praesumuntur legitime facta donec probetur in contrarium.*

---

1 Transcript p 18.
2 The plaque that is there now is hard to miss. At the time of sale was it smaller? Or screened by vegetation? This is one of the innumerable puzzles of the case.
3 'Is there any person in possession or occupation of the subjects or any part of them adversely to the interest of the applicant?'
4 Transcript p 56.
5 Transcript p 59.
6 Transcript p 60.

The duty of disclosure

One of the most important aspects of the decision is its elaboration of an applicant's duty to the Keeper. We do not know in detail how the buyers' solicitors viewed matters,[1] but here is a passage from a letter they wrote to their clients after settlement but before lodging the form 1:

> Another issue might arise here. This is the attitude of the Keeper of the Land Register. In due course your title deeds will be scrutinised and a land certificate will be issued. If he agrees with the view that the wording in the verbal description in the older title deeds of Ashfield[2] is sufficiently vague to allow him to conclude[3] that the tomb is within the ownership at Ashfield House then there will be no difficulty.

No doubt many conveyancers take a broadly similar attitude on first registrations: 'We'll see if the Keeper accepts it. If he does, well and good.' One of the expert witnesses, Donald Reid, is reported by the Tribunal as having said that 'he had often given the same sort of advice'. In a sense that approach is quite right. But the Tribunal stresses that the Keeper must be dealt a full hand. There is a duty of disclosure. This point comes out with particular clarity in the Tribunal's discussion of the letter by the buyers to their solicitors shortly after settlement, telling them about the plaque asserting the Council's ownership. That was a piece of information that the solicitors should have mentioned in the form 1. Put another way, it is not enough to show the Keeper the good bits and pass over the bad bits in silence. If there are bad bits they must be disclosed. Not to disclose them may be judged to amount to carelessness, or indeed in extreme cases, fraud. It is not enough to take the view that, if the Keeper wishes to make a requisition, he is free to do so.

Land registration application forms are often compared to insurance application forms, and rightly so. Everyone knows that keeping quiet about important facts may mean that the insurance policy is invalid. Keeping quiet on a land registration application form may also have adverse effects. Although the objective in a conveyancing transaction is to achieve registration without exclusion of indemnity, that, in itself, is not enough. Needless to say, the Keeper keeps the application forms so that if problems crop up later he can see what was said and, equally importantly, what was *not* said.

In insurance law, a familiar issue is whether the duty to disclose is to be judged from the standpoint of the 'reasonable insured' or that of the 'reasonable insurer'. The two approaches can lead to different results. The answer for non-life insurance is 'reasonable insurer' and for life policies 'reasonable insured'.[4] Although the Tribunal does not put it in exactly this way, in substance it is saying that the duty of disclosure required of an applicant is not what the applicant or

---

1 Though see their letter to their clients mentioned at p 19 of the transcript.
2 'Ashfield' is 1 Chamberlain Road.
3 This seems to be saying that the vaguer the title, the more likely that ownership can be inferred. The logic is unclear.
4 The position is different in English law where the answer is always 'reasonable insurer'.

the applicant's solicitor considers relevant but what the Keeper can reasonably be expected to consider relevant:[1]

> [T]he ... duty of care ... requires consideration by the solicitor, not what the solicitor makes of the ...[2] information, but whether the Keeper might regard the information as material and whether its non-disclosure might lead to inaccuracy.

There is something that might be called 'conveyancer's tic/tick' in which the 'correct' ticks are made on the forms. The objective is a land certificate with no exclusion of indemnity. But if there has been non-disclosure, a land certificate is a house built on sand. The clients may think that they are getting a guaranteed title but that may be an illusion, and it may be difficult, later on, to explain to the client just why the 'guaranteed title' was not what it seemed.

Whilst the advent of the modern land registration system has brought many benefits, there may also have been drawbacks. It can be argued that there has been a decline in the standard of examination of title. In the old days, the recording of a deed in the Sasine Register, though necessary, was not sufficient: if the title was bad, it was bad. So one checked carefully. Today there is an illusion that if the Keeper accepts an application without exclusion of indemnity, that is all that matters. It is not all that matters. The Tribunal takes the view that an applicant owes a duty to the Keeper not to cause the Land Register to be inaccurate.[3] When – as is almost always the case – the application is handled by a solicitor on behalf of the applicant, the solicitor is, on the client's behalf, bound by that duty.[4] By uncritically accepting the position as stated in the PDR, the buyers' solicitors in *McCoach* were 'abdicating the responsibility of the purchaser to take care that the title submitted for registration would not produce an inaccuracy'.[5]

The problem of remedy

When the buyers were registered as proprietors of the micro-park, they did indeed acquire ownership of it: this is the Keeper's Midas touch. But what was the result when, in July 2006, the Keeper rectified the Register by deleting the micro-park from the title sheet for 1 Chamberlain Road? Although the Act does not say so, presumably the effect was that the buyers lost ownership. In the event, the buyers were unsuccessful in their appeal against this decision, but what if it had succeeded? The Tribunal discusses this point and takes the view that the result of a successful appeal would have been that the Keeper's decision would have been reversed, so that the micro-park would have been added once again to the title sheet for 1 Chamberlain Road. If that is right, then the buyers would have

---

1 Transcript p 58.
2 The word we have omitted here is 'new'. At this point the Tribunal happens to be dealing with the information from the plaque, but the concept is of general application.
3 Transcript p 41, and cf p 58.
4 Transcript p 41. Whether the solicitor may also have an independent duty, and not merely a vicarious one, is not an issue raised in the case.
5 Transcript p 52.

acquired ownership of the micro-park for a second time. Whilst that may well be correct, it is not a position free from difficulty. Two points may be made.

In the first place, it would mean that there exists an additional method in which the Land Register can be changed – what might be called 'restoration'. That is a method hitherto not recognised. If restoration is a competent procedure where there has been an unlawful *rectification*, then why should it not be equally available where there has been an unlawful *registration*? But if it is, then that has some remarkable implications. For example, the City Council could have appealed against the Keeper's original registration decision so as to reverse it by 'restoration'.[1] Given that that would not be a 'rectification', the protection given by section 9 to a buyer in possession would not apply.

In the second place, it was undisputed that the Land Register, in showing the buyers as owners of the micro-park, had been inaccurate. 'Restoration' would thus have involved the Tribunal *ordering the Keeper to make the Land Register inaccurate*. Now, there are some odd things in the law of land registration, and perhaps this is one of them. But common sense, at least, must rebel.

Where from here?

Assuming that there is no appeal, or that if there is an appeal it does not succeed, one wonders what will follow. If the micro-park was included in the missives,[2] then *prima facie* there would be a damages claim against the seller for breach of contract, though such a claim might have disappeared if the missives had the typical two-year supersession clause. Of course, if the missives provided that the seller did not warrant title to the micro-park, the question of liability would not arise. The terms of the missives are not known to us. Nor do we know whether the seller granted absolute warrandice in the disposition in respect of the micro-park. If she did, then presumptively she would now be liable. In that event, an interesting question might arise as to whether she might in turn have a claim against her solicitors. We can offer no view on that, but we can add a footnote: even if she were to have such a claim, the quantum of damages might turn out to be nil (see another of this year's cases, *Hay v Gourley McBain*[3]). At least two other possible claims might exist. One would be by the buyers against the Keeper for indemnity under section 12(1)(a) of the 1979 Act. But if the Tribunal's finding of carelessness is correct, then such a claim would surely fail.[4] The other would be a claim by the buyers against their solicitors. Here again we are not in a position to offer any view, except to comment that the quantum of any such claim would presumably be reduced by the amount of the buyers' warrandice claim (if any) against the seller. We offer these comments for the sake of completing the discussion: naturally we are not saying that in fact there was any breach of duty to their clients by either law firm. Such matters are outwith our knowledge of the case, which is limited to what is set out in the Tribunal's opinion.

---

1 We thank Richard Miller for this point.
2 Which is likely but not quite certain. See above.
3 2008 SLT (Sh Ct) 101.
4 Land Registration (Scotland) Act 1979 s 12(3)(n).

Variant plot endings

If the buyers had been successful in the appeal then the Register would have been restored to its inaccurate state. Where would that have left the City Council? It would have been involuntarily expropriated. Arguably, therefore, it would have been entitled to recover the value of the property from the buyers, either under the law of delict (*damnum injuria datum*) or under the law of unjustified enrichment.[1] Put another way, the buyers would have acquired the Council's property and so arguably would have been obliged to pay the Council a fair value for it. If that is right, then if the buyers had been successful in this action it might not have been wholly good news for them. Of course, an alternative for the Council would have been to claim from the Keeper under section 12(1)(b) of the 1979 Act. But that would not make any real difference to the buyers because, on paying the Council, the Keeper would have been subrogated to the Council's rights (if any) against the buyers.[2] One could also argue that, if the Register had not been rectified, the original seller (instead of, or together with, the buyers) would have been liable to the Council for having sold the Council's property.

Or take another variant plot ending. Suppose that, soon after buying, the buyers had resold to X. X's title would probably have been unchallengeable, because the inaccuracy would not have been his fault.[3] Does that mean that the question of who bears the loss depends on chance? Does it mean that, since the buyers did not sell at once, they bore the loss (though perhaps with the possibility of recovery), whereas if they had sold immediately they would not have suffered? That seems an arbitrary result. But if the buyers were personally liable to the Council (see above) that arbitrary result would not follow.

All this, however, is to speculate. The interaction of the modern land registration system with the law of delict and the law of unjustified enrichment is full of obscurities that may take decades to resolve.

COMMON AREAS

Introduction

2008 saw two cases on problems arising out of conveyances of *pro indiviso* shares of common areas in residential developments: *Turnberry*[4] and *PMP Plus*.[5] It is to be feared that a major issue has appeared in the conveyancing world. Conveyancing

---

1 This would be – to use a German term that has established itself in the academic world – the *Eingriffkondiktion*.
2 Land Registration (Scotland) Act 1979 s 13(2).
3 Even if he had known about it. See *Dougbar Properties Ltd v Keeper of the Registers of Scotland* 1999 SC 513.
4 *Turnberry Homes Ltd v Keeper of the Registers of Scotland* 11 June 2008, Lands Tribunal, available at http://www.lands-tribunal-scotland.org.uk/decisions/LTS.LR.2007.01.html. The Tribunal comprised J N Wright QC and I M Darling FRICS.
5 *PMP Plus Ltd v Keeper of the Registers of Scotland* 2009 SLT (Lands Tr) 2. The Tribunal comprised Lord McGhie, J N Wright QC and I M Darling FRICS.

practice in new-build cases may have to change, and repercussions from existing titles may continue for years to come.[1]

First, the scene should be set. NewBuildCo Ltd buys some land and develops it as a residential estate, selling off the units as and when they are completed. Most of the development will be individual units to be conveyed to individual buyers, but some of it will be common areas. For example there may be landscaping, paths and roadways, a playpark and so on. Not least important, there may be a common parking area. What, in terms of title, is to happen to these areas? There seem to be three possibilities, although our impression is that the third is the most usual in practice.

(1) The developer retains the common areas. That seems risky from the standpoint of the various buyers. Strictly, they have no right to use or even enter the areas in question. And even if a servitude is granted, as it sometimes is, it is unlikely to be legally effective, for there is no such thing as a general servitude of use (although a servitude of parking is permitted).[2] In short, the areas are the developer's, to do with as it pleases – and what pleases the developer may not please the individual buyers.

(2) At first the developer retains the common areas but on completion of the development conveys to an entity that will maintain these areas. This possibility itself divides into three: (2a) the disponee is an association representing the individual buyers;[3] (2b) the disponee is a factoring company; (2c) the disponee is the local authority.

(3) The developer conveys the common areas to the owners of the individual units to be held as common property. So if there are 40 units, each is supposed to have a 1/40 share.[4]

Though we give the example of a residential development, much the same sort of thing can also happen in commercial developments. In *Turnberry* there was a muddled mix of (2b), (2c) and (3). In *PMP Plus* (3) was attempted – but the actual result was (1). In what follows we deal mainly with (3).

In practice the common areas are often described in a deed of conditions, with the split-off dispositions then containing words of conveyance by reference to the deed of conditions.[5] In other words, whilst the dispositive act itself is the

---

1 K Ross, 'There may be trouble ahead' (2008) 53 *Journal of the Law Society of Scotland* Jan/48 anticipated some of the problems.

2 D J Cusine and R R M Paisley, *Servitudes and Rights of Way* (1998) paras 3.71 and 3.77. It is thought that the position has not been altered by s 76 of the Title Conditions (Scotland) Act 2003. English law is more accommodating, at least in respect of common areas in housing estates: see *In Re Ellenborough* [1956] Ch 131. For servitudes of parking, see *Moncrieff v Jamieson* 2008 SC (HL) 1. The question of the fixed list of servitudes is discussed at pp 107–10 above.

3 But only an association with legal personality, such as the owners' association under the statutory Development Management Scheme (for which see p 69 above), can hold title to land.

4 Of course, it can be more complicated. For example, it may be that one chunk of common area will be exclusive to only some of the units. Such complications can be ignored for present purposes.

5 A deed of conditions cannot itself operate as a disposition. But a subsequent disposition can convey by means of express reference to the deed of conditions.

disposition, the description of the common areas is in the deed of conditions. Sometimes the developer has finalised the site layout by the time of the deed of conditions (or first sale) and so already knows exactly where the common areas are to be. In that case, the disposition to the first, and every subsequent, buyer can not only have a plan showing the individual unit sold but can also include or refer to a plan showing the common parts. Such a disposition conveys a *pro indiviso* share to a precisely plotted common area. An example where the site layout will typically be complete at the outset is the sale of public-sector housing. In such cases the sorts of problems that we discuss here will not normally arise.

But in most cases the estate layout has not been finalised by the time of the first sale, and indeed may not be finalised until much later on. Developers usually want freedom. In the early stages NewBuildCo Ltd may not yet have decided where to locate all the units. 'Flexibility' is the word one comes across. In practice this tends to mean that the developer is hoping to obtain a variation in the planning consent so as to squeeze extra units onto the site. So what usually happens in practice in case (3) is that the split-off dispositions to the individual buyers contain a plan of the individual property but no plan of the common areas. Instead the developer conveys, or purports to convey, something on the lines of 'a right in common with the other proprietors in the said development to such other parts of the said development as shall not be disponed by us and our successors as individual dwellinghouses' or 'a right in common with the other proprietors in the said development to such parts of the said development as may be laid out by us and our successors as paths and amenity areas'. In *PMP Plus*, for example, the split-off dispositions said this:

> a *pro indiviso* share with all the proprietors of all other dwellinghouses and flatted dwellinghouses erected or to be erected on the Development known as Festival Park, Glasgow being the whole development of the subjects registered in the Land Register of Scotland under Title Number GLA 69039 (hereinafter referred to as 'the Greater Development') in and to those parts of the Greater Development which on completion thereof shall not have been exclusively alienated to purchasers of dwellinghouses or flatted dwellinghouses, which said parts comprise or shall comprise inter alia the boundary walls, quay wall and jetty, walkways, railings, fences, hedges and other walls enclosing the Greater Development, footpaths, sewers, drains, water supply pipes, electric mains, underbridge, car parking areas, parking area accesses, lay-bys, any embankments and access steps, the entrance drives, service roads, pathways, ornamental garden ground, play areas and other areas of open space and others so far as these serve and are common to all dwellinghouses, flatted dwellinghouses or others erected on the Greater Development (hereinafter referred to as 'the said common parts')....

Until fairly recently, few saw any legal difficulty in this sort of thing. In the Sasine Register the split-off deed was recorded and that was that. When the Land Register came in, a problem evidently arose. Given that the Land Register is map-based, how could property be registered without mapping? The practical answer arrived at by the Keeper was based on the fact that the A Section (Property

Section) of a title sheet has two parts. The first is the title plan. The second is the part giving a verbal description. The verbal description may be brief – just a few words – or it may be long, with all sorts of useful information. Its function is to supplement the title plan. The Keeper's practice in these cases was and is to make use of the verbal part of the Property Section to set out the *pro indiviso* share to *another* property, ie the common area. Thus there was, so to speak, 'registration without mapping'. Over the years countless such registrations have taken place, as in *PMP Plus* and *Turnberry*.

To include in a title sheet what are sometimes called 'incorporeal pertinents', such as the benefit of a servitude, clearly makes sense. But to include 'corporeal pertinents' – land *elsewhere* – is open to question, and to do so without mapping is even more open to question. But of that, more later.

PMP Plus: what happened and what was held

The Festival Park development

We begin with *PMP Plus*, which was chronologically the second of the cases but is much the more important. Mavisbank Quay is in central Glasgow and is on the Clyde, just by the 'Squinty Bridge'. It was redeveloped as part of the Clyde Waterfront Regeneration scheme, under the name of Festival Park, the development site extending to about 6.8 hectares. To begin with the developer was Laing Homes Ltd but the development was later sold to Persimmon Homes (West Scotland) Ltd. The latter company for some reason did not complete title,[1] so the various deeds were granted by Laing with Persimmon's consent.[2] We mention this point merely as background information: it has no particular bearing on the issue before the Tribunal.

We have already quoted from one of the split-off dispositions. Some of the early ones said 'a one two hundred and ninety first share' of the common areas while the later ones did not specify the share. But in broad terms all the dispositions were very similar. The Keeper accepted all without question: in other words, he registered buyers in respect of both (a) their individual units, which were properly mapped, and (b) *pro indiviso* shares of an area which, apart from the fact that it lay somewhere within the whole development, was unidentified.

The sale to PMP: stage 1

While the development was ongoing, Persimmon/Laing considered selling about 0.15 hectares of the development – we will call this 'the site' – to PMP Plus Ltd, which wished to build a medical centre. The Keeper was approached about this in 2001. Would he be prepared to register PMP given that the site was arguably within the common area? His reply was:

---

1 At the time of writing the Land Register continues to show Laing, not Persimmon, as the proprietor of GLA 69039.
2 See paras 7 and 22 of the Tribunal's opinion.

On completion of the development the right in common of the proprietors of the subjects registered under Title Number GLA 74132[1] will crystallise to a defined area in common with the other two hundred and ninety proprietors of dwellinghouses and flatted dwellinghouses as set out in the Property Section of the Title Sheet: until that time the developer would appear free to alienate areas as provided for in the Deed of Conditions.

Now, this is remarkable, in more than one way.[2] In the first place, it is an admission that, insofar as they showed a *pro indiviso* share to the common area, all the title sheets of individual buyers were invalid. By accepting these dispositions, the Keeper had, it seems, been making the Land Register inaccurate. The purchasers of the individual units might think they had a right to the common area, and the title sheet said they had such a right, but they had no such right. The logical consequence, duly accepted in this letter, is that Laing/Persimmon was still the owner. And since it was still the owner it had the power to dispone as it saw fit.[3] In the second place, the idea that ownership could somehow be transferred by an off-register event months or years after the registration of the disposition is an odd one. As will be seen, when the case came before the Tribunal the Keeper adopted a somewhat different position, and in particular he abandoned this 'crystallisation' argument: he accepted that a split-off conveyance either takes effect at the time of registration or not at all, ie that if it does not take effect at once then it cannot take effect later by 'crystallisation'.

The sale to PMP: stage 2

Though the Keeper had given the green light to a sale to PMP, the traffic did not move. No disposition was yet granted. When Laing/Persimmon finally did grant a disposition to PMP (the disposition was dated 17 October 2006), matters had changed. The Keeper thought that by this stage the development might be complete. On the basis of his crystallisation argument, completion would mean that ownership would have vested in the various individual buyers, so that Laing/Persimmon would no longer own the common area. And if it no longer owned, it could not dispone. Actually at this stage not all 291 split-off dispositions had been registered, so that even if 'completion' had happened, it would follow from the Keeper's approach that Laing/Persimmon still owned a small share of the common area – eg 5/291. In that case it could have given PMP title to (eg) a 5/291 share but no more. Standing the doubt about whether completion had happened, it was uncertain, on the crystallisation argument, whether Laing/Persimmon

---

1 This was an individual property in the development, little different from the others as far as the issue is concerned.

2 We should perhaps say at this point that whilst one speaks of 'the Keeper' adopting this or that position, the reality is more complex. What is said by one staff member at Registers of Scotland is normally what another staff member would have written, but there can be exceptions. Likewise in litigation one says that 'the Keeper's position was' when in reality it is the position taken by counsel. That position may bind the Keeper in that case, and will usually represent his general view, but not necessarily in every respect.

3 That might breach the *personal* rights of the various individual buyers. But personal rights are one thing and real rights another.

owned (a) 100%, or (b) only a small (eg 5/291) share. So the Keeper's response to the 2006 disposition was to say that he would accept it for registration, but with exclusion of indemnity.

That response is understandable, given the Keeper's·crystallisation theory. But even on that basis it was problematic. If completion of the development had happened, and accordingly Laing/Persimmon owned only a small (eg 5/291) share, then the 286 other owners would have been expropriated in the event of registration of the disposition. Why? Because of the Keeper's Midas Touch: the rule that registration confers ownership.[1] So if the Keeper thought that completion had happened, the result of his willingness to register PMP would have been to create a large-scale inaccuracy in the Land Register. If X grants a disposition to Y and X has no power to dispone, the Keeper's response should not be to register Y with exclusion of indemnity, but not to register him at all.[2]

Sale of what to whom when?

It may be noted, before going on with the story, that prior to 'completion' Laing/Persimmon was free, in terms of the split-off deeds, to use any part of the unbuilt land to build houses and flats and then sell them. Once completion happened, that would (in terms of the split-off deeds) no longer be possible. That argument, however, goes round in a circle, for as long as Laing/Persimmon could still build new houses and flats and sell them, the development was definitionally not 'complete'. Hence there is a logical puzzle about whether this development could ever have been 'completed'.

Sale of unbuilt land for *other* purposes, as to PMP, would also be barred, in terms of the split-off deeds, after 'completion' (if that ever could happen). And as will be seen, when the sale to PMP took place, arguably completion had happened. But equally a sale to PMP *before* completion would have been barred because the area thus sold would not be an area that 'shall not have been exclusively alienated to purchasers of dwellinghouses or flatted dwellinghouses'. In other words, the individual unit buyers were to acquire, as co-owners, everything that was not alienated to other individual unit buyers. PMP was not an individual unit buyer, because the site was for non-residential use. But this line of reasoning seems not to have been developed in the case. In any event, it is based on the wording of the split-off deeds, and as will be seen those deeds were held not to work.

The appeal to the Tribunal

PMP was happy that the Keeper was prepared to register it as 100% owner of the site but unhappy at the exclusion of indemnity. If the Keeper excludes indemnity, a disgruntled applicant can appeal to the Lands Tribunal under section 25 of the Land Registration (Scotland) Act 1979, and that is what PMP did.

---

1 Ie the fact that registration is constitutive of the right even if the deed on which registration is based is defective. See Land Registration (Scotland) Act 1979 s 3(1)(a), and p 127 above.

2 There can be certain exceptions to this general principle.

PMP's argument to the Tribunal

According to PMP, the development was not complete at the time of its own application for registration, far less at the time of registration of the prior split-off dispositions. The common area being thus undefined at the time of registration, *none* of the buyers had a real right to it. The idea of subsequent crystallisation was rejected. It followed that Laing/Persimmon was still the owner and so could dispone. There existed no basis for excluding indemnity.[1]

The Keeper's three principles

The Keeper advanced three 'principles'. These were accepted by PMP, and whilst the Tribunal does not seem to have endorsed them expressly, the impression is that it did so in fact. These principles – which seem to us sound – are of considerable importance. It is doubtful whether all conveyancers sufficiently appreciate them. Indeed, the first principle was not accepted by the Keeper until the case itself. We quote the three principles as summarised by the Tribunal:[2]

> The first principle is that it is not possible to convey an area of land ascertainable only under reference to an uncertain future event. A conveyance operates *de praesenti* and the real right is acquired on registration. In terms of s 3(1),[3] registration has the effect of vesting a real right in the person registered as entitled to the interest as at the time of registration. Except in certain circumstances which have no application to the present, the legislation does not envisage creation of a real right otherwise than by such registration. The Register makes no provision for a postponed vesting of a real right.
>
> The second principle is that it is an essential requirement of the scheme of the Register that property is sufficiently described by reference to the Ordnance map. An application for registration is not to be accepted unless it is 'sufficiently described' to enable the Keeper to identify it by reference to the Ordnance map. It is potentially misleading to say that the Keeper is given a discretion in this matter. In relation to each application he has to make a decision as to whether the land in question is 'sufficiently described'. The Keeper should not accept an application for registration of land that is not sufficiently described to enable him to identify it by reference to the Ordnance Map.
>
> The third principle is that in the absence of a sufficient description of property, a purported conveyance of that property would be ineffective. The essence of that proposition was accepted although there was some question as to the appropriate terminology. Once the Keeper has registered a title, it will have the protection of the Register but there will still be a question as to what is covered. Whether such a title is properly to be described as 'void' in relation to particular subjects may be doubted but there was no dispute that it would not give a valid title in relation to subjects not adequately covered by the description.

The first principle is an acceptance that the crystallisation argument does not stand up. Subject to certain ifs and buts, a conveyance takes effect either at

---

1 Paragraph 52.
2 Paragraphs 56–58.
3 Of the Land Registration (Scotland) Act 1979.

registration or not at all.[1] The Tribunal states this rule in connection with the Land Register, but it is equally true of the Sasine Register.

The second principle is about the 1979 Act and says (to repeat the Tribunal's words) that 'the Keeper should not accept an application for registration of land that is not sufficiently described to enable him to identify it by reference to the Ordnance Map'. Note that this does not say that the Keeper must *actually* map every property, but only that he *could* do so: 'enable' is the verb used.[2] That distinction may seem a fine one, but as will be seen it is in fact large and important.

Though the Keeper's third principle has a grandiose academic name, the 'specificity principle', it is really just common sense. If Jack owns 10 hectares and he grants to Jill a disposition of 'one hectare (the location of which will be agreed between me and my said disponee), being part and portion of my estate of Dunroamin registered in the Land Register of Scotland under title number REN 123456789', then that is a bad conveyance. To the question – 'which hectare?' – there is no answer. The Keeper would reject such a deed. For the Land Register there would be the obvious point that the unidentified property could not be mapped.[3] But equally the Keeper would reject it for the Sasine Register.[4] That which cannot be identified cannot be transferred.[5] You can transfer something: you cannot transfer something-or-other. In *PMP Plus* the identification of the common area was impossible until the development was completed.

The Keeper's argument to the Tribunal

The Keeper abandoned his crystallisation argument. Instead he ran two different arguments.[6] The first was that, even before completion of the development, it was reasonably clear what the common area was to be. Hence the specificity principle was satisfied from the start, and each of the individual buyers accordingly had valid *pro indiviso* shares in the common area. The second was an *esto* argument: *esto* the first argument was not accepted, nevertheless the development had now been completed, and the most recent split-off deeds (ie those after completion but before the lodging of PMP's registration application) therefore *did* carry with them valid *pro indiviso* shares. The Keeper noted that Harper Macleod, acting for the Festival Park Residents Association, had stated that the development was complete.

On the first argument, Laing/Persimmon owned only a small fraction of the site. On the *esto* argument, Laing/Persimmon owned most shares in the site but not all. In either case, Laing/Persimmon was not able to give a good title to

---

1 The ifs and buts mean that this principle is not – unlike the specificity principle – an absolute one.
2 This word comes from s 4(2) of the 1979 Act.
3 Land Registration (Scotland) Act 1979 ss 4, 6.
4 *Macdonald v Keeper of the Registers* 1914 SC 854.
5 The same applies to the grant of subordinate real rights. For example, if Jack purported to grant to Jill a standard security over one unidentified hectare, that would be invalid.
6 See para 53. We pay tribute to Keeper's counsel for his frankness in acknowledging that the situation was 'a mess' (para 70).

291/291 shares in the site. Here again, however, one sees a certain inconsistency in the Keeper's position: on his own arguments he should not have been offering to register PMP as *sole* owner.

The Tribunal's decision

Neither of the Keeper's arguments prevailed. As for the first argument, the Tribunal agreed with PMP that 'the intention was clearly that the common parts were only to be defined at some future point after the start of the development'.[1] That being so, the split-off conveyances carried no share in the common parts, and the title in the Land Register was likewise invalid, to the same extent.[2] As for the second argument, that required a decision as to whether, at the time that PMP submitted its application for registration, the development was complete. In the Tribunal's view, that point had not yet arrived:[3]

> [W]here it is agreed that there were still houses for sale, and therefore alienations to take place, at the time when the appellants' application for registration was presented, determination of the extent of the common parts had not yet occurred at that time.

Accordingly, the Keeper had been wrong to exclude indemnity in respect of PMP's title.

The logic of the decision is hard to fault. At the time of writing it is not known if there is to be an appeal. Although the decision was limited to the 1/3 acre site that PMP wished to acquire, it would seem to apply equally to the whole of the common areas in the development.

Exception to the Keeper's Midas touch

As already mentioned, the Keeper has the Midas touch: by section 3 of the 1979 Act, everything he registers turns to valid. But there can be exceptions. Section 3 itself adds a proviso, and the Tribunal invokes it:[4]

> Section 3(1) only confers title 'insofar as the right ... is capable, under any enactment or rule of law, of being vested as a real right'. A title which purports to convey subjects which have not been identified except by reference to future actings is not capable of effect under any rule of law cited to us.

It may be that the proviso in the statute actually does not cover this type of case. The proviso says that rights of a *type* that cannot be real are outwith the scope of section 3. But a share of a common area is a type of right (*pro indiviso* ownership) that *is* capable of being a real right. At all events, the Tribunal's view

---

1 Paragraph 75.
2 Just to be clear: nobody was suggesting that there was any problem about the titles to the individual units. Only the title to the common areas was in question.
3 Paragraph 92.
4 Paragraph 101.

that the Keeper's Midas touch cannot apply to this type of case seems right, whether or not it comes under the umbrella of the statutory proviso.[1]

The Keeper's 'offside goals' argument

The Keeper had another argument. *Esto* Laing/Persimmon was still the undivested owner of the common area, the various buyers of the individual units would still be able to challenge PMP's title on the basis of what is often called the offside goals rule, ie the rule that if X is under an obligation to grant a real right to Y but instead, and in breach of that obligation, grants a real right to Z, and Z was aware of Y's prior personal right, Y may be able to reduce Z's title.[2] If the various individual buyers did not have real rights (as PMP argued) then presumably they had personal rights, and PMP knew of those rights. Hence the offside goals rule could operate against PMP. That being so, the Keeper argued, he was entitled to exclude indemnity.

This argument was not dealt with at this stage of the case and a further hearing was due to take place in March 2009. Whatever the outcome of that further hearing, it will not change the decision reached by the Tribunal that the titles of all the individual buyers to the common area were invalid.

PMP Plus: exploring the implications

Prescription?

Although a decision about a single development in Glasgow, *PMP Plus* casts doubt on the ownership of common parts in housing estates throughout the country. In the search for solutions, one obvious thought is positive prescription. Granted that no right in the common parts is conferred by the split-off writs, can such a right not be acquired 10 years down the line by the running of prescription? That is unlikely. In the first place, positive prescription requires possession. What of the childless couple who never set foot in the playpark? And few people may actually step into the planted areas. There is a well-known principle, *tantum praescriptum quantum possessum*, which means that a prescriptive title cannot go beyond what has been possessed. Further, even if there is possession, proving it may be difficult. Most serious of all is the fact that positive prescription does not run on indemnified titles,[3] and most titles are indemnified. That, in this respect, an unindemnified title is preferable to an indemnified one is curious, but such

---

1 Cf the case where a disposition is registered in favour of a company that turns out not to exist, either because there was no such company, or there was such a company but it was dissolved before the conveyance. This type of case crops up from time to time. Nobody would suggest that the company must be the owner of the property even though there *is* no company.
2 See eg *Rodger (Builders) Ltd v Fawdry* 1950 SC 483. For extended accounts, see K G C Reid, *The Law of Property in Scotland* (1996) paras 695–700; D A Brand, A J M Steven and S Wortley, *Professor McDonald's Conveyancing Manual* (7th edn 2004) paras 32.52–32.62.
3 Prescription and Limitation (Scotland) Act 1973 s 1 (as amended) provides that, for the Land Register, positive prescription runs only on titles for which indemnity has been expressly excluded.

is the law.[1] However, after 20 years a servitude right might be acquired at least in respect of parking.[2]

Indemnity?

If a buyer's title to the common areas is void, might indemnity be due from the Keeper? Section 12(1)(a) of the 1979 Act provides that the Keeper must compensate someone who suffers loss as a result of rectification. Suppose, then, that PMP sought and obtained rectification of the Register so as to remove the 1/3 acre site from the 291 individual title sheets. What would have been lost? The answer is nothing, for the title to the common areas was already void. So an indemnity claim against the Keeper would seem to have no basis.

Another possible ground for the Keeper to resist liability would be to argue that the inaccuracy was caused wholly or substantially by the applicant's 'carelessness' in submitting a (partially) invalid disposition.[3] On the other hand, if that person later dispones to someone else, the carelessness argument seemingly could not be pled by the Keeper against the disponee.[4]

Rectification?

Might the 291 owners seek rectification against PMP in respect of the site, by the deletion of PMP's name and replacement by their own names? It is difficult to see any basis for such a rectification. Rectification presupposes inaccuracy,[5] and given what the Tribunal held it would seem that the Register, in showing PMP as owner of the site, was accurate. PMP took a valid disposition from the owner, Laing/Persimmon.

As already mentioned, the more likely move is for PMP to seek rectification of the 291 individual title sheets. There would be no obvious defence. If the title sheets were all invalid insofar as they showed the individual buyers as co-owning the site, then presumably they were all inaccurate. And the various buyers were not protected as 'proprietors in possession' of the site[6] because they were not proprietors, and presumably were not in possession either, at least by this stage.

In the foregoing the underlying assumption is that the various individual units have not changed hands so that they are still owned by the first buyers. If a later buyer is involved, matters become more complex. But before looking at that case, another issue must be considered.

---

1 See further Scottish Law Commission, Discussion Paper on *Void and Voidable Titles* (Scot Law Com DP 125 (2004); available at www.scotlawcom.gov.uk) paras 3.4 ff.
2 As pointed out to us by one seminar attender whose name, alas, we missed. But while a right to park could be acquired, there is no servitude right of use. See D J Cusine and R R M Paisley, *Servitudes and Rights of Way* (1998) paras 3.71 and 3.77.
3 Land Registration (Scotland) Act 1979 s 12(3)(n). The fact that the Keeper would also have been careless does not, it seems, prevent reliance on the applicant's carelessness: see *McCoach v Keeper of the Registers of Scotland* 19 December 2008, Lands Tribunal, discussed above at pp 00–00.
4 *Dougbar Properties Ltd v Keeper of the Registers of Scotland* 1999 SC 513, discussed in *Conveyancing 1999* pp 71–72.
5 Land Registration (Scotland) Act 1979 s 9(1).
6 Under LR(S)A 1979 s 9(3)(a).

Validity of maintenance obligations?

If purchasers do not receive ownership of the common area, are they nevertheless liable for its maintenance? Certainly the deed of conditions is likely to impose such an obligation as a real burden. Whether the burden is valid and enforceable is less certain. Section 3 of the Title Conditions (Scotland) Act 2003 begins:

> A real burden must relate in some way to the burdened property. The relationship may be direct or indirect but shall not merely be that the obligated person is the owner of the burdened property.

It is important to note that, while the burdened property is the individual unit, the maintenance obligation relates to a quite different property (the common area), and a property in respect of which the obligated person has neither ownership nor even a right of use. At best, that person has the slight benefit – for as long as the area remains undeveloped – of a view of grass and other landscaped areas. He can look but he cannot touch. Is that enough to satisfy section 3? Can it really be said that a burden to maintain such an area is related, even indirectly, to the individual unit which is purported to be burdened? There is much to be said for the view that it is not.

Must the Keeper map?

Section 6(1)(a) of the 1979 Act directs the Keeper to make up and maintain the title sheet of an interest in land by entering therein 'a description of the land which shall consist of or include a description of it based on the Ordnance Map'. The word 'include' makes it clear that as well as the OS-based title plan the Keeper can include supplementary data. But whether he makes use of that option or not, the description must be 'based on the Ordnance Map'. Does that mean: no registration without mapping? The answer would seem to be affirmative. So is the Keeper in breach of his statutory obligations in purporting to register land without mapping it? The answer is presumably 'yes', although there might be exceptions. One candidate exception is where there is tenemental property. Here the Keeper often just red-edges the 'steading' and supplements that with a verbal description of the tenemental unit in question. What about common areas for non-tenemental properties? From a common sense starting point, an exception for tenements seems persuasive, but an exception for common areas for non-tenemental properties seems less persuasive. And in either case can the exception be reconciled with section 6? We are able to offer no confident answers.

This issue was not before the Tribunal in *PMP Plus*. But the Tribunal was clearly not wholly happy with the idea of registration (or purported registration) without mapping. 'Central to the scheme is a map based register' it says,[1] and it hints that it regards the issue as an open one. Thus, referring to certain earlier cases, it says:[2]

---

1 Paragraph 36.
2 Paragraph 96.

They illustrate that the concept of a description without reference to extraneous material is well understood. It might well be thought to be a central feature of a map based registration system. In a slightly different context Lord President (Rodger) in *MRS Hamilton v The Keeper*[1] said that it was intended that 'both the proprietors of the interests and third parties should be able to rely on the register to tell them all that they need to know at any given moment about any particular interest in land'. However, as parties have not joined issue on this point, we do not require to decide whether and to what extent the central requirement of a map based description permits exception or whether any registered title whose physical extent cannot be ascertained without reference to extraneous material is necessarily ineffective or restricted in effect.

If the Keeper must map but does not do so, what then?

In the *PMP* case the Keeper registered without mapping and the result was a nullity. But it was a nullity because the area in question was not merely unidentified but unidentifiable. That leaves open the question of what happens if the Keeper registers, without mapping, an identifiable area of land – ie an area that can be identified on the ground but not from what the Register itself says. Is that a valid registration or not? To the extent (if at all) that the Keeper is allowed to register without mapping, the answer is 'valid'. But to the extent (if at all) that the Keeper is not allowed to register without mapping, the answer may be 'void'. But it is impossible to be confident on this point and, as will be seen from the quotation above, the Tribunal expressly leaves the issue open.

Might second-hand buyers be in a better position?

Suppose X buys a property, with a *pro indiviso* right to the common area. The common area is unidentifiable so that, on the basis of *PMP Plus*, X's title is invalid. Later, when the estate is complete, X dispones to Y. Is Y in a better position, always assuming (as seems likely)[2] that the Keeper is willing to register Y in respect of the common areas as well as the individual unit? The answer is: 'perhaps'. As the estate is complete, it is finally possible to give meaning to the words, by now in the title sheet, which describe the common area. So the disposition from X to Y will not fail on the ground that the common area is unidentifiable – even if identification requires the assistance of evidence extrinsic to the deed. But two difficulties remain. The first was the subject of the previous paragraph: if the Keeper must map the common areas but fails to do so, the title might not be valid even although such areas are identifiable. If that is the law, it is fatal to the position of successors such as Y. The second arises from X's lack of title. As X had no share in the common areas, any conveyance to Y in respect of those areas is *a non domino*. At one level that might not matter, for (subject to the first difficulty) the Keeper's Midas touch will confer a title on Y. But the Register is then inaccurate and can, in principle, be rectified at the instance of the original developer. If, however, Y

---

1 *MRS Hamilton Ltd v Keeper of the Registers of Scotland (No 4)* 2000 SC 271 at 277B.
2 At the time of writing no statement on this point, or on any other arising out of *PMP Plus,* had been made by the Keeper.

can show that he has (shared) possession of the common areas then he may be protected against rectification, as a proprietor in possession.[1]

What has just been discussed relates to the common areas in general. But what of the particular site conveyed to PMP Plus? Then the 'proprietor in possession' argument would not work because presumably it would be PMP Plus that would be in possession of the site, and not the individual buyers. In such a case, however, one might have 'title shuttlecock'. Each time an individual unit was conveyed, the buyer of that unit might acquire a 1/291 share of the site by virtue of the Keeper's Midas touch.[2] Thus PMP's title would ebb slowly away. Then as and when PMP Plus sold the site, the site buyer would acquire a 100% title again. Title shuttlecock is absurd, but it could result from a combination of (a) the Keeper's Midas touch, and (b) the fact that the same land has been included in different title sheets.[3]

The Sasine Register

What about the Sasine Register? The first and third principles put forward by the Keeper are common law principles and apply equally to the Sasine Register. *PMP Plus* suggests, if only by implication, that there may be many invalid *pro indiviso* rights in the Sasine Register. One difference, in this connection, between the Sasine Register and the Land Register is that in the former positive prescription will normally run, provided that there is possession, whereas in the Land Register positive prescription will usually not run, as already mentioned, because in the new register prescription does not run on indemnified titles and most titles are indemnified.[4]

Immediate implications

How should conveyancers respond to *PMP Plus*? It is still of course early days, and at the time of writing no statement has been issued by the Keeper. Still, some preliminary thoughts can be hazarded. What is clear from the decision is that a conveyance of a *pro indiviso* share is indeterminate and can confer no real right. If NewBuildCo Ltd is selling new houses and the disposition contains a conveyance of a share in an unidentifiable common area, the seller is being paid for nothing. And even if the area later becomes identifiable, that does not help at least the initial purchaser. That has to be explained to the client and, if there is a lender, it has to be explained to the lender. The explaining may not be easy.

Future implications: the problem of new developments

The discussion thus far assumes that the conveyancing will continue to be done in the future in the same way as at present. But it seems reasonable to suppose

---

1 Land Registration (Scotland) Act 1979 s 9(3)(a).
2 Whether this could happen depends on how the 'mappable or mapped' issue is answered: see above.
3 A striking example of this phenomenon is presented by the facts of *Safeway Stores plc v Tesco Stores Ltd* 2004 SC 29. For a discussion of the 'title shuttlecock' aspects of this decision, see *Conveyancing 2003* pp 94–96.
4 Prescription and Limitation (Scotland) Act 1973 s 1.

that things will now have to be done differently. The question is: in what way? The Tribunal, aware of the problems, offered some ideas, though expressly disclaiming any view as to their soundness. We quote:[1]

> There was some discussion of possible methods of giving a real right in all potential common parts while reserving the necessary flexibility. One might be to grant a title to a share of all the unbuilt land with a commitment, express or implied, that the first title holder would not object to subsequent title sheets being recorded with indemnity. The subsequent titles would gradually eat away at his title until eventually he would be left with the parts that were not alienated to others. This possible approach was tentatively suggested by the Tribunal in course of the discussion and adopted on behalf of the Keeper as a valid technique. Indeed, we understood Mr Dewar[2] to adopt it as an alternative theoretical analysis of what had happened in the present case. As discussed below, we are satisfied that an intention to adopt such an approach cannot be spelled out of the titles in this case. It may, perhaps, be an approach which could be refined and used in certain circumstances. Another way of dealing with the matter might be for parties to agree that purchasers would get their title in two stages. They would get a title to their own dwellinghouse at the outset and a title to the common parts would be given to all proprietors once the extent of these parts was identified. The title might be taken in trust for them at that stage. *Candleberry Limited v West End Homeowners Association*[3] appears to include an example of common parts being held by a homeowners' association. A third possibility might be to register the title to the common parts without indemnity and allow the matter to be resolved by prescriptive possession in the fullness of time. Such an approach seems contemplated by the *Practice Book* at para 5.63 although it must be said that it is not entirely easy to reconcile this approach with the obligation imposed on the Keeper by s 4. In any event, this process would appear also to involve a two stage approach to the register before a good title was obtained. We express no view as to the soundness of any of these approaches. They were touched on before us and tend to illustrate the difficulties. Our concern is with the specifics of the present case.

This is interesting but we confess to having doubts. Method 1 seems to be that the first person to buy a unit would be granted (a) his individual unit plus (b) a *pro indiviso* share to all the rest of the development. The second person to buy a unit would then be granted (a) his individual unit plus (b) a *pro indiviso* share to all the rest of the development. This conveyance would of necessity trespass on the rights of the first buyer, so this second disposition would have to be with the first buyer's consent 'express or implied'. We doubt whether this would work in practice. The concept is that the first and later buyers grant a mandate – in effect a power of attorney – to the developer, authorising the developer to dispone part of the property belonging to the individual buyer. There are two difficulties. In the first place, this would be a mandate to convey heritable property that would be (i) improbative, (ii) unsigned, and (iii) perhaps merely implied. That is

---

1 Paragraph 65.
2 Counsel for the Keeper.
3 2006 SC 638.

something that is unlikely to appeal to conveyancers.[1] In the second place, even if the mandate is initially valid (which is arguable), it is precarious. What if the buyer sells? Why should the mandate bind the new owner? What if the first buyer has a feud with NewBuildCo and withdraws his consent? What if he dies? What if he is sequestrated?[2]

Method 2 is that each split-off disposition is only of the unit itself. When the estate layout is fixed, a second round of dispositions is granted to all the various individual owners, conveying to them a *pro indiviso* share in the common area. This would work.[3] The drawback is that it is cumbersome and, because cumbersome, costly.

The Tribunal mentions a variant of method 2 which is that, when the estate layout is fixed, there is a single conveyance to an association to hold in trust for the various individual owners. That is simpler and cheaper in conveyancing terms, but involves the ongoing expense of an association to hold the title to the common area. It will work best in conjunction with the statutory Development Management Scheme, which is due to become available in 2009, because under that Scheme the owners' association is a body corporate and so can hold title to common areas in its own name.[4]

Method 3 is for the Keeper to ignore the 1979 Act, register the invalid shares with exclusion of indemnity, and wait for positive prescription to solve the problem (if it can). This, even if it works, is not wholly satisfactory.

It is worth adding that another solution is for the developer to have the estate layout complete before the first sale. Is that so unreasonable? It is what happens in many countries. If the developer does not do that because of the hope of persuading the planners to allow more units on site, is that reasonable as far as the earlier buyers are concerned?

Postscript to *PMP Plus*: the quantum worry

The *PMP Plus* decision may cause insomnia, so we are reluctant to make things worse. But there is a connected issue, not focused in *PMP Plus* itself, that we have to mention, however reluctantly. Some of the break-off deeds specified the quantum of *pro indiviso* share: 1/291. But others did not. We quote what one of us has written:[5]

> A well-drawn grant will indicate the respective sizes of the shares.... Where the grant is silent, there is a presumption of equality of shares, so that a conveyance of

---

1 There might also be an argument that a mandate to grant a conveyance of heritable property *must* be signed as a matter of law, and not merely as a matter of acceptable practice. This raises some tricky issues which we will not go into here.

2 In *Turnberry*, discussed below, the Tribunal and the Keeper had reservations about the mandate approach.

3 Assuming that the developer is still the owner at that stage, still solvent and still willing to co-operate.

4 Title Conditions (Scotland) Act 2003 part 6. For a full discussion of the Development Management Scheme, see Scottish Law Commission, Report on *Real Burdens* (Scot Law Com No 181 (2000)) part 8. The proposed timetable for the introduction of the Scheme is discussed at p 69 above.

5 K G C Reid, *Law of Property in Scotland* (1996) para 22.

a house to 'A and B' will, in the absence of any indications to the contrary, confer on each of A and B a one half *pro indiviso* share. In large housing developments ... the developer may face the difficulty of not knowing at the time when the first houses are sold how many houses the development will ultimately contain. In this situation it is particularly important to specify the size of the shares ... even if the final result is that proprietors receive shares of different sizes, and a disposition which takes refuge in an unspecified grant of common property may fail *quoad* the common parts on the grounds that the granter did not know the size of the share he was granting and thus lacked the necessary intention to transfer ownership.

To this problem there *is* a simple solution. The early buyers can be given a very small specified fraction (eg 1/400). That leaves the developer with future flexibility. As far as the individual buyers are concerned, the exact quantum seldom matters. A 1/400 share is just as good as a 1/40 share when it comes to, say, pushing one's children on the swings in the playpark.

Conclusions

The *PMP* decision has shone light into a messy corner. The practical issues and the theoretical issues are both very difficult. What we have written above is merely provisional, and certainly non-exhaustive. Nobody is to blame for the mess, but the mess is there nonetheless. Solicitors acting for buyers, solicitors acting for developers, and the Keeper are all going to have to do some hard thinking about where to go from here.

The Scottish Law Commission, whose final report on land registration is due in 2009, is considering an idea in which a developer would be able, at the end of the development, to lodge a plan with the Keeper showing the common area. By statute the effect would be to vest a *pro indiviso* share in the various individual owners. This would functionally be like a series of conveyances (as in method 2 above) but would be simpler and cheaper. The Commission is also considering the possibility of conferring on the Lands Tribunal a power, in specified types of case, to map the common area itself and then register the map in the Land Register. These ideas, if they go ahead, may help.

The *Turnberry* case

The *Turnberry* case[1] was decided by the Tribunal earlier in the year. Its facts were in general terms similar to the facts in *PMP Plus*. Two differences can be noted at the outset. One was that the original intention was to convey some of the unbuilt area to a single entity, Greenbelt, though at the end of the day that never happened. The other is that the sale of the area in dispute happened when the developer became insolvent. In *PMP Plus* there was no insolvency, but insolvency is one of the major themes in this field. As well as differing in respect of certain factual matters, *Turnberry* differed from *PMP Plus* in that the arguments in the

---

1 *Turnberry Homes Ltd v Keeper of the Registers of Scotland* 11 June 2008, Lands Tribunal, available at http://www.lands-tribunal-scotland.org.uk/decisions/LTS.LR.2007.01.html.

latter case – which was also the later case – were not advanced. Had they been, the result would presumably have been different.

A developer granted *pro indiviso* rights to an indeterminate common area in a development called 'Beechwood' in Motherwell. Later the developer, or to be more precise the developer's receiver, sold a chunk of the development to another developer (Turnberry Homes Ltd), for inclusion in a neighbouring development called 'Briarwood'. As in *PMP Plus* the Keeper was willing to register the buyer. As in *PMP Plus*, he excluded indemnity on the basis that individual owners of the Beechwood houses might have *pro indiviso* shares in the site in question. As in *PMP Plus* the buyer appealed to the Lands Tribunal against this exclusion of indemnity. But the outcome was different. The Tribunal rejected the appeal. The reason for the different outcome seems to have been simply that the appellant, Turnberry, did not run the same argument as was later to be run in *PMP Plus*.

Clause 7 of the Beechwood deed of conditions said:

In relation to the Development 'Common Parts' means the Development under exception of all of the plots conveyed or to be conveyed to individual proprietors and shall include any amenity play areas, boundary fences, walls, railings and hedges enclosing the same and common access roads, pavements, footpaths, visitor car parking spaces and all sewers, drains, pipes, cables and common lighting. Each proprietor within the Development shall have an equal *pro indiviso* right of property in common with all the other proprietors within the Development to the Common Parts except to the extent that the same or any part thereof may be taken over by or sold or conveyed to the Local Authority or other party with a view to the maintenance obligations being taken over by such party.

Clause 10, an unappetising and indigestible sentence running to 753 words, said:

(One) Whereas the Grantors may decide to convey to The Greenbelt Group of Companies Limited[1] or any associated company[2] of the said the Greenbelt Group of Companies Limited or its successors[3] (hereinafter referred to as 'GGC or its foresaids') any area(s) of open space/landscaped areas and play areas within the Development (hereinafter referred to as the 'Open Ground') and whereas GGC or its foresaids are or will be taken bound in terms of the Disposition granted or to be granted in their favour in respect of the Open Ground to manage and maintain the Open Ground as a landscaped open space and as a play area in accordance with a Management and Maintenance Specification comprised in the Schedule annexed and executed as relative to such conveyance to GGC or its foresaids subject to such variations to the said Specifications as may be agreed in writing from time to time between GGC and all the proprietors within the Development (all of which works and other matters comprised from time to time in such management and maintenance are hereinafter referred to as 'the Management Operations') all proprietors within the Development are hereby taken bound and obliged in all time coming to contribute to the whole

1 A visit to the Companies House website fails to disclose the existence of such a company.
2 We wonder whether this means 'associated company' as that expression is used in the Companies Acts.
3 We wonder what 'successors' means in this context.

costs of the Management Operations on a pro rata basis as aftermentioned and to pay and make over to GGC or its foresaids such annual sums (plus Value Added Tax exigible thereon) as represent the pro rata share applicable from time to time the relevant dwellinghouse of the total annual costs of effecting the Management Operations as aforesaid for the relevant year, which pro rata share shall in the case of each dwellinghouse be calculated by reference to the total number of dwellinghouses constructed or permitted to be constructed within the Development with each dwellinghouse bearing annually a proportion of the said costs which is equivalent to the numerical proportion or fraction which the relevant dwellinghouse bears to the total number of dwellinghouses constructed or permitted to be constructed within the Development, (and so that and by way of illustrative example only, if the said total number of dwellinghouses amounts to ninety seven (97), each dwellinghouse shall bear a one ninety seventh share of the said costs annually), and which pro rata share shall be payable in all time coming annually in advance by all proprietors within the Development to GGC or its foresaids; (Two) the costs of effecting the Management Operations to be paid by Proprietors pursuant to sub-clause (One) of this Clause shall not be permitted to increase in any one year by a margin or amount which exceeds in the relevant increase (if any) for that year in the rate of inflation as measured by the UK Index of Basic Materials and Fuels as published by the Financial Times, London; (Three) all proprietors within the Development are hereby bound and obliged not to deposit refuse upon or otherwise exercise any rights which they may have over the Open Ground in such a manner as to cause nuisance or prejudice to the Open Ground or any part thereof or to prejudice or adversely affect the efficient and economic carrying out by GGC or its foresaids of any part of the Management Operations; (Four) to the extent, if any, to which it may in law be necessary, for the purposes of enabling GGC or its foresaids, validly to enforce the foregoing land obligations, there is hereby conferred upon GGC and its foresaids a jus quaesitum tertio for enforcement of the foregoing provisions of these presents in a question with all proprietors within the Development (Five) for the avoidance of doubt, the provisions of this Deed of Conditions, with the exception of this Clause TENTH, are intended to regulate ownership and occupation of dwellinghouses and therefore such provisions, with the exception of this Clause TENTH are hereby disapplied from application to the Open Ground; (Six) the whole of the foregoing conditions and obligations contained in this Clause are hereby declared to be real reservations, burdens, conditions and land obligations affecting each and every dwellinghouse within the Development with the intent to confer upon GGC or its foresaids as proprietors of the Open Ground express right title and interest jus quaesitum tertio to enforce performance of same against all proprietors within the Development or any one or more of them, and as such are appointed to be inserted in all Dispositions and other deeds or instruments relating to any dwellinghouse within the Development otherwise the same shall be null and void.

Both of these clauses seem to contemplate the possibility that the developer could, after disponing *pro indiviso* shares of the common area to the individual buyers, nevertheless dispone the common area to other parties.

Could either of these provisions form a basis for the conveyance to Turnberry? Turnberry did not seek to found on clause 7, which contemplates the possibility of a conveyance to 'the Local Authority or other party with a view to the maintenance obligations being taken over by such party'. Perhaps that was because Turnberry was not taking over the maintenance obligations. Or perhaps it was because clause 7 may only be saying that a *pro indiviso* share may be conveyed to the local authority etc: the precise meaning of the second sentence of Clause 7 is hard to determine.

Instead Turnberry based its position on clause 10(5), which, it argued, had the effect of excluding the 'Open Ground' from the 'Common Parts' and so left the developer with undivested ownership of the 'Open Ground', which 'Open Ground' was said to include the area sold to Turnberry. There were difficulties in this argument, one of which was that clause 10 was dealing with transfer to GGC, and Turnberry was not GGC. The Tribunal so held: 'The natural meaning of all the operative parts of Clause Tenth, including Clause Tenth (5), is that they only apply in the event of a transfer to Green Belt.'[1] It followed that 'the conveyances to individual proprietors, which include conveyance of the rights specified in the deed of conditions, took it out of the appellants' power to convey (at least without the consent of those individual proprietors whose titles were registered) the subjects of appeal to the appellants, there being no authority for that in the deed of conditions'.[2] Accordingly the appeal failed.

The Tribunal in its opinion says this, on the mandate issue, which was mentioned earlier in connection with *PMP Plus*:[3]

> We are not so certain of the position if Wilson[4] had, after one or more individual conveyances, sought to transfer to Green Belt. The deed of conditions might appear to allow for this possibility. On behalf of the Keeper, however, Mr Dewar submitted that as soon as there was a conveyance to an individual house owner it was no longer possible for the developer to convey common parts to anyone else. There would seem to be force in that submission, but it also seems to produce some practical difficulty.... The question is perhaps whether a developer can, at the same time as providing that individual proprietors will receive rights *pro indiviso* in the common parts, effectively reserve a right subsequently to withhold or withdraw some of the land. Perhaps the Keeper is right and such a result has to be achieved in another way. However, as we are unable to construe the deed of conditions as reserving a right to dispose of land otherwise than in accordance with Clause Tenth we do not consider it necessary to decide this question in this case and wish to reserve our position on it.

Finally, as has already been mentioned, Turnberry did not seek to argue, as PMP did, that the conveyances of *pro indiviso* shares to the individual buyers were all invalid. Had it done so, the outcome of the case is likely to have been different.

---

1 Paragraph 27.
2 Paragraph 29.
3 Paragraph 30.
4 That is to say, the company that had been the developer of the Beechwood estate.

❧ PART V ❧
TABLES

TABLES

CUMULATIVE TABLE OF DECISIONS ON VARIATION OR DISCHARGE OF TITLE CONDITIONS

This table lists all opposed applications under the Title Conditions (Scotland) Act 2003 for variation or discharge of title conditions. Decisions on expenses are omitted. Note that the full opinions in Lands Tribunal cases are often available at http://www.lands-tribunal-scotland.org.uk/records.html.

Restriction on building

Name of case	Burden	Applicant's project in breach of burden	Application granted or refused
Ord v Mashford 2006 SLT (Lands Tr) 15; *Lawrie v Mashford*, 21 Dec 2007	1938. No building.	Erection of single-storey house and garage.	Granted. Claim for compensation refused.
Daly v Bryce 2006 GWD 25-565	1961 feu charter. No further building.	Replace existing house with two houses.	Granted.
J & L Leisure Ltd v Shaw 2007 GWD 28-489	1958 disposition. No new buildings higher than 15 feet 6 inches.	Replace derelict building with two-storey housing.	Granted subject to compensation of £5,600.
West Coast Property Developments Ltd v Clarke 2007 GWD 29-511	1875 feu contract. Terraced houses. No further building.	Erection of second, two-storey house.	Granted. Claim for compensation refused.
Smith v Prior 2007 GWD 30-523	1934 feu charter. No building.	Erection of modest rear extension.	Granted.
Anderson v McKinnon 2007 GWD 29-513	1993 deed of conditions in modern housing estate.	Erection of rear extension.	Granted.
Smith v Elrick 2007 GWD 29-515	1996 feu disposition. No new house. The feu had been subdivided.	Conversion of barn into a house.	Granted.

155

Name of case	Burden	Applicant's project in breach of burden	Application granted or refused
Brown v Richardson 2007 GWD 28-490	1888 feu charter. No alterations/new buildings.	Erection of rear extension.	Granted. This was an application for renewal, following service of a notice of termination.
Gallacher v Wood 2008 SLT (Lands Tr) 31	1933 feu contract. No alterations/new buildings.	Erection of rear extension, including extension at roof level which went beyond bungalow's footprint.	Granted. Claim for compensation refused.
Blackman v Best 2008 GWD 11-214	1934 disposition. No building other than a greenhouse.	Erection of a double garage.	Granted.
Faeley v Clark 2006 GWD 28-626	1967 disposition. No further building.	Erection of second house.	Refused.
Cattanach v Vine-Hall, 3 Oct 2007	1996 deed of conditions in favour of neighbouring property. No building within 7 metres of that property.	Erection of substantial house within 2 metres.	Refused, subject to the possibility of the applicants bringing a revised proposal.
Hamilton v Robertson, 10 Jan 2008	1984 deed of conditions affecting 5-house development. No further building.	Erection of 2nd house on site, but no firm plans.	Refused, although possibility of later success once plans firmed up was not excluded.
Cocozza v Rutherford 2008 SLT (Lands Tr) 6	1977 deed of conditions. No alterations.	Substantial alterations which would more than double the footprint of the house.	Refused.

Other restriction on use

Name of case	Burden	Applicant's project in breach of burden	Application granted or refused
Church of Scotland General Trs v McLaren 2006 SLT (Lands Tr) 27	Use as a church.	Possible development for flats.	Granted.
Wilson v McNamee, 16 Sept 2007	Use for religious purposes.	Use for a children's nursery.	Granted.

Name of case	Burden	Applicant's project in breach of burden	Application granted or refused
Verrico v Tomlinson 2008 SLT (Lands Tr) 2	1950 disposition. Use as a private residence for the occupation of one family.	Separation of mews cottage from ground floor flat.	Granted.

Flatted property

Name of case	Burden	Applicant's project in breach of burden	Application granted or refused
Regan v Mullen 2006 GWD 25-564	1989. No subdivision of flat.	Subdivision of flat.	Granted.

Sheltered and retirement housing

Name of case	Burden	Applicant's project in breach of burden	Application granted or refused
At.Home Nationwide Ltd v Morris 2007 GWD 31-535	1993 deed of conditions. On sale, must satisfy superior that flat will continue to be used for the elderly.	No project: just removal of an inconvenient restriction.	Burden held to be void. Otherwise application would have been refused.

Miscellaneous

Name of case	Burden	Applicant's project in breach of burden	Application granted or refused
McPherson v Mackie 2006 GWD 27-606 rev [2007] CSIH 7, 2007 SCLR 351	1990. Housing estate: maintenance of house.	Demolition of house to allow the building of a road for access to proposed new development.	Discharged by agreement on 25 April 2007.

Applications for renewal of real burdens following service of a notice of termination

Name of case	Burden	Respondent's project in breach of burden	Application granted or refused
Brown v Richardson 2007 GWD 28-490	1888 feu charter. No buildings.	Substantial rear extension.	Refused.

Name of case	Burden	Applicant's project in breach of burden	Application granted or refused
Council for Music in Hospitals v Trustees for Richard Gerard Associates, 5 Feb 2008	1838 instrument of sasine. No building in garden.	None.	Refused.

Servitudes

Name of case	Servitude	Applicant's project in breach of burden	Application granted or refused
George Wimpey East Scotland Ltd v Fleming 2006 SLT (Lands Tr) 27 and 59	1988 disposition. Right of way.	Diversion of right of way to allow major development for residential houses.	Granted (opposed). Claim for compensation for temporary disturbance refused.
Ventureline Ltd, 2 Aug 2006	1972 disposition. 'Right to use' certain ground.	Possible redevelopment.	Granted (unopposed).
Graham v Parker 2007 GWD 30-524	1990 feu disposition. Right of way from mid-terraced house over garden of end-terraced house to the street.	Small re-routing of right of way, away from the burdened owner's rear wall, so as to allow an extension to be built.	Granted (opposed).
MacNab v McDowall, 24 Oct 2007	1994 feu disposition reserved a servitude of way from the back garden to the front street in favour of two neighbouring houses.	Small re-rerouting, on to the land of one of the neighbours, to allow a rear extension to be built.	Granted (opposed).
Jensen v Tyler 2008 SLT (Lands Tr) 39	1985 feu disposition granted a servitude of way.	Re-routing of part of the road in order to allow (unspecified) development of steading.	Granted (opposed).

CUMULATIVE TABLE OF APPEALS 2008

This lists all cases digested in *Conveyancing 1999* and subsequent annual volumes in respect of which an appeal was subsequently heard, and gives the result of the appeal.

Aberdeen City Council v Wanchoo
[2006] CSOH 196, 2007 SLT 289, 2006 Case (16) *affd* [2008] CSIH 6, 2008 SLT 106, 2008 Case (11)

Adams v Thorntons
2003 GWD 27-771, OH, 2003 Case (46) *affd* 2004 SCLR 1016, 2005 SLT 594, IH, 2004 Case (44)

Aerpac UK Ltd v NOI Scotland Ltd
31 March 2004, OH, 2004 Case (1) *affd* [2006] CSIH 20, 2006 GWD 18-365, 2006 Case (7)

Anderson v Express Investment Co Ltd
2002 GWD 28-977, OH, 2002 Case (5) *affd* 11 Dec 2003, IH, 2003 Case (13)

Armstrong v G Dunlop & Sons' JF
2004 SLT 155, OH, 2002 Case (48) *affd* 2004 SLT 295, IH, 2003 Case (39)

Bank of Scotland v Forman
25 July 2005, Peterhead Sheriff Court, A59/99, 2005 Case (36) *affd* [2007] CSIH 46, 2007 Case (48)

Barker v Lewis 2007 SLT (Sh Ct) 48, 2007 Case (7) *affd* 2008 SLT (Sh Ct) 17, 2008 Case (17)

Bell v Fiddes
2004 GWD 3-50, OH, 2004 Case (8) *affd* [2006] CSIH 15, 2006 Case (13)

Bell v Inkersall Investments Ltd
[2005] CSOH 50, 2005 Case (28) *affd* [2006] CSIH 16, 2006 SC 507, 2006 SLT 626, 2006 Case (59)

Ben Cleuch Estates Ltd v Scottish Enterpise
[2006] CSOH 35, 2006 GWD 8-154, 2006 Case (61) *rev* [2008] CSIH 1, 2007 Case (47)

Burnett v Menzies Dougal
2004 SCLR 133 (Notes), OH, 2004 Case (42) *rev* [2005] CSIH 67, 2005 SLT 929, 2005 Case (40)

Burnett's Tr v Grainger
2000 SLT (Sh Ct) 116, 2000 Case (21) *rev* 2002 SLT 699, IH, 2002 Case (19) *affd* 2004 SC (HL) 19, 2004 SLT 513, 2004 SCLR 433, HL, 2004 Case (24)

Cahill's Judicial Factor v Cahill
2 March 2005, Glasgow Sheriff Court, A2680/94, 2005 Case (49) *affd* [2006] CSIH 26, 2006 GWD 19-409, 2006 Case (88)

Caledonian Heritable Ltd v Canyon Investments Ltd
2001 GWD 1-62, OH, 2000 Case (69) *rev* 2002 GWD 5-149, IH, 2002 Case (61)

Candleberry Ltd v West End Homeowners Association
12 October 2005, Lanark Sheriff Court, A492/5 *affd* 2006 GWD 21-457, Sh Ct, 2005 Case (9) *rev* [2006] CSIH 28, 2006 Hous LR 45, 2006 Case (15)

Caterleisure Ltd v Glasgow Prestwick International Airport Ltd
2005 SCLR 306, OH, 2004 Case (21) *rev* [2005] CSIH 53, 2005 SLT 1083, 2005 SCLR 943, 2005 Case (15)

Cheltenham & Gloucester plc v Sun Alliance and London Insurance plc
2001 SLT 347, OH, 2000 Case (63) *rev* 2001 SLT 1151, IH, 2001 Case (73)

City Wall Properties (Scotland) Ltd v Pearl Assurance plc
[2005] CSOH 139, 2005 GWD 35-666, 2005 Case (32) *affd* [2007] CSIH 79, 2007 Case (43)

Conway v Glasgow City Council
1999 SCLR 248, 1999 Hous LR 20 (Sh Ct) *rev* 1999 SLT (Sh Ct) 102, 1999 SCLR 1058, 1999 Hous LR 67, 1999 Case (44) *rev* 2001 SLT 1472, 2001 SCLR 546, IH, 2001 Case (51).

Glasgow City Council v Caststop Ltd
2002 SLT 47, OH, 2001 Case (6) *affd* 2003 SLT 526, 2004 SCLR 283, IH, 2003 Case (6)

Grampian Joint Police Board v Pearson
2000 SLT 90, OH, 2000 Case (18) *affd* 2001 SC 772, 2001 SLT 734, IH, 2001 Case (17)

Hamilton v Mundell; Hamilton v J & J Currie Ltd
20 November 2002, Dumfries Sheriff Court, 2002 Case (13) *rev* 7 October 2004, IH, 2004 Case (11)

Harbinson v McTaggart 2006 SLT (Lands Tr) 42, 2006 Case (69) *affd* under the name of *Allen v McTaggart* [2007] CSIH 24, 2007 SC 482, 2007 SLT 387, 2007 Hous LR 29, 2007 Case (40)

Henderson v 3052775 Nova Scotia Ltd
2003 GWD 40-1080, OH, 2003 Case (58) *affd* [2005] CSIH 20, 2005 1 SC 325, 2005 Case (47) *rev* [2006] UKHL 21, 2006 SC (HL) 85, 2006 SLT 489, 2006 SCLR 626, 2006 Case (86)

Inverness Seafield Co Ltd v Mackintosh
1999 GWD 31-1497, OH, 1999 Case (19) *rev* 2001 SC 406, 2001 SLT 118, IH, 2000 Case (13)

Jones v Wood
27 October 2003, Dumfries Sheriff Court, 2003 Case (52) *affd* [2005] CSIH 31, 2005 SLT 655, 2005 Case (42)

Kaur v Singh (No 2)
1999 Hous LR 76, 2000 SCLR 187, 2000 SLT 1324, OH, 1999 Case (34) *affd* 2000 SLT 1323, 2000 SCLR 944, IH, 2000 Case (26)

Kingston Communications (Hull) plc v Stargas Nominees Ltd
2003 GWD 33-946, OH, 2003 Case (35) *affd* 17 December 2004, IH, 2004 Case (31)

Labinski Ltd v BP Oil Development Co
2002 GWD 1-46, OH, 2001 Case (16) *affd* 2003 GWD 4-93, IH, 2003 Case (17)

Little Cumbrae Estate Ltd v Island of Little Cumbrae Ltd
April 2006, Glasgow Sheriff Court, 2006 Case (73) rev [2007] CSIH 35, 2007 SC 525, 2007 SLT 631, 2007 Hous LR 40, 2007 Case (42)

McAllister v Queens Cross Housing Association Ltd
2001 Hous LR 143, 2002 SLT (Lands Tr) 13, 2002 Case (26) *affd* 2003 SC 514, 2003 SLT 971, IH, 2003 Case (28)

Minevco Ltd v Barratt Southern Ltd
1999 GWD 5-266, OH, 1999 Case (41) *affd* 2000 SLT 790, IH, 2000 Case (36)

Moncrieff v Jamieson
2004 SCLR 135, Sh Ct, 2003 Case (20) *affd* [2005] CSIH 14, 2005 SC 281, 2005 SLT 225, 2005 SCLR 463, 2005 Case (6) *affd* [2007] UKHL 42, 2008 SC (HL) 1, 2007 SLT 989, 2007 SCLR 790, 2007 Case (3)

Neumann v Hutchison
2006 GWD 28-628, Sh Ct, 2006 Case (17) *rev* 2008 GWD 16-297, Sh Ct, 2008 Case (12)

Peart v Legge
2006 GWD 18-377 *affd* 2007 SCLR 86, Sh Ct, 2006 Case (18) *rev* [2007] CSIH 70, 2008 SC 93, 2007 SLT 982, 2007 SCLR 86, 2007 Case (5)

Robertson v Fife Council
2000 SLT 1226, OH, 2000 Case (84) *affd* 2001 SLT 708, IH, 2001 Case (82) *rev* 2002 SLT 951, HL, 2002 Case (69)

Royal Bank of Scotland plc v Wilson
2001 SLT (Sh Ct) 2, 2000 Case (53) *affd* 2003 SLT 910, 2003 SCLR 716, 2004 SC 153, IH, 2003 Case (40)

Scottish Youth Theatre (Property) Ltd v RSAMD Endowment Trust Trustees
2002 SCLR 945, OH, 2002 Case (3) *affd* 2003 GWD 27-758, IH, 2003 Case (8)

Souter v Kennedy
23 July 1999, Perth Sheriff Court, 1999 Case (69) *rev* 20 March 2001, IH, 2001 Case (81)

Spence v W & R Murray (Alford) Ltd
2001 GWD 7-265, Sh Ct, 2001 Case (9) *affd* 2002 SLT 918, IH, 2002 Case (1)

Stephen v Innes Ker
[2006] CSOH 66, 2006 SLT 1105, 2006 Case (67) *affd* [2007] CSIH 42, 2007 SC 501, 2007 SLT 625, 2007 Case (41)

Stevenson v Roy
2002 SLT 445, OH, 2002 Case (67) *affd* 2003 SC 544, 2003 SCLR 616, IH, 2002 Case (54)

Superdrug Stores plc v Network Rail Infrastructure
2005 SLT (Sh Ct) 105, 2005 Case (35) *rev* [2006] CSIH 4, 2006 SC 365, 2006 SLT 146, 2006 Case (62)

Tesco Stores Ltd v Keeper of the Registers of Scotland
2001 SLT (Lands Tr) 23, 2001 Case (30) *affd* sv *Safeway Stores plc v Tesco Stores Ltd* 2004 SC 29, 2004 SLT 701, IH, 2003 Case (25)

Thomas v Allan
2002 GWD 12-368, Sh Ct, 2002 Case (7) *affd* 2004 SC 393, IH, 2003 Case (22)

Warren James (Jewellers) Ltd v Overgate GP Ltd
[2005] CSOH 142, 2006 GWD 12-235, 2005 Case (26) *affd* [2007] CSIH 14, 2007 GWD 6-94, 2007 Case (35)

Wilson v Dunbar Bank plc
[2006] CSOH 105, 2006 SLT 775, 2007 SCLR 25, 2006 Case (77) *rev* in part [2008] CSIH 27, 2008 SC 457, 2008 SLT 301, 2008 Case (62)

Wilson v Inverclyde Council
2001 GWD 3-129, OH, 2001 Case (29) *affd* 2003 SC 366, IH, 2003 Case (27)

TABLE OF CASES DIGESTED IN EARLIER VOLUMES BUT REPORTED IN 2008

A number of cases which were digested in *Conveyancing 2007* or earlier volumes but were at that time unreported have been reported in 2008. A number of other cases have been reported in an additional series of reports. For the convenience of those using earlier volumes all the cases in question are listed below, together with a complete list of citations.

Ben Cleuch Estates Ltd v Scottish Enterprise
[2008] CSIH 1, 2008 SC 252

Credential Bath Street Ltd v Venture Investment Placement Ltd
[2007] CSOH 208, 2008 Hous LR 2

Gallacher v Wood
2008 SLT (Lands Tr) 31

Hamilton v Dumfries and Galloway Council
[2007] CSIH 75, 2008 SC 197, 2008 SCLR 101

Hamilton v Robertson
2008 SLT (Lands Tr) 25

McDonald v O'Donnell
[2007] CSIH 74, 2008 SC 189, 2008 SCLR 93

Moncrieff v Jamieson
[2007] UKHL 42, 2008 SC (HL) 1, 2007 SLT 989, 2007 SCLR 790

Peart v Legge
[2007] CSIH 70, 2008 SC 93, 2007 SLT 982, 2007 SCLR 86